SHELBY AND AC COBRA

OTHER TITLES IN THE CROWOOD AUTOCLASSICS SERIES

SHELBY AND AC COBRA

BRIAN LABAN

THE CROWOOD PRESS

First published in 2015 by
The Crowood Press Ltd
Ramsbury, Marlborough
Wiltshire SN8 2HR

www.crowood.com

British Library Cataloguing-in-Publication Data
A catalogue record for this book is available from the British Library.

ISBN 978 1 78500 003 4

All images other than those identified as having been supplied by The Motoring
Picture Library, Beaulieu, are from the author's own photographic archive or
were sourced on-line, and credited to the original copyright holder where that
information is known. For any other image, every effort has been made to discover
the identity of and to contact the original copyright holder, but where this has
not been possible, the publisher and author would be grateful to acknowledge any
further information.

Dedication
To Peter Brook – who will understand why …

Typeset by Jean Cussons Typesetting, Diss, Norfolk

Printed and bound in India by Replika Press Pvt. Ltd.

CONTENTS

INTRODUCTION

Carroll Shelby, 'father of the Cobra', died on 10 May 2012, aged eighty-nine. Through most of his life, including his racing career, he had suffered heart problems, and in recent years had had both heart and kidney transplants, but rarely stopped working. In anything resembling its 1960s guise, AC Cars, midwife to Shelby's baby, had passed on long before Shelby did. But the Cobra name (and various more or less faithful pastiches of the 'authentic' Cobra) outlived both of them. In fact the Cobra thrived, to the extent of reaching a '50th Anniversary' Series in 2014, marketed by the modern Shelby company and carrying the magical 'CSX' chassis number prefix that Shelby (and others) always argued was the true identifying mark of any 'genuine' Cobra.

The Cobra itself was (and is) a mechanically simple, race-bred, old-school sports car, and one of the most successful competition cars in motor sport history – albeit with an extraordinarily convoluted commercial and political history, dominated by conflicting claims to its parentage, by recurrent litigation about its title, and by multiple challenges to the right of kit-car and replica builders even to copy its essence.

WHAT'S IN A NAME?

Even the title of this book reflects the contention. Shelby himself was very helpful in researching *AC Cobra – The*

The absence of Shelby's name and the steering wheel shifted to the right (by an artist, not an engineer) indicate a brochure for the European 289 – but every inch the definitive Cobra.

INTRODUCTION ■

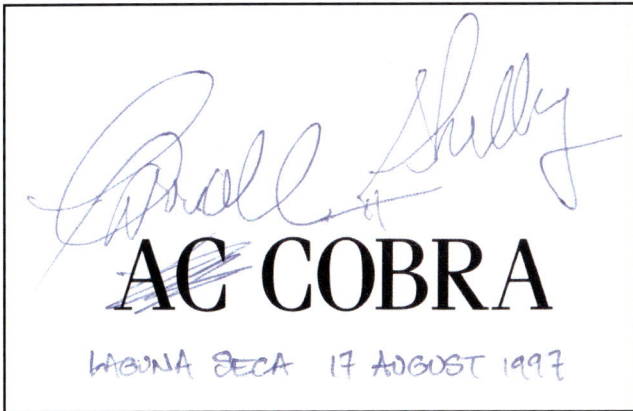

Shelby himself was always adamant about what his car was called. He signed a copy of the original edition of this book at Laguna Seca in 1997, with subtle editing.

Complete Story, published in 1991, but he never liked the original title. Much as he respected AC's role, to Shelby, a Cobra was always a Shelby Cobra. By the time that edition was published, Shelby's relationship with the later AC regime (and especially with Brian Angliss, who ran the company from 1982 to 1986) had degenerated almost to the point of open warfare. And maybe he had a point: while taking nothing away from AC at the time, without Shelby there would have been no Cobra.

The Cobra was conceived and created in the early 1960s, and in essence it was made possible by Shelby's vision, the Ford Motor Co.'s money, and AC's manufacturing skills, shepherded by Shelby when none of the three would have produced the car individually.

At the time, the exact name wasn't high on anyone's agenda compared to making the car happen. Shelby's motive was to fulfil his idea of putting a big American engine into a sporty European chassis; Ford's was to support their 1960s marketing mantra of 'Total Performance', on and off track; AC's was simply to survive in the perilous business of being a small-volume specialist car-maker that had just lost vital supply chains.

Shelby (plus Ford) and AC were almost literally worlds apart, on opposite sides of the Atlantic; and probably just as far apart in terms of business philosophies and personalities. Shelby was the brash, larger-than-life Texan, sometime chicken farmer, retired racer, middling engineer, consummate self-promoter; Ford was the motor sport-obsessed corporate giant, with deep pockets but mainly bought-in

race-engineering talent; AC was the small, artisan, staunchly British sporting car builder who did almost everything by hand and didn't make as many cars in a year as Ford did in a morning.

POWERED BY FORD

Ford's interest in having their name on the car extended only as far as wanting it discreetly to carry the evocative 'Powered by Ford' tag. In the USA, few among Ford's target market for the Cobra would have known the AC name from a hole in the ground, and certainly wouldn't have gone out of their way to buy one, even with a US V8 under the bonnet. British driver Tommy Cole (tragically killed at Le Mans in 1953) is credited with starting that particular transplant trend in the early 1950s by being the first to shoehorn a Cadillac V8 into a British Allard chassis; all-American

The Father of the Cobra with offspring. The Cobra was the halo car, the Shelby Mustangs in the background were the money-makers that spun off from Ford's investment.

7

Backers Ford were always surprisingly reticent about their direct involvement in the Cobra, at least in terms of badging, but look and you would find it.

sporting hero Briggs Cunningham also squeezed a 5.5-litre Cadillac V8 into the first Healey Silverstone to reach the USA. But without a big manufacturer like Ford to back and sell the concept, motor sport aficionados aside, neither Allard nor Healey were beating the US buyers off with a stick. Ditto in the UK – anybody who knew the Shelby name

probably knew him as a former driver with Aston Martin, who had given that even more English sports car maker victory at Le Mans in 1959.

So in 1963, when the Cobra went into production, it had a seemingly fairly trivial identity crisis, being labelled at various times and in different markets as Shelby Ford AC Cobra, Shelby AC/Cobra (for some reason including the forward slash), AC Cobra, Shelby Cobra, and in later incarnations even Ford Cobra. The only immutable bit was 'Cobra' – a name that Shelby claimed came to him in a dream, which he wrote down on a notepad, and which Ford and AC were both happy to go along with.

While the precise title dispute rumbled on even fifty years later, there has never been much argument about the car's place in the sports car pantheon: the Cobra is an icon.

Simplicity, far from being a limitation, became its underlying and defining strength. It put a large-capacity but not especially sophisticated, mass-produced US V8 engine into

The Cobra couldn't have existed as a competition car without the street car to provide the numbers, but the street car benefited in almost every respect from the racer – in this case a light and lithe early 289 and the muscular full race 427 in Shelby colours.

The Cobra never went away: this is the celebration CSX4000 series 289 FIA.

a suitably uprated version of an equally uncomplicated but clearly competent European-style chassis – under a body again made beautiful by its simplicity.

It was such an obvious marriage: lots of affordable power, not much weight, minimal frills. It was by no means the first time it had been done, but Shelby, Ford and AC finally showed how to do it properly, and the Cobra became much more than the sum of its parts.

As a road car (this in the early 1960s) it redefined the upper levels of straightline performance – not so much in top speed, given its original aerodynamic limitations, but certainly in terms of ferocious acceleration, where it actually mattered more. It came to fulfil both Ford and Shelby's underpinning motor sporting ambitions at all levels of sports car and endurance racing. From day one it began to give the previously dominant Corvettes and Jaguars a very hard time in American club racing, quickly carried its winning ways back to Europe, and eventually took the ultimate prize by beating Ferrari in the Manufacturers category of the World Sports Car Championship.

COBRAS BEYOND THE COBRA

One place where the (genuine) Cobra didn't set the record-

books ablaze was in terms of production volumes – although it would look like a runaway best-seller along-side the likes of the Allards and Healeys. In its first, indisputably Shelby-fostered incarnation (pre-AC MkIV and subsequent continuations), the Cobra only lasted seven years from first production 260 to final European-spec (AC-badged) 289. The original-generation roster (again pre-MkIV) details 655 leaf-spring 260s and 289s, 348 coil-spring 427s (the majority of which were actually 428-powered), and twenty-seven Europe-only coil-sprung AC MkIIIs. That's 1,030 cars in all. Then there are the follow-ons, from Shelby and from various incarnations of AC (via Autokraft), of both sanctioned and disputed title.

There are the (mainly Shelby-built) cars with 'run-on' versions of the original, magical CSX nomenclature, and the (mainly AC-built) ones without; there are cars built long after Cobra production ostensibly ended in 1969, including Shelby's CSX4000 and 6000 Series 427 Cobra S/C roadsters from the late 1990s, through to the CSX7000 Series FIA 289 race-car re-creations, and the limited edition '50th Anniversary' of 2014.

Most controversially of all, there are the legions of replicas and recreations, some every bit as good as the real thing in terms of nuts and bolts but in no way the real thing in terms of provenance; some truly awful, but almost all generically dubbed 'Cobra', begging questions of imitation and flattery – though Shelby was hardly ever flattered.

The true intrigue of the Cobra is the unique union of Carroll Shelby, AC Cars and the Ford Motor Co., of motor sport in the 1960s, and of big engines in small cars. It encompasses key characters in the wings: the Hurlock brothers, who controlled AC at the crucial time and had the courage to take on Shelby's ideas; John Tojeiro, designer of the 'surrogate' AC Ace (if Shelby was father of the Cobra, Tojeiro was its grandfather); racer and test driver Ken Miles, who took the Cobra prototypes by the scruff of the neck and tested and tuned them until they worked; Pete Brock, who created the Ferrari-beating Daytona coupé; Lee Iacocca, who held the reins at Ford in the days of Total Performance; Ford's Dave Evans, who gave Shelby the engine to make his dream a reality; and Phil Remington, who Shelby respected possibly most of all, as both brilliant engineer and down-to-earth administrator.

Spotted by Shelby in 1961 (and possibly before that as their Le Mans golden days overlapped), the Ace was a good-looking, fine-handling sports car. Launched in 1953, it had revitalized AC's image and turned them back into a sporting marque. Initially it had AC's own 6-cylinder engine. From 1956 it was offered with the well-regarded 6-cylinder Bristol engine, but by early 1961 as Bristol (slightly ironically) switched to American Chrysler V8 power, the Ace was a car looking for another engine.

So far as the car itself is concerned, that's where the Cobra story starts; but the bigger picture begins best with the man who was looking for a car when it mattered, the man who had the vision and the essential can-do philosophy, the 'father of the Cobra' himself.

Without the Ace, here at AC's spiritual home of Brooklands, there would have been no Cobra.

CHAPTER ONE

CARROLL SHELBY BEFORE THE COBRA

Carroll Hall Shelby was born on 11 January 1923 in Lees-burg, Texas, a tiny, remote community of barely 200 people at the time, on the Louisiana and Arkansas Rail-way, 120 miles (193km) northeast of the rather larger city of Dallas. His parents were local people, and church-going Baptists. Leesburg's founders may have been a bit optimis-tic in 1873 when the tiny settlement opened a post office, but in 1923 Shelby's father Warren Hall Shelby was a Texas mailman, who made most of his deliveries by horse-drawn buggy. When he was around three, Carroll's mother Eloise (née Lawrence) gave Carroll a sister.

It was a back-country life, but a reasonably comfortable one. The US mail paid Shelby's father enough for him to buy his first (second-hand) car just before Carroll reached his fifth birthday – a dark-green 1925 Willys Overland tour-er with folding top, artillery wheels, manual gearshift and wood-rimmed steering wheel. It was hardly sporty, but a virtually identical model appeared in Willys Overland public-ity shots in 1923, sign-written on the open bodywork with the boast: 'This Stock 1923 Overland – First Car To Reach Lake Tahoe (Via Placerville)', a short but brutal trek through the mountains between California and Nevada in the days when the American road network was still pretty sketchy.

Shelby Sr loved cars and Carroll picked up the bug, watch-ing his father tinkering with the Overland engine, or sitting on his knee holding the steering wheel. Warren obviously liked Overlands (built in Toledo, Ohio) and in 1928 bought a slightly sportier Overland Whippet, with a 2.2-litre 4-cyl-inder engine and wire wheels, which made an even deeper impression on the boy.

Then, in 1930, the family moved to Dallas, where Warren was promoted to postal clerk and Carroll started attending Woodrow Wilson High School. He was a sickly child, and by age nine or ten he was showing signs of the heart problems

that would dog him through his life, meaning he was often prescribed afternoon bed rest in his pre-teen years.

By the time he was around fourteen, though, the prob-lems seemed to have eased. Shelby had started to grow taller and stronger, and while he tired easily he was living a more normal teenage life, still fascinated by cars, and now by aeroplanes, too.

His father had helped young Carroll learn to drive, in a scruffy 1934 Dodge; by 1938 he had a car of his own, reg-istered in his father's name, as Carroll (at just fifteen) still wasn't old enough legally to own it himself. That, and most of the other cars he occasionally got to drive, had tricky manual 'crash' gearboxes, so he learned one useful driving

Modest four-wheel beginnings for the boy from Leesburg, Texas, in the late 1920s.

Warren Hall Shelby, Texas mailman and father of Carroll, had an affinity for Overlands, built in Toledo, Ohio – rugged and dependable with just a hint of sporty.

The boy had a brief flirtation with flying, and apparently dressed the part.

skill for a future racing driver quite early – how to double-declutch.

WHEELS AND WINGS

Racing was already creeping into Carroll's consciousness as his father took him to the dirt-track races at the local 'bull-ring' ovals. When his father couldn't take him, he'd go on his own, and get involved in a bit of fetching and carrying for the racers.

Alongside that came a growing interest in flying. Rural Texas was scattered with small airfields and private landing strips, and young Shelby started odd-jobbing at some of those, too. That occasionally allowed him to sit in a cockpit, and eventually his indulgent father paid for his first joy ride, in a Ford Trimotor. Shelby admitted that it frightened him to death, but again he had the bug. He negotiated passenger rides whenever he could, and after graduating from Woodrow Wilson High in 1940 he enrolled on an aeronautical engineering course at the Georgia School of Technology.

By this time he had also worked as a motorcycle delivery rider for a local drugstore, using an Excelsior bike. But he wasn't good on two wheels, and while he never hurt himself badly he eventually grew sick of falling off, and quit his job

Appropriately enough for his future connections, Shelby's first joy ride, sponsored by his father, was in a Ford Trimotor – in this case, also appropriately, a mail plane.

on the spot. From then on, he would stick to four wheels, always with the option of a bit more serious flying.

Around 1939 Shelby met Jeanne Fields at a Baptist church social, and married her in December 1943, just after his father had died, from the heart problems that Carroll probably inherited from him. By December 1944 they had a daughter, Sharon Anne, and Shelby's life had moved on quite dramatically. He never completed the course at Georgia Tech; as World War II started to draw America in, Shelby had joined the United States Army Air Corps; in November 1941 he started training at San Antonio Aviation Cadet Center (later to become Lackland Air Force base). Between his new military career, his courting of Jeanne and his mother's reduced financial circumstances, any ideas of getting more involved in motor racing were temporarily pushed into the background.

A QUIET WAR

With the help of a friendly recruiting sergeant (and before the realities of war kicked in), Shelby organized a posting near to his mother and wife-to-be's homes, at Randolph Field, a vast base around 15 miles (24km) from San Antonio, opened in 1931 and still America's primary flight training facility. In his Basic Flying Training Squadron, Carroll Shelby combined his training with less glamorous duties – including moving tons of chicken manure from an old farm to flower beds around the base's Spanish Colonial-style buildings. Moving chicken manure would have a resonance in the Shelby story a few years later.

He also drove a fire truck on the base for a few months, until with the war in Europe under way he finally got his chance to fly regularly. His pre-flight training started at Randolph in November 1941 and in September 1942, as a sergeant, he was transferred to Ellington Field, this time near Houston. In his training days he used to fly over his fiancée's family farm, occasionally dropping letters and once even landing to take Jeanne (and her mother!) for a highly unofficial joy-ride. Shelby was never a slave to the rule book.

In December 1942 he was commissioned as a second lieutenant, but that was as far as his promotions went, and he neither saw active service nor did much travelling: the

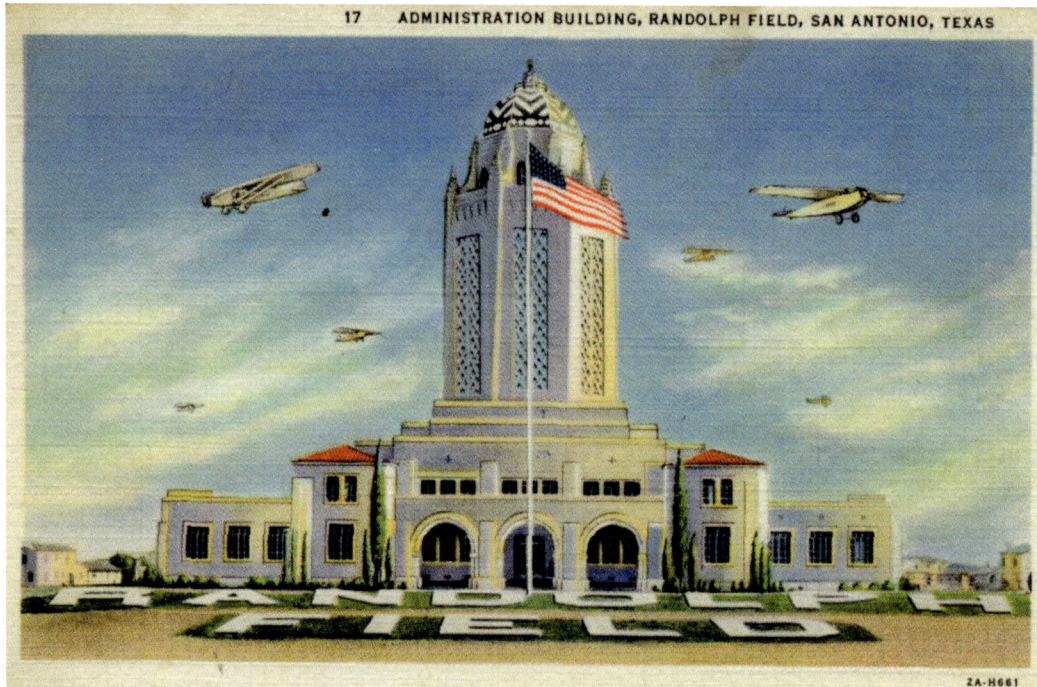

17   ADMINISTRATION BUILDING, RANDOLPH FIELD, SAN ANTONIO, TEXAS

Shelby's first Army Air Corps posting was Randolph Field, with its famous colonial-style buildings, and conveniently close to home in Dallas.

furthest he went in his four-and-a-half years of military flying was the Gulf of Mexico.

His time as a military pilot (and later instructor) wasn't without its adventures. As well as the unsanctioned diversions to Jeanne's family farm, he crashed in the desert during a simulated bombing run. He got his student pilots out of the plane while it was still in the air, then hung on as long as he could himself before bailing out too – to face a long walk home.

A bit like falling off motorbikes, it helped get the flying bug out of his system, so by the time he left the service in 1945 he had no ambition to carry on as a commercial pilot. Unfortunately, he had no particularly relevant training to do anything else either, so his immediate post-war career options were strictly limited – although the birth of Carroll and Jeanne's first son, Michael Hall Shelby, in November 1946, and younger brother Patrick Burke Shelby in October 1947, meant he needed some way of paying the bills.

With long-time friend Bailey Gordon, Carroll went into the ready-mixed concrete business, starting with one truck each but quickly building up a fairly substantial business, with more trucks and employing a number of other drivers.

In 1947 Shelby expanded into his own trucking operation, mainly carrying timber for the building industry. While that was a successful move, he was always aware of the

possibility of a slump in the building business, which could have taken him with it; so with a little help from his oil-man father-in-law he sold out of the trucking business and went into oil.

Like many of Shelby's early career paths, that didn't last long. Starting from the bottom during 1948 and working as a 'do-anything' roughneck, he soon found that there was little money and few prospects in that area of the business, so it was time for another change. This one would become a famous part of the Shelby story.

For all his apparent butterfly tendencies, he wasn't afraid of hard work, or of seeking outside advice. Determined to be successful at something, he now submitted himself to a series of aptitude tests, which for some reason suggested that he would be best suited to working with animals. A Shelby legend was about to take shape.

CHICKEN FARMER TO RACER

At the time, chicken farming was a growing industry in this part of Texas; there was government finance on offer to help would-be entrepreneurs get started in the business. And Shelby had his Air Corps experience with at least one aspect of chickens.

The chicken-farmer overalls started out of expediency but became a trademark, and even in later life Shelby was happy to play up to it.

Typically, he didn't go for half measures. His first batch was 20,000 birds and in the first three-month cycle he made around $5,000 profit, which was a promising start. But it was too good to last, and his second batch of birds was wiped out by disease. His money and business plans went with them, sending him back to scratching a meagre living by odd-jobbing, while raising a few pheasants and Irish setters on the old chicken farm.

More as a hobby than as a job, Shelby now got involved with cars again, specifically working on a backyard-built, ladder-framed racer with a Ford flathead V8 and home-made body, owned and built by an old school friend, Ed Wilkins. Then one thing led to another.

In January 1952, Shelby (now a father of three) raced the car in a drag race meeting at Grand Prairie Naval Airbase, near Dallas Fort Worth. Without much to beat, and without the complication of having to go round corners, Shelby won quite easily, prompting Wilkins to give him a chance on the next step of the motor sport ladder, in a proper circuit race. The car was an imported MG TC – British sports car of choice for a post-war generation of US servicemen returning from Europe, and MG's big contribution to Britain's desperate post-war export drive, when earning dollars was top of the wish-list.

In his first circuit race, at Norman, Oklahoma in May 1952, Shelby won his class again, in an event sanctioned by

In the early postwar years, the MG T Series was one of Britain's key exports to the USA, and the way into motor sport for many a would-be driver – including Shelby.

the newly formed Sports Car Club of America. The SCCA was another catalyst; without it there wouldn't have been any serious racing in the USA at the time. The Club was founded in 1944, essentially as an enthusiasts' social club, but in 1948 it started to sanction and organize races across the country. By 1951 it had created the SCCA National Sports Car Championship, and although the SCCA followed a strictly amateur code until 1962, the organization itself was

thoroughly professional. In that first race at Norman, Shelby was helped by the early leader spinning off, but later on the same day he won again, still with the TC but against several much more powerful Jaguar XK120s. As quickly as that, Carroll Shelby was a racing driver, and quite a promising one.

He won again in August, with a borrowed XK120 in Okmulgee, Oklahoma. In November, already attracting driving opportunities from better-funded car owners, he won a 50-mile (80km) race at Caddo Mills, Texas, driving a Cadillac-Allard (as conceived by Tom Cole) owned by wealthy sportsman Charles Brown of Monroe, Louisiana.

Among the people he beat that day was Masten Gregory, from Kansas City, another future Le Mans winner, GP and Indy 500 driver, who became a lifelong friend to Shelby. It was Gregory's first race and, like Shelby, he drove an Allard, in Gregory's case with a Mercury V8. Gregory was famous throughout his racing career for his thick-lensed glasses, but Shelby later described him as 'the fastest American ever to go over there and race a Grand Prix car'. A few years later they would be racing GP cars against each other.

Their backgrounds were very different. Gregory's family made a fortune in the insurance industry and his Allard was paid for from his share of his family inheritance. Shelby, on the other hand, was still barely scratching a living from the farm, and drove throughout the 1953 season as an amateur. Most of the time he drove various examples of the fearsome Cadillac-Allards, first for Charlie Brown, then for Roy Cherryhomes of Jacksboro, Texas – who paid Shelby's expenses (which was a small step in the right direction) while Shelby rewarded him with nine wins from nine starts.

Among those was a race at Eagle Mountain Naval Airbase. Redundant military runways featured in a high proportion of America's early post-war races, not just because there were literally hundreds of them but because of another fortuitous SCCA connection. General Curtis E. LeMay was famous as the man who shaped US bombing strategy through World War II, oversaw the Berlin airlift, and became USAF Chief of Staff in the early 1960s. LeMay was also a huge sports car racing enthusiast, and facilitated access to many disused (and even active) airbases for the SCCA's early races.

Long before Shelby and AC put a Ford V8 into the Ace and created the Cobra, people were putting US V8s into British Allards – in this case a Cadillac engine, with Sydney Allard driving.

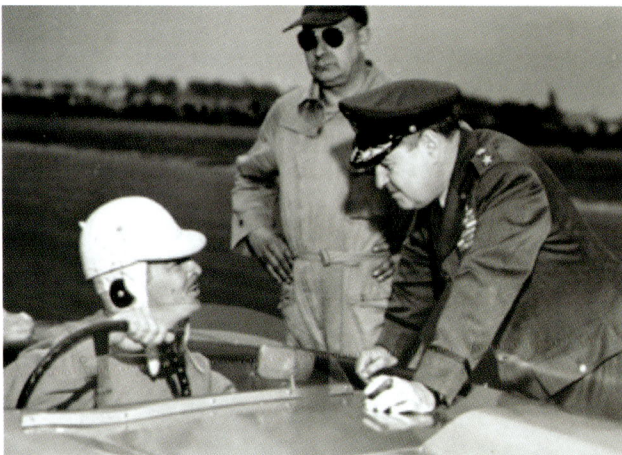

Curtis LeMay was better known as the architect of American air power during World War II, but he was also a committed sports car racing enthusiast, and supporter of the SCCA.

THE SHELBY TRADEMARK

Eagle Mountain was one of those, and it was where Shelby appeared for the first time in what was to become his trademark outfit – his striped dungarees: 'I'd been working on the

First time around: the dungarees in Shelby's
heyday, here in the pit lane at Goodwood.

city, combining two long, parallel out-and-back straights on the Avenida General Paz linked by short 180-degree loops at each end, with a bigger loop part-way along one of the straights into the Autodromo Oscar Alfredo Galvez, in a city park.

Cherryhomes supplied the familiar Cadillac-Allard and paid Shelby's expenses but didn't go to the event, while Shelby's co-driver, airline pilot Dale Duncan (who also happened to be Masten Gregory's brother-in-law) took care of the travel arrangements. Duncan also put out a carburettor fire while the car was in the pits, improvising when no fire extinguisher was available; suffice it to say that the first stage of the fire-fighting involved climbing up onto the bonnet of the car and unbuttoning his overalls...

The race was punctuated by accidents and won by a works Ferrari 375 Plus driven by 1950 World Champion Giuseppe Farina with Umberto Maglioli, at an average of almost 90mph (145km/h). Shelby and Duncan survived to finish tenth overall and to win the amateur division – and the Kimberly Cup, donated to the SCCA by 'Gentleman Jim' Kimberly, millionaire sportsman, racing enthusiast, and the Kimberly of Kimberly-Clark, makers of Kleenex. They finished four places ahead of Gregory, also in his first 'overseas' race. 'Gentleman Jim' was one more member of this early SCCA coterie. As a driver he won the Club's National

farm when I realized I was due to race. It was a hot day so I didn't bother to change. I found the overalls cool and comfortable, and I won the race, too. I became identified with them and after that I just wore them all the time.'

If Shelby dressed like a chicken farmer, he looked increasingly like a serious racing driver. In January 1954 his career took another step with his first race outside North America, in the Mil Kilometres de la Ciudad de Buenos Aires, where Shelby was one of four SCCA drivers invited by the Automobile Club of Argentina.

It was another indicator of the growing revival of motor racing after the War – the first ever South American round of the FIA's World Sports Car Championship and a considerably more important race than anything Shelby had done to date. It ran on a 5.9-mile (9.5km) circuit inside the

Shelby inevitably went through the Allard phase
in his early career, in this case in a typically race-
modified J2X, with first wife Jeanne on the pit crew.

The man who took Shelby to Europe, John Wyer, Aston Martin racing boss and 'Death Ray' even to his friends, for the unflinching stare.

Championship; as SCCA President he was a staunch advocate of the original amateur code – while ensuring that everything he was involved with was ultra-professional.

The Mil Kilometres would be Shelby's last race in Cherryhome's Allard, but the start of something far bigger for his longer-term racing prospects. Again, it involved some Shelby serendipity. Aston Martin works driver (and European rising star) Peter Collins was staying at the same hotel as Shelby, was impressed by his performance (or maybe his dungarees) and introduced him to Aston Martin's visiting race director, John Wyer.

Wyer was sufficiently impressed by what he had seen and heard of Shelby to offer him another big step up, with an expenses-paid drive for Aston Martin at Sebring, Florida, in March 1954 – by any standards, a very serious race.

Sebring, almost inevitably, was based on another massive redundant bomber base (formerly Hendricks Field) and held its first, six-hour race on New Year's Eve 1950. In 1952 it started the tradition of a 12-Hour endurance race, which soon became a round of the Sports Car World Championship, widely regarded as second only to the 24 Hours of Le Mans as a test of car and drivers, and taken very seriously by both American and European teams.

In 1954, Shelby jumped at the opportunity to race there, and although he was forced out when the rear axle broke after seventy-seven laps, he had been quick enough to convince Wyer that he had real potential. What's more, Shelby was now racing against the best drivers in the sport, from Europe as well as the USA. The 1954 Sebring 12-Hour race was won by Stirling Moss and Bill Lloyd in an OSCA entered by Briggs Cunningham; Mike Hawthorn would win in 1955 (in a D-Type Jaguar) and Juan Manuel Fangio in 1956 (for Ferrari) and 1957 (for Maserati) – a very illustrious winners list.

EUROPE CALLS

So Wyer invited Shelby to Europe to drive the Aston DBR, providing he could pay his own expenses; and while he obviously couldn't do that himself, Shelby's growing reputation meant he now knew both Americans and Europeans who might help.

That also meant that the Aston Martin opportunity wasn't Carroll Shelby's only option. At the time he was considering another offer from a west Texan oil millionaire, Guy Mabee. While Shelby didn't take up that offer, it may have planted a seed in his mind. Eight years before the Cobra would appear, Mabee's plan was to build an American sports car to beat the Europeans at their own game. In 1953 he had built a 200mph (320km/h) special for his son Joe to drive at the Bonneville Speed Trials. Part of his plan was to have Shelby develop a road-going sports car around the same basic layout of tubular chassis, front beam axle and a big Chrysler V8. You can certainly see the train of thought.

Bolstered by Jeanne's encouragement in spite of the obvious financial challenges, Shelby chose the Aston Martin deal and the chance to race in Europe – while keeping Mabee in the equation, as he helped Shelby finance the trip, and tentatively agreed to buy an Aston from the works team for Shelby to run in races where the team hadn't entered him themselves. The unspoken potential bonus was that Shelby would be able to pick up ideas for Mabee's planned car from the best that Europe could offer at the time.

In the event, Mabee didn't buy the Aston, and Wyer, fully aware of Shelby's personal financial position, declined his new driver's honourable but totally impracticable offer to buy the car himself. This also said a good deal about the urbane and pragmatic Wyer, who would become arguably the biggest influence of all in Shelby's progression up to and far beyond the Cobra.

RIGHT: **If Shelby hadn't been transported to Europe by Wyer and Aston, his future might have been steered by Guy Mabee, Texan millionaire and builder of racing and record-breaking specials.**

BELOW: **In April 1954, *Motor Racing* magazine marked Shelby's first race in Europe, at Aintree in a DBR3, with the cover photograph recording his second-place finish.**

Leaving Jeanne at home, Shelby arrived in Europe in April 1954 and started his European racing career in an Aston DBR3 in a wet race at Aintree. Finishing second to Duncan Hamilton (who had won Le Mans in 1953) was a respectable result that helped Shelby persuade Wyer to let him race at the biggest endurance race of all, at Le Mans, in June, to partner Belgian journalist and racer Paul Frère (a future winner himself, in 1960).

It wouldn't be an auspicious Le Mans debut for the tall Texan, but through no fault of his own. Le Mans was (and is) the jewel in the global sports car crown, and by 1954 Aston Martin were taking it seriously – though at this stage in their Le Mans campaign they were still overshadowed by Jaguar, Ferrari and potentially by ever-threatening American wild card, Cunningham. They should have faced Maserati, too, but Maserati's works cars were eliminated before they arrived, after a road accident on the way to the race. Expected entries from Lancia and Mercedes-Benz stayed away, too, and Austin-Healey withdrew in protest at the inclusion of 'prototypes' in the entry, which made it virtually impossible for the smaller, production-based teams to expect much success.

What was left was enough to make a strong race of it: Aston Martin entered four works DB3Ss (two open and two

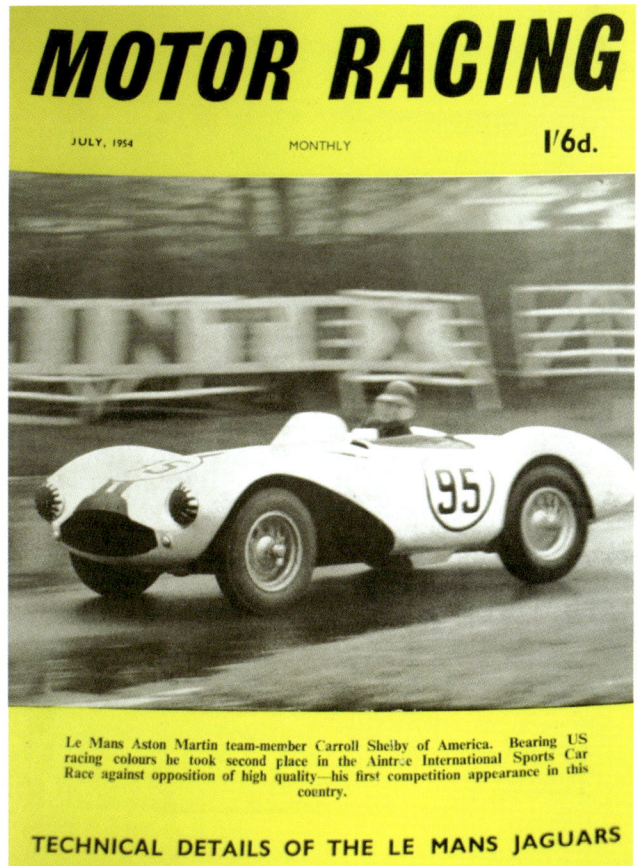

MOTOR RACING
JULY, 1954   MONTHLY   1'6d.

Le Mans Aston Martin team-member Carroll Shelby of America. Bearing US racing colours he took second place in the Aintree International Sports Car Race against opposition of high quality—his first competition appearance in this country.

TECHNICAL DETAILS OF THE LE MANS JAGUARS

closed cars) plus one 'Lagonda' (effectively a V12-engined DB3S), and there was also a privately entered DB2/4. They faced three of Jaguar's ground-breaking D-Types, plus a privately entered C-Type, and five Ferraris – including one entered by Cunningham alongside his two C-4Rs.

It rained for most of the race, often torrentially, and no one got close to the battle between Jaguar and Ferrari, eventually won (by just 2.5 miles/4km) by Ferrari durability over Jaguar speed. None of the five Astons (or the Lagonda) finished. Shelby's Le Mans baptism had a particularly

JOHN WYER – THE MAN FROM ASTON

By recruiting Shelby into the Aston Martin team and bringing him to Europe, John Wyer laid one of the key foundation stones in the Cobra story; and he would continue to play an influential part in Shelby's life through the Cobra's birth and beyond.

Had it not been for Wyer, it's highly unlikely that Shelby would have come to Europe in 1954, and while he might have joined forces with Guy Mabee and forged a different path in America, it wouldn't have ended with the authentic Cobra.

If Wyer hadn't been as influential as he was, Shelby wouldn't have made the European contacts that he did. By the time Shelby went to Aston Martin, Wyer was already well established there – a hard taskmaster, nicknamed 'Death Ray' for his famously hard stare, but undoubtedly one of motor sport's most respected team managers.

He was born in 1909 in Kidderminster, in the British Midlands, where his father was a Sunbeam distributor; in 1927 Wyer was apprenticed to Sunbeam (who only three years earlier had been GP winners), sparking his love of motor racing while still at school.

Aston Martin entered Wyer's world in 1947, after he joined race-preparation company Monaco Engineering in Watford, where one of his first jobs was team-managing new Monaco director Dudley Folland's 2-litre Aston in sports car races around Europe. In 1949 that took Wyer to Le Mans for the first time, when Folland raced his Aston with Anthony Heal, of the Heal's store family. That introduced Wyer to new Aston Martin proprietor David Brown, who in March 1950 offered him the job of racing manager for Aston and Lagonda. What was meant to be a one-year appointment would last for more than thirteen – right up to 1963.

As Development Engineer, Wyer oversaw road car design, as well as a fledgling racing programme based on race-prepared road cars. By 1951 (having recruited pre-war Auto Union designer Eberan von Eberhorst), Wyer had evolved purpose-built cars like the DB3 and DB3S. With right-hand man Reg Parnell he also recruited many fine drivers, including Stirling Moss, Peter Collins, Tony Brooks, Roy Salvadori – and Shelby.

Limited time and resources often forced conflicts between Aston's racing and road car needs (even the ill-starred GP car), so the 1950s were rollercoaster years. The DB2 came third at Le Mans in 1951, but it was four years before Aston had another finisher there. Other high spots included GT class wins in the Mille Miglia in 1951 and 1952, a hat-trick of Goodwood Nine-Hour wins, three Nürburgring 1000km wins, second places at Sebring in 1953, Le Mans in 1955, 1956 and 1958, a 1953 TT one-two, even numerous rally wins. Through it all, though, Le Mans continued to elude them – until 1959.

That was the glory year for Wyer and Aston, as Salvadori and Shelby (five years after Wyer first brought him to Europe) finally won the 24 Hours outright in the DBR1, and steered Aston to the World Sports Car Championship – helped by another win in the Tourist Trophy, at Goodwood, and victory for Stirling Moss in the Nürburgring 1000km with a borrowed DBR1 supported by Wyer.

Winning let David Brown withdraw Aston Martin from racing at the top before the costs hurt even more, but left Wyer with a gap in his life, not helped by the frustration of running Aston's road-car side. In April 1963, during a business trip to California, he visited Shelby (supposedly just socially), and in Shelby's office he met Ray Geddes, the young Ford executive overseeing the commercial links between Ford and Shelby. Geddes was already involved in Ford's planned entry into motor sport, and persuaded Wyer to talk to his Ford colleague Don Frey. In Wyer's words, 'that decision was to change my life'.

When Wyer's Aston contract expired in June 1963, he didn't renew it, but almost immediately joined Ford's multi-million-dollar GT40 programme – squarely aimed at Le Mans. Wyer oversaw the programme from concept, through creating the car (in the UK), its difficult Le Mans debut in 1964 (where Salvadori pulled out of the driving squad before the race), via an even more difficult 1965, to develop the cars to the point where they finally won, in 1966, with Bruce McLaren and Chris Amon. That was after a terse memo circulated in Ford HQ in Dearborn

dramatic ending. During the night, he brought his open car (in the same white and blue American racing colours as the Cunninghams) into the pits to complain of a wobble in the steering. When the mechanics jacked the car up, a front wheel fell off, taking the broken stub-axle with it – possibly

saying simply 'Henry expects you to win'. It should also be pointed out that the first win didn't come from Wyer's MkI GT40s but from the MkII, developed by Shelby American and engine specialists Holman & Moody.

Shelby, while in effect racing against Wyer, remained a close ally, co-ordinating European and US elements of the GT40 programme while his US-based team led technical development of the car. In 1965 the GT40s appeared in Shelby colours, while Shelby worked with Wyer on building the 'customer' GT40s, until Shelby left the programme in 1967 – when Ford withdrew from sports car racing after their second Le Mans win.

Wyer's Ford contract ended in 1966, but he stayed close to the programme, and to Shelby. With John Willment, Wyer formed JW Automotive and took over Ford Advanced Vehicles, to supply GT40 technical support for the next three years and to support private GT40 owners in international sports car racing, again regularly in contact with Shelby.

At Sebring in January 1966 (before Ford achieved its first Le Mans win) Wyer was introduced to a potential GT40 road car customer, Grady Davis; and although it meant little to Wyer at the time, Davis was Executive Vice President of the Gulf Oil Company.

From being a potential customer, Gulf became Wyer's patron. Within a year, Wyer and Davis evolved a Gulf-sponsored sports car programme, wearing the iconic pale blue and orange livery. Wyer revelled in Grady's enthusiasm, and Gulf's rapid decision-making allowed him quickly to evolve the distinctive, narrow-roof Mirage from the GT40, which became a great endurance car in its own right. When Wyer and Gulf did win Le Mans for the first time, in 1968, it was with a 'conventional' GT40 driven by Rodriguez and Bianchi. They won their second Le Mans in 1969, with Ickx and Oliver in another GT40, and added a third in 1975, with Derek Bell, Ickx, and the Gulf-Ford Cosworth GR8.

Having also been instrumental in the Gulf-Porsche Le Mans campaign (made famous in the Steve McQueen film *Le Mans*), Wyer retired in 1976 to Scottsdale, Arizona, which was kinder to his lifelong asthma than Europe, and died in 1989.

Shelby's first taste of the greatest endurance race in the world, Le Mans, was in 1954, with the Aston Martin in white and blue American racing colours. It was an interesting debut.

as a result of Shelby having been off the circuit and into the scenery earlier in the race.

But Shelby started to come good in Europe, and even to see some reward for the adventure. Sharing a 'semi-private' Aston with regular team driver Graham Whitehead at the Supercortemaggiore GP at Monza, he finished fifth and won his first professional purse, $2,000 – enough to send something home even after his expenses. His final outing in his first European season was at Silverstone in July, when he finished third behind Collins and Roy Salvadori in an Aston one-two-three. Importantly, he'd done enough to justify Wyer's backing.

On the down side, by the time he returned to America in August the Mabee project was on hold so Shelby was in effect unemployed, until Cherryhomes temporarily came to the rescue by paying Shelby to drive his Jaguar C-Type in two late-season races.

FOR THE RECORD

Fortunately, Shelby's new European contacts then offered another lifeline, as Donald Healey asked Shelby to join a record-breaking programme at Bonneville, whose driving team would also include no less a motor sport giant than

A record-chasing expedition to Bonneville in 1954 started a lifelong friendship between Shelby and car-builder Donald Healey, on the right, in overalls.

former outright Land Speed Record-holder Captain George Eyston – who had recorded over 357mph (575km/h) at Bonneville in 1938.

That was with the mighty six-wheeler 36.5-litre Thunderbolt streamliner, but the Healey team would be chasing class records with the production-based Healey 100S, in supercharged and unsupercharged forms and in one car with a special streamliner body. Shelby had a strong friendship with Healey and once described him as 'a kindred spirit'. The Bonneville partnership was a huge success: the team took more than seventy Class D records and Healey himself joined the exclusive Bonneville '200mph Club' – interestingly enough alongside Joe Mabee's earlier qualification in the Mabee Special.

In a different world, Shelby's friendship with Donald Healey might have opened the door for Healey, not AC, to build the Cobra, but by the time the opportunity arose, Healey was tied to the British Motor Corporation, and it wasn't BMC's kind of deal.

Shelby did carry on driving for Healey, though, sharing a works car with another of the Bonneville record-breaking team, Roy Jackson-Moore, in the 1954 Carrera Panamericana road race. By general consensus this near 2,000-mile (3,200km) road race, conceived in 1950 to celebrate the opening of the Pan-American Highway, was one of the toughest, most dangerous races in the world, as Shelby found out the hard way.

He arrived too late to practise, or even properly to recce the challenging route through the mountainous country on the borders of Mexico. The only experience Shelby had of the course before he started the race was driving a short section of it in the wrong direction from Mexico City to the start in Tuxtla Gutiérrez.

The 1954 Carrera Panamericana would be the last, partly because it had already claimed so many lives itself in just five years, but the 1955 Le Mans disaster was the final straw, bringing a lot of rethinking into motor sport at the time. By 1954, as European teams like Ferrari, Lancia and Mercedes-Benz had started to contest the originally rather low-key Carrera, speeds on the almost completely unprotected public roads were becoming quite terrifying. In 1954, eventual race winner Umberto Maglioli in a Ferrari completed the final, 227-mile (365km) stage at an average of 138mph (222km/h).

By that time, Shelby was already long gone, and lucky not to become another tragic Panamericana statistic. Just 109 miles (175km) into the race he crashed heavily into a concrete road marker north of Oaxaca. The car went end-over-end several times and most of the passenger side, including the wheels and metal tonneau cover, were torn away. The only reason Jackson-Moore was not in the car at the time was that having frightened each other to death even getting to the start, the drivers had agreed (as the rules allowed) to fly between their driving stints rather than passenger each other.

Shelby was seriously hurt. He had badly broken his arm and shattered his elbow, but had to wait seven hours for an ambulance to reach the remote spot and take him to hospital. While he was waiting he was consoled by two spectating girls from Brooklyn who had seen the accident, and by several locals offering enough beer and Mexican brandy to take at least some of the pain away. Some time afterwards Shelby apologized to Donald Healey, joking that an attractive Mexican girl had caught his eye. But there wasn't much to joke about, as the shattered elbow in particular would give rise to complications even after Shelby had been taken home. He spent eight months either undergoing operations or in plaster casts before he was anything like properly healed.

To add insult to injury (literally) the Mexican authorities refused to let Shelby out of the country for a full week after the accident. They needed him to explain the whereabouts of two missing Austin-Healey wheels that were on the import documents for the car but evidently not on what little was left of it when it was presented for export.

Remarkably, his slow recovery didn't stop Shelby racing; by January 1955 he was driving again, cast and all. Ever resourceful, he devised a system of swapping his full cast for a lightweight glass-fibre one just before a race, with the hand of his damaged arm taped to the steering wheel for support. In March, still not fully healed, he co-drove a 3-litre Ferrari 750 Monza with American future world champion Phil Hill in the Sebring 12 Hours – universally acknowledged as one of the most physically punishing races on the calendar. They actually thought they had won, but after a protest from Jaguar and eight days of checking the lap charts by the race authorities, they were confirmed in second place, by just 25 seconds, although they did win the Index of Performance.

FACE TO FACE WITH FERRARI

Fortunately for Shelby, he found another important American sponsor (and another kindred spirit), an extremely wealthy west-coast construction man and racing enthusiast, Tony Paravano. Paravano was also a prolific buyer of Ferraris, and had decided to add maybe fifteen more to the ten he already

Shelby drove an Austin-Healey in the Carrera Panamericana road race in 1954, and was lucky to survive this very large accident, costing him eight months of recuperation.

owned. He wanted Shelby to race them, and told him he could decide which was most suitable for what event, on a race-by-race basis. By September, Shelby was well established with Paravano, and they set off to Europe together, on one of Paravano's regular Ferrari-buying expeditions.

Now Paravano was clearly a good Ferrari customer, generally thought of as a good man, who later became a strong champion for professional drivers' rights. But like many others before and after him, Paravano was apparently not Enzo Ferrari's type. In particular, Paravano was guilty of the ultimate sin in Enzo's eyes, of modifying both bodywork and mechanical underpinnings of his Ferraris if he thought he could squeeze more out of them. They had 'a full and frank discussion' and Paravano took his not-inconsiderable custom down the road to Maserati, who were a bit less sensitive.

So Shelby's first direct experience of Enzo Ferrari was an interesting one, and would have considerable echoes in his own later dealings with the autocratic Commendatore. In short, Shelby immediately saw Ferrari as arrogant and domineering, the sort of man it would be very satisfying to beat with an all-American sports car sometime in the future.

His relationship with Paravano was a lot happier, and he drove all kinds of cars for him during 1955, not just the Ferraris – including a Formula 1 Maserati 250F in the Syracuse Grand Prix in October, where he finished sixth and became a genuine GP driver.

In sports cars, Shelby drove a Ferrari 121LM at Oulton Park but retired; and his co-driver Gino Munaron crashed their Ferrari 750 Monza in the Targa Florio. But Shelby was also free to drive for others, and did, finishing ninth overall and winning the 1500cc class in the Tourist Trophy at Dundrod – in a Porsche 550 Spyder shared with his old friend Masten Gregory, also now well established in Europe.

Back in the USA, Shelby won a race at the Seattle Seafair with one of Paravano's Ferraris, adding to a tally of more than ten US race wins in 1955. Then he ended this season just as he had the previous one, with a large accident. This one was at Palm Springs and at least Shelby wasn't hurt, but Paravano's Ferrari didn't come out of it nearly so well, after climbing over the back of an Oldsmobile Special.

Nevertheless, 1956 would be the biggest year so far for Shelby, further increasing his reputation with many good results, and his experience by driving an incredible list of cars. His latest benefactor was John Edgar, a son of the family that owned the Hobart Manufacturing Co., world-famous manufacturers of weight scales and associated equipment. Edgar also made a substantial income from other

investments, and was another Ferrari enthusiast. Shelby started driving for him in May 1956 and at various times in 1956 drove a catalogue of Ferraris, including a 4.9-litre 375 Plus, 2-litre Testarossa 500, 4.4-litre 121LM, and another single-seater, Luigi Chinetti's ex-Formula 1, ex-Indianapolis 375, which Shelby used to win the Mount Washington and Grant's Despair hillclimbs.

FRIENDS IN HIGH PLACES

He won at Pebble Beach and Fort Worth in Ferraris. He also won races in an Alfa Romeo Veloce special for Max Hoffman – another of America's legendary links with Europe. With his main dealership in Park Avenue, New York, Austrian-born American citizen Hoffman was a huge enthusiast for European sports cars and was almost single-handedly responsible for opening the import market for several major marques after the war, including Porsche, VW, BMW and Mercedes. A flamboyant salesman, brilliant businessman and outstanding judge of what the market wanted, by the early 1950s Hoffman was importing around half of Porsche's total production into America, with a corresponding influence on what kind of car they built and a strong friendship with the family.

While Ferry Porsche was on a visit to America around 1952, Hoffman suggested that the company needed a proper badge, and sketched one on the back of a napkin in a New York restaurant. It incorporated the crest of the house of Wurttemberg, the black prancing horse of the city of Stuttgart and the Porsche name. Tidied up by Porsche themselves, it became the official Porsche emblem, and still is. It was Hoffman who suggested a sporty special edition of the 356 for America, which became the iconic Speedster.

Most famously of all, it was Hoffman who suggested to Mercedes-Benz in 1953 that they turn

John Edgar was another of Shelby's wealthy US backers, providing all kinds of Ferraris in the mid-1950s when Shelby was driving almost anything with wheels in both Europe and the USA.

Shelby the Aston Martin team driver at Sebring in 1956, where he finished fourth with Roy Salvadori – his future Le Mans winning partner.

their 300SL racer into a road-going supercar (arguably the first true supercar). He countered Mercedes' arguments that the cost would be absolutely prohibitive by placing a firm order for 1,000 cars if they would build them. That's how the legendary 300SL Gullwing came to make its debut at the 1954 New York Motor Show.

This was the kind of company that Carroll Shelby, son of a Texas mailman and sometime chicken farmer, was now moving in: Kimberly, Mabee, Paravano, Edgar, Hoffman – men with money and influence, but also men with an enthusiasm for all kinds of racing, for sports cars in general, and for European sports cars in particular.

Unlike all but a handful of American drivers, Shelby's own European experience was also growing. In 1956 he renewed his contract with Aston Martin, and opened his 1956 season by finishing fourth at Sebring in March, sharing a works DB3S with Roy Salvadori – another driver who would become a major figure in Shelby's story.

Then, having safely and successfully negotiated around twenty races during the season, Shelby completed an

unfortunate hat-trick by rounding out a third successive year with a fairly serious accident – this time breaking his shoulder while playing beach football with a coconut during the annual Nassau Speed Weeks in December.

Importantly, Shelby was becoming 'known', and was named *Sports Illustrated*'s 1956 Sports Car Driver of the Year, with his photograph on the magazine's cover.

He was doing a modest amount of promotional work and paid tyre-testing as well as racing, but combined with his frequent travelling, still wasn't making a regular enough income to avoid the inevitable strains on his marriage and family life.

That led to another major step in the road towards the Cobra, as Shelby also opened a car dealership in 1956 – Carroll Shelby Sports Cars Inc., in Dallas.

Yet again, he had well-connected backing, from Dick Hall, an oil man from Abilene, Texas, whose brother Jim Hall later built the Chaparral sports racing cars that gave America some high-profile racing success in Europe at much the same time as the Cobra.

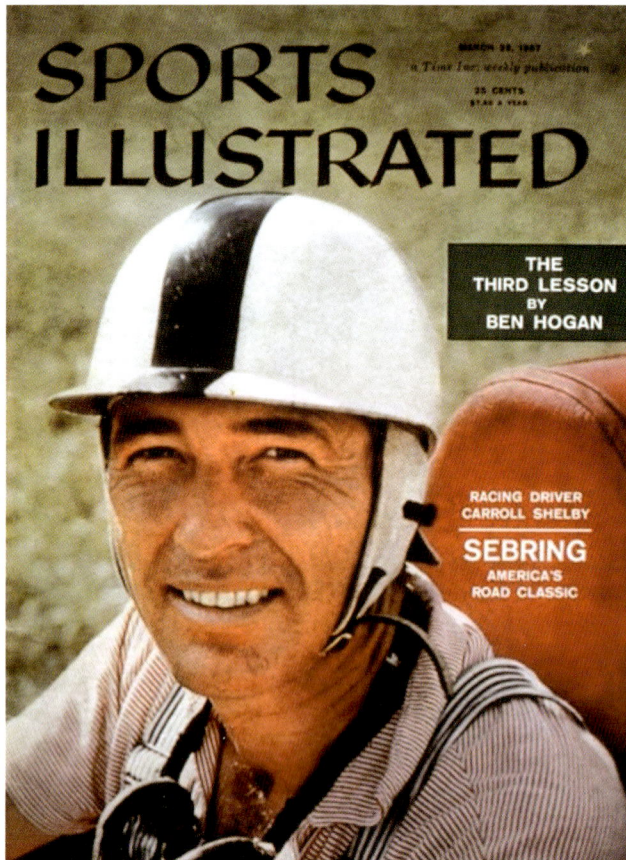

By 1957, Shelby had achieved enough to be recognized by America's sporting press.

Shelby knew Hall through driving his Ferrari Monza in a couple of races (everybody with any money and a fondness for sports cars in 1950s America had at least one Ferrari), and they had talked about getting into the sports car sales business in Dallas, where there was little or no serious competition. Of course, they went for European cars, including MGs and Healeys at the lower end and Maseratis on the more exotic spectrum. They even sold Rolls-Royces from their premises at 5611 Yale.

Arguably, even at that early stage, Shelby should have capitalized more on his growing name, but in a familiar pattern he never found time among his other commitments, especially the racing, to devote more of it to the fledgling business. Instead, in 1957 he started racing again for John Edgar, and took second place (behind multiple world champion Juan Manuel Fangio's Maserati) in Edgar's 375 Plus in the inaugural Cuban GP.

FERRARI'S DARKER SIDE

Shelby had already been back to Europe, not to drive but on another Ferrari-buying foray for Edgar, and another confrontation with Ferrari himself. This time, while discussing the possibility of a works drive for Ferrari, Shelby discovered at first hand that in spite of everything, Ingegnere Ferrari had little respect for Shelby's credentials and the attempt to forge a possible working relationship was therefore almost entirely one-sided. According to legend, Shelby walked out on the conversation with the parting shot that one day he would be back 'to whip Ferrari's ass'. It may also have been another of those pivotal days in the journey to the Cobra.

Lack of empathy with Ferrari notwithstanding, 1957 became Shelby's best year to date as a driver, albeit with mixed emotions. For openers, he shared a works Maserati 300S with Salvadori at Sebring but was disqualified for refuelling too early; and soon after, the possibility of a GP drive for Maserati in Europe (alongside Moss and Fangio) fizzled out. But back home, mainly with Edgar's new 300S and 450S Maseratis, Shelby had a great year, winning nineteen races

Alongside the racing, Shelby was building his business base, including his first sports car dealership, Carroll Shelby Sports Cars, in Dallas (and apparently selling Morris Minors!).

Shelby based his racing school, and original Cobra headquarters, at Riverside Raceway, created by John Edgar. This is a parade lap on the opening day – with an Ace in the pack.

and his second SCCA Championship. He also went one step further in the *Sports Illustrated* pantheon, as overall Driver of the Year.

His racing season, however, came to a premature and dramatic end on the first lap of practice for the inaugural meeting at the new Riverside circuit in September. Riverside was another project backed by Edgar and largely hacked out of the rocky Southern California desert by his construction company, John Edgar Enterprises, as a 'proper' European-style road-racing course, very different from the old, flat airfield circuits.

Shelby survived the accident and admitted it was down to simple driver error, but he suffered severe back and facial injuries and had to have three vertebrae fused together by his doctors, and seventy-two stitches in his face, mainly tacking his nose back on, followed by a long regime of plastic surgery. Motor racing in the 1950s really was dangerous.

That was in September, but incredibly Shelby was racing again by November, back at Riverside in the same (rebuilt) car. And he won, spectacularly fighting back through the field after a first-lap spin, to beat Dan Gurney's Ferrari.

But the end of that season was the (amicable) end of Shelby's association with Edgar, while his marriage to Jeanne was also heading towards eventual divorce in 1960. He remarried very soon afterwards to actress Jan Harrison, but that marriage only lasted a matter of months. Against that background, he started to look back to Europe – this time, he

later admitted, as much as a means of studying sports car design as simply for racing.

Maybe he was already becoming more cynical about that. Early in 1958 he was prevented from running in the Indianapolis 500 by a rule that said two 'rookie' drivers couldn't qualify for the race in the same car. The owner of the car that was supposed to give Shelby his Indy debut never intended to race it himself but had already taken the obligatory 'rookie' tests in it, so that was the end of Shelby's opportunity. Having failed to shift the organizers' position, Shelby explained what he thought of them and their rules in basic Anglo-Saxon terms, and never went back to The Brickyard (at least as a driver).

He did go back to Aston Martin, although he had a disappointing year with them. At Sebring he retired with a broken gear linkage; he took third place at Spa, retired from the Nürburgring 1000km with another transmission problem, took third again in the Tourist Trophy at Goodwood, but missed Le Mans because of illness.

With his marriage failing, he lived most of the season in Europe – not in Britain for the Aston Martin connection, but in Modena, in the heart of the Italian motor sport industry. He learned to speak Italian, and drove Maserati 250Fs in a couple more Grands Prix for the Centro Sud team and for Temple Buell, with a best of fourth place in the Italian GP at Monza, where he shared the car with old friend Masten Gregory, as you could in those days.

Possibly distancing himself from home, he also sold his interest in Carroll Shelby Sports Cars to the Halls, although he continued his friendship with them, and was happy for them to continue using the company's original name.

1959 – LE MANS WINNER

Against all this, Shelby was happy to stay in Europe for 1959, and it was one of the most important decisions he ever made. He occasionally drove Buell's GP Maserati again, without achieving much as the car was increasingly outdated, but he also had another Grand Prix opportunity, as Aston Martin made a brief foray with the DBR4/250 F1 car.

In his autobiography, *The Certain Sound: Thirty Years of Motor Racing*, Shelby's mentor John Wyer wrote 'David Brown had always wanted a Formula One car and was beginning to be a bit restive about the success being achieved by his fellow millionaire Tony Vandervell, with the Vanwall'. By the end of 1957 it was an open secret that Aston, under Wyer's guidance, was working on a GP car, but the project wouldn't be a great success. In a nutshell, the single-seaters were essentially based on the sports cars (certainly in terms

The biggest day of Shelby's racing career, outright winner of Le Mans in 1959, with Roy Salvadori. Dungarees on top of the world, Aston Martin boss, David Brown, behind the girl.

Aston Martin had a brief foray into F1, and took Shelby with them, but the front-engined **DBR4/250** was outdated even before it appeared, and was quietly retired.

of engines) but held back by the priority of making the sports car programme work.

The first version of the DBR4 was testing by New Year 1958, and Wyer always believed that had it been ready to race that year it could have given the dominant Ferraris and Vanwalls a run for their money; but proprietor David Brown insisted on concentrating on the sports cars, where new rules had opened the genuine possibility of winning at Le Mans.

The GP car appeared in 1959, with a full programme planned after a non-championship debut in the International Trophy race at Silverstone, where Salvadori finished a promisingly close second to Brabham's Cooper – a result that was flattering only to deceive.

The two F1 cars were to be driven by Salvadori and Shelby, but they struggled from the start, missing races and having all manner of problems in the ones they got to. Shelby's only finishes were eighth in Portugal and tenth in Italy. An updated car (DBR5) appeared for 1960 but it was too little, too late, against the new rear-engined generation.

Shelby had already stopped driving it by then, but sports cars were a completely different story, and 1959 was the pinnacle of Shelby's (and Aston's) racing career.

For all concerned, the highlight was Le Mans in June, when Aston had their revenge for recent near misses, including second places overall in 1955, 1956 and 1958. In classic late-1950s Le Mans style, Shelby and Salvadori, sharing one of the three works DBR1s, committed to not being the fastest pairing in the race but consistently quick enough, and there when it finished, as faster cars eliminated themselves.

Moss, in the fastest DBR1, powered into an early lead, goading the Ferraris into self-harm, although the initial Aston-Ferrari battle lasted well into the race. By around one-third distance, with the Moss/Fairman Aston slowed by engine problems and most of the other hares faltering or failing in one way or another, Shelby and Salvadori had a two-lap lead from the sole surviving works Ferrari. Overnight, the Aston had what the drivers thought was a chassis problem but which turned out to be tyre-shredding; and by early morning the Ferrari had clawed into a three-lap lead – with the Trintignant/Frère Aston backing up in third.

Shelby and Salvadori stuck to Plan A, quick but cautious, the Ferrari faltered with barely four hours to go, the Aston cruised back into the lead and stayed there until 4pm – with their team-mates, Trintignant and Frère, an equally self-disciplined second.

The 2-litre class-winner was a much-modified AC Ace, and it's quite possible that Shelby, tousle-haired, in his distinctive chicken-farmer striped dungarees, hugging the girls and swigging champagne from the bottle, took a good look at the AC.

It was by far the biggest win of his career and by far the biggest pay-day. Having agreed before the race to pool whatever winnings they jointly delivered and share them out equally, each Aston driver took home around $8,000. The win also brought a brief blaze of international celebrity and a new sideline for Shelby endorsing various products. That included some clean-cut ads for the Gillette razor company, some of them dubbed from Shelby's Texan drawl into comic-book English. They were well-paid and fun to do, but short-lived. More important, Shelby, as with the Ace, was now diligently filing away ideas and contacts for what was a coalescing long-term plan – to be a sports car manufacturer.

CALLING TIME

That overlapped with his retirement from racing, as 1960 would be Shelby's last season as an active driver. He had, more or less unnoticed, driven most of Le Mans 1959 fighting the effects of dysentery. More seriously, he had driven with a nitroglycerine capsule under his tongue – an emergency back-up in case of any recurrence of his still on-going heart problems (although he may have forgotten to mention that to the team).

Shelby at his aggressive best, right on the limit in his final race for Aston Martin, at Goodwood in 1959, where the Tourist Trophy decided the Sports Car Manufacturers Championship. The car won the race, but Stirling Moss had taken it over from Shelby after a pit fire had sidelined his own DBR1. Aston won the championship.

Shelby did some races with more conventional medication in 1960, including winning with a Maserati T61 Birdcage at Riverside in May and Castle Rock in June en route to the USRRC Drivers' Championship. He drove all sorts of other cars, including Lance Reventlow's Scarab, another all-American attempt at beating the Europeans at their own game. But his heart problems were becoming more insistent with the continuous strain of racing, general overwork and the combination of family and financial pressures. It was time to stop.

He took the plunge in December, after finishing fifth in the Riverside GP with the Birdcage. He retired with few regrets and plenty of plans, especially for his sports car project.

With that in mind, and with his divorce finalized, he had moved to California, largely to be near the hot-rod/custom-car building community where there was the talent and facilities to build his planned car to his own specifications. He had a small but growing Goodyear racing-tyre distributorship, and shared workshop space in legendary hot-rod builder Dean Moon's tuning establishment. It was space enough to work on turning his ideas into reality – an inexpensive US sports car to compete with the best European imports. In time, maybe even the fastest sports car in the world.

His contacts list continued growing. Setting up the Carroll Shelby School of High Performance Driving, at Riverside, he employed Pete Brock and John Timanus as instructors, both with their parts to play very soon now in the Cobra story. Most vitally of all, in 1961, through his Goodyear racing-tyre connections, Shelby was about to have a chance meeting with a Ford racing engineer who later turned out to have the key to what would become the Shelby AC/Cobra Powered by Ford. The pieces were falling into place.

CHAPTER TWO

A SPORTING HERITAGE

By the time Carroll Shelby walked away from life as a racing driver, AC Cars (as it had become) had been building motor vehicles for almost sixty years, and had become known for some excellent sporting models. It was still a small company, however, surviving rather than thriving, having been propped up for a long time by products far removed from sports cars. Shelby, with time on his hands and ideas for a particular kind of car, needed a partner like AC; but AC, with their prospects drastically damaged by the loss of a key supplier, equally urgently needed a saviour like Shelby and the connections he could bring.

The relationship that developed between Shelby and later incarnations of AC Cars in particular would become turbulent, but without the mix of AC's sporting background and Shelby's timely mission to find a collaborator, the Cobra would never have happened as it did.

How it all began. The Autocarrier was a practical, affordable three-wheel alternative to the four-wheel delivery van, and sold around the world – in this case in Australia.

AC's roots were far from either Texas or world title-winning sports cars. When Autocars and Accessories Ltd was founded in West Norwood (near the iconic Crystal Palace in southeast London), in 1904, the motorcar was in its infancy. And the enterprise didn't start with passenger cars, sporting or otherwise. They first built the Autocarrier, a small, low-cost, three-wheeled delivery truck, as an alternative to the horse and cart for small businesses who didn't need or couldn't afford a four-wheel van.

THE BUTCHER AND THE ENGINEER

The unlikely partnership behind the company was John Weller, a talented engineer, and John Portwine, owner of a chain of butchers' shops. Portwine provided the initial £200 working capital and could obviously make good use of the Autocarrier for his own shops; Weller had already designed and built a motorcycle, plus the technically interesting 20HP 4-cylinder Hitchon-Weller car, exhibited at the nearby Crystal Palace Motor Show in 1903. It was later built by the Hitchon Gear and Automobile Co of Accrington, Lancashire, and sold under the name Globe – but soon sidelined by Weller's partnership with Portwine.

Weller's Autocarrier tri-van was simple, but ideal for purpose. It had two, tiller-steered wheels at the front, under cycle-type mudguards flanking a spacious carrying box. The single rear wheel (again with simple cycle mudguard) was driven through a hub-mounted two-speed epicyclic gearbox and clutch, by a long chain from the air-cooled 631cc single-cylinder engine, mounted under the driver's exposed and rudimentary bench seat.

It sold well, priced from £80, with customers including the Great Western Railway Co., Associated Newspapers in Fleet Street, and well-known London stores Selfridges and Maples. Goodyear used the Autocarrier for delivering

The Sociable was the passenger-carrying version of the Autocarrier, and first of the AC sporting line in this two-seat 'forecar' layout.

THE A.C. TRICAR.

tyres to wealthy automobile owners, and one customer built a fleet of more than seventy Autocarriers. It even found an export market, with sales as far flung as China and Argentina.

The AC initials first appeared in 1907, when the company was renamed Auto Carriers Ltd – the first of many changes of company identity over the decades to come. A year later,

the partners expanded into the passenger-car market – a modest beginning, with a passenger-carrying version of the Autocarrier, the AC Sociable.

The first versions, with simple basketwork bodywork, had a forward-facing passenger seat where the carrying box normally sat, ahead of a motorcycle-type saddle (instead of the basic bench) for the driver, and tiller steering. That

A long road ahead to the Cobra, but the Sociable tricar was a useful tool in early Trials.

With full weather protection, the Sociable was a very acceptable family runabout, with the tax advantages of prevailing tricar legislation, and an enthusiastic following.

continued when the passenger was relocated alongside the driver, with a footwell where the original seat had been, but still with essentially the same three-wheel, rear-drive layout.

The Autocarrier and Sociable sold side by side until the outbreak of World War I in 1914, in sufficient numbers to let the company grow quite substantially. By the time it was reorganized again as Auto Carriers (1911) Ltd, capital had grown to £25,000, and the same year (1911) the company moved to bigger premises in Thames Ditton, Surrey. They would still be based there as the Cobra story evolved, and into the early 1980s.

The move to Thames Ditton was partly prompted by considerable demand for the versatile and robust Autocarrier from the British army. In August 1910 *Motor Cycling* featured an Autocarrier adapted for military purposes; and the 25th London Cyclist Regiment acquired a small fleet, some equipped with Maxim guns, some as ammunition carriers.

FROM THREE WHEELS TO FOUR

The three-wheel Autocarrier stayed in production until 1915; but by 1913 AC had added their first four-wheel offering, a pretty and quite sporty light-car (in the tax-advantaged regulatory meaning), powered by a French-made 10HP 1094cc 4-cylinder Fivet proprietary engine. Reflecting Weller's talent for innovation, it had an aluminium-cased three-speed gearbox in unit with the back axle, and a disc-type transmission brake.

Fewer than 100 had been built before the war halted passenger car production, but the company continued its growth, making shells and fuses for the military, as well as special versions of the Autocarrier for use in the field in the early years.

They announced their first postwar car a couple of weeks ahead of the Armistice, in October 1918, and were ready to resume production as soon as hostilities ended. Their ambition had clearly survived the war as well as their factory. When the car went into production in 1919 it was similar to the pre-war four-wheeler but with a larger Fivet engine. That lasted only as long as the supply of engines from the Paris Billancourt factory, which wasn't long, then AC switched to a British-built 1.5-litre 4-cylinder 11.9HP Anzani unit.

Much as Shelby would eventually give a lifeline to AC, AC gave a lifeline to the struggling British Anzani. AC's initial order for 2,000 engines gave Anzani urgently needed funds, while Weller and Portwine became directors of British Anzani, as well as of AC. That lasted until September 1922, by which time the founders had been joined on the AC board by new directors S.F. Edge, Lt Col. John S. Napier and Thomas Gillett.

That was a defining move for AC's future, as all three of the new directors had decidedly sporting inclinations. Australian-born Selwyn Francis Edge had been one of the biggest names in the early motoring world. Living in Britain since he was three (in 1871), Edge had become a pioneer bicycle racer, pioneer motorist, racing driver, record breaker and speedboat racer. But he didn't compete only for fun, he was widely credited as the British motor industry's first public relations specialist, promoting everything he did with a rare fervour. Much of that was with Napier cars, Edge

The next inevitable step was from three wheels to four, and had happened before the outbreak of World War I with the 1913 10HP, the next link in the chain.

AC probably wouldn't have survived the turbulent 1920s without the support of Selwyn Francis Edge (in the car), a controversial figure, but staunch supporter of AC's sporting direction.

having had a close (but often acrimonious) relationship with Napier since the turn of the century, when he was also credited with creating the first 6-cylinder automobile engine, underpinning all Napier's early achievements.

He took part in the 1900 1000-Miles Trial, in four Gordon Bennett Cup races (winning outright in 1902), and set single-handed 24-hour distance records at Brooklands in 1907. His stormy relationship with Napier officially came to an end in 1912, but stipulated that Edge couldn't be involved with any other motor manufacturer for seven years. During that time (most of it conveniently covered by the war), Edge became Controller of Military Machinery to the Ministry of Munitions, with distant echoes of Shelby, as a gentleman pig-farmer in Sussex.

In his military role he may have noticed the Autocarrier, but he certainly noticed AC, and started to buy a growing shareholding as soon as his Napier severance terms allowed. Edge, Napier and Gillett first joined the AC board in February 1921, and by that year AC was quite a large company, with 900 employees and capital of £330,000.

A SPORTING TURN

After Weller and Portwine resigned in 1922 (Weller

citing 'irreconcilable differences' with the new regime), Edge was in effect in complete control of AC's future directions. Shortly afterwards he transferred production of the Anzani engine to his own Cubitt factory (which also made bodywork for AC cars) in Aylesbury, Buckinghamshire. Ironically, they never did complete the initial order of 2,000 'Anzani' engines for AC, but did start to supply engines to another new company, just down the road from AC, in Kingston, Surrey.

That was Frazer-Nash, founded in November 1922, destined to become a major rival to AC in racing, and as manufacturers of very British sporting cars. In the immediate run-up to the birth of the Cobra, Frazer-Nash and AC would be among several small British sports car companies using the 6-cylinder Bristol engine. The final twist that led directly to the Cobra was that supplies of the Bristol engine (to AC as well as to anyone else) dried up after Bristol themselves switched to using a big American V8 – beating the Cobra into production as a successful 'hybrid', but opening the door by doing it.

As it appeared in 1919, the first postwar AC had a 1496cc 6-cylinder engine designed by John Weller – which, quite remarkably, stayed in production for more than forty years.

Another key to AC's long-term future was the introduction of their first 6-cylinder engine, designed by John Weller and its roots still traceable even in this 1948 descendant.

With Brooklands on the Thames Ditton doorstep, record breaking was an excellent shop window for **AC**, including the very specialized 100mph single-seater streamliner of 1922.

In its original form, in 1919, it produced 35bhp; by the time it was finally retired in 1963 (after the Cobra had appeared), its capacity had grown to 1992cc (that happened in 1922!) and output to 103bhp, in the Cobra's forerunner, the Ace.

As well as being extraordinarily long-lived, it underpinned almost all AC's evolution as a manufacturer of truly sporty cars, initially under Edge's guidance, aided by fellow board member Thomas Gillett, who was already an accomplished competition driver and now played a central role in AC's up-coming record-breaking activities.

With Edge's and Gillett's experience (and with the Brooklands track virtually on AC's doorstep), the company had ample opportunities for publicity-grabbing record attempts, and made the most of them with both 4- and 6-cylinder cars. They also ventured further afield, to the Montlhéry track near Paris for more record runs, and started to rack up multiple wins in races, rallies, hillclimbs and reliability trials.

Weller had already developed a number of 4-cylinder engine variants for AC's record-breakers, including ohc 8- and 16-valve units. In 1921, before Weller left the company, Harry

Hawker (of the Hawker aviation family) used a special version of Weller's original 1.5-litre engine in a single-seater chassis to lap Brooklands at over 100mph (160km/h), while land-speed record contender Kaye Don set further 100mph production car records at Brooklands in 1922.

Further from home, **AC director Thomas Gillett** extended the record-breaking tally with a new 24-hour record at Montlhéry, just outside Paris, with the 6-cylinder single-seater in 1925.

The Hon. Victor Bruce and Mrs Bruce were also
prominent **AC** drivers, their exploits inevitably
including record breaking, as here in 1927 with
a stripped version of the production car ...

At Montlhéry in 1925, a 6-cylinder AC set a world
24-hour record at an average of 82.6mph (132.9km/h). In
December 1927 another took records for up to 15,000
miles (24,000km), in spite of overturning and losing 15 hours
for repairs!

The Montlhéry car was driven by another great British
sporting motorist (Edge knew how to attract them) the Hon.
Victor Bruce, with Mrs Bruce. In 1926, with W.J. Brunell,
Bruce used a 6-cylinder AC tourer to win the Monte Carlo
Rally. It was the first time a British car had ever won the
event (first held in 1911, interrupted by World War I, but
back in fine style by 1924). In the days when 'The Monte' was
a long-distance winter endurance run, with routes converg-
ing on Monte Carlo from starting points all over Europe, it
was also the only time it was ever won from the far-flung
British starting point of John O'Groats.

... and in 1926, when the Hon. Victor, with **W.J.
Brunell**, made **AC** the first ever British winners of
the Monte Carlo Rally, enduring wintry conditions
from a northerly start at John O'Groats.

A COMMERCIAL KNIFE-EDGE

That was the good news; the bad news was that in spite of
all the sporting success, and the quality of the cars delivering
it, the company was going through severe financial and management traumas. There were fundamental disagreements
between Weller, Portwine and the new regime under Edge,
not least over non-fulfilment of the Anzani engine contract
– which contributed to British Anzani going into liquidation
in 1925 (although Weller and Portwine had actually left both
AC and Anzani boards by 1922). Also in 1922, with Edge now
established as Chairman and Governing Director, the company name was changed again, from Auto Carriers (1911) Ltd
to the simpler AC Cars Ltd.

After the Monte Carlo win, the victorious car
came back to the works in Thames Ditton,
which was still a fairly modest base by 1927.

-the Cars with the
3 YEARS' GUARANTEE

There is admittedly no prettier car on
the road than the A-C, and the amazing
guarantee that covers all models shows
how great is their makers' confidence in
the sound QUALITY that permeates
them through and-through. See them
at Olympia—and be convinced

SEE THEM AT
OLYMPIA
Stand
No. 176

PRICES from £295
All types of bodies. We are now prepared to
supply a second door on open 2-seater bodies at an
extra charge of £5.

AC CARS. Limited.

THAMES DITTON, SURREY
Full range of A-C Cars at
55/56, PALL MALL, LONDON S.W.1
Full Catalogue on request.

We can sup-
ply reliable
second-hand
A-C Car.

By any name, even with Edge's unstinting support, it was struggling. By the mid-1920s, Vauxhall Motors (with a considerable sporting history of their own) owned a substantial stake in AC, and might have propped the company up further; but in October 1925 Vauxhall was absorbed into the giant American General Motors Corporation, which had little interest in bailing out a small and obscure British sports car maker, especially given plenty of financial challenges of their own in the mid-1920s Depression years.

Keeping the faith, Edge bought all Vauxhall's 80,000 AC shares, increasing his own cumulative investment in the company to £135,000, but the problems continued. With virtually no development budget, AC were falling behind the opposition in technical terms simply because they couldn't afford to keep up. Quick as some ACs were, front-wheel brakes were still only an option as late as 1927, and right up to 1933 AC only offered three-speed gearboxes. Having absorbed too much money for too long, the 4-cylinder model hardly sold at all, and went out of production in 1927, leaving just the sixes.

The company was restructured yet again in 1927, when Edge formed AC (Acédès) Ltd. That in turn went into liquidation in 1929 when Edge and Gillett, both having lost their substantial personal investments, left. For the time being, car production stopped, leaving just the service department, which added a spot of colour at least, by producing two

TOP: **A pretty car with a generous three-year guarantee was how AC presented its wares in this 1925 pre-Motor Show press advertisement, but the sporty slant is still obvious.**

LEFT: **AC did seem to have a thing about pretty girls in their pretty cars, this time in 1923, in a particularly good-looking version of the two-seater with polished aluminium bodywork.**

With World War II approaching, AC's cars had come a long way from the open roadsters to this very handsome fixed-head coupé from 1938, and they were selling well.

special AC 6-cylinder engines to drive the generators on the R100 airship.

ENTER THE HURLOCKS

In 1930 the virtually redundant Thames Ditton factory was bought by two brothers, Charles and William Hurlock. Initially, they had no plan to revive AC car production but wanted to use the works as a depot for their existing business, selling and servicing cars and commercial vehicles from a base in Brixton, southeast London.

Some thirty years later, it would be Charles, with William's son Derek, who would have the vision to listen to a tall Texan by the name of Carroll Shelby when he offered them an American V8 to turn their little Ace sports car into something he wanted to call the Cobra.

The path started when the service manager at the surviving part of the company assembled a car (from existing parts) for William Hurlock. Hurlock liked his one-off AC and convinced enough of his friends how much he liked it for AC to restart a small run of replicas in the early 1930s – each built to a firm order from parts already in stock.

While well aware of the limitations of the existing, long-outdated chassis (and in particular its woefully antiquated three-speed gearbox), William Hurlock realized that in Weller's 6-cylinder engine (old as it was, but now up to 66bhp in its sportiest triple-carburettor form) they could have such a car to take to the next Motor Show at Olympia.

From there, AC's car-building operation revived quite quickly, if never to earlier levels, with a pre-war workforce barely one-tenth its early 1920s peak and a total output of fewer than 650 cars between resumption of production and the outbreak of World War II.

Of necessity, most parts were bought in from outside suppliers, but that was by no means unusual for a manufacturer of AC's size (or even many larger companies). For instance, AC fitted Weller's ohc 6-cylinder engine, now in unit with a four-speed ENV gearbox, into a modified Standard 16 chassis and clothed it in their own bodywork, offering several different styles including two- and four-door saloons, coupés, tourers and a short-wheelbase sports car. From 1935 they added the option of a Wilson pre-selector gearbox, and from 1935 you could have an AC with a synchromesh 'box.

Some famous names first appeared on the cars of this period, like Ace and Acédès, Aceca and Greyhound – high-quality cars in the higher-medium price range, and invariably handsome. Starting with a standardized body/chassis combination to keep costs under control, AC offered customers a wide enough range of mechanical and trim options to mean that every personalized car could in effect be unique.

THE SPORTING LEGACY

As for the path to the Cobra, there was one other crucial factor. Like Edge, Weller and Portwine, the Hurlock brothers were keen motor sport enthusiasts – in their case mostly for rallying (which was rather different in the 1930s from what it is today). Rallying, however, gave reborn AC valuable headlines: in 1933 an all-female team of AC sports-tourer drivers won the RAC Rally, led by Kitty Brunell (daughter of AC's 1926 Monte Carlo winner W.J. Brunell); and in 1935 T.V. Selby only narrowly missed giving AC another Monte Carlo win.

The Weller engine went from strength to strength. In the Arnott-supercharged UBS- and UBSS-engined 16/80 and 16/90 sports cars (introduced in 1937 in long- and short-wheelbase variants) the 'old' six gave as much as 95bhp, marking these out as attractive 'off-the-shelf' competition cars, especially for amateur drivers on a modest budget.

They took the AC name further afield again: by 1937 AC were among the first British manufacturers to export to America, and they exhibited at that year's New York Show.

Unfortunately, just as they were getting back into their stride, the outbreak of World War II in September 1939 brought car production to a halt again as the company switched back to wartime production. This time it was nothing if not varied, ranging through six-pounder guns, flamethrowers, undercarriages for troop-carrying gliders, fire-pump trailers, and bodywork for Ford and Bedford fire engines. Sowing the seeds for another association that would last well beyond the war, AC also began to make aircraft parts for Fairey Aviation.

The 16/80 Sport was another 1938 offering, and still had a life in various kinds of competition, but as World War II approached, the high-end sporting image had slipped a little.

ON AIR MINISTRY APPROVED LIST
CONTRACTORS TO HER MAJESTY'S GOVERNMENT

AC CARS L^{TD}

MANUFACTURERS OF AC CARS

REGISTERED OFFICES AND WORKS
THAMES DITTON, SURREY
ENGLAND

OUR REF. MGW/EES   YOUR REF. DHTLJ/BB

ALL COMMUNICATIONS TO BE ADDRESSED TO THE COMPANY AND NOT TO INDIVIDUALS

29th October, 1957

The letterhead is actually postwar, but it still reveals the vital links that had kept the company alive, 'On Air Ministry Approved List', and as 'Contractors to Her Majesty's Government'.

Such ongoing contracts would keep AC afloat, but delayed any return to car manufacture until late 1947. When AC did come back, inevitably perhaps, they re-booted the good old Weller engine again, initially in good-looking two- and four-door saloon variants. Late in 1949 they introduced their first postwar sports tourer, the rather bulbous Buckland

– in effect an open version of the 2-litre saloon, but one that played a direct part in the line to the Ace and Cobra, through its body builder, Ernie Bailey.

Both Buckland and saloons sold into the late 1950s, in ever decreasing numbers. Occasional rallying successes apart, AC's sporting reputation was also slipping badly by now, while the opposition was getting stronger, particularly from the likes of newcomer Jaguar, who would quickly build a reputation for selling exceptionally fast and stylish sports cars like the XK at prices that the rest of the industry couldn't hope to match. Between 1951 and 1957 Jaguar also cemented its reputation with five outright Le Mans wins.

AC couldn't hope to compete either on-track or off. Nice as the saloons, in particular, were, the underpinnings were inescapably getting long in the tooth. While Weller's amazing engine was still able to hold its own in most company, the saloon chassis still had the same non-independent cart-spring suspension that had served ACs since well before the war, while the opposition was hitting a far more sophisticated postwar stride.

SUPPORTING ACTS

Perversely, poor car sales were less of an issue for AC than they had once been, with several new and profitable strings to their bow. Their Fairey Aviation contracts were large and ongoing; most famously, in the 1950s they had won a

Twenty-six years after winning the Monte Carlo Rally, ACs were still competing, but both cars and event had changed, and there wouldn't be any more outright contenders from AC.

A very uncharacteristic lifeline: the three-wheel Petite was the 'able-bodied' version of the big-selling invalid car that helped keep the company afloat through difficult times.

It's a Gift
for every Golfer

BAG BOY
THE WORLD'S FINEST GOLF CART

THE gift every Golfer appreciates, for it avoids the drudgery in
golf. Bag Boy is the only Golf Cart with Independent
Suspension and air cushion (or pneumatic) tyred wheels to protect
the clubs from jolts . . . . . . and more, for with a touch on the
patent release, the wheels retract round the bag, the adjustable
handle comes down, and in six seconds it is ready to pack away in
almost the size of the golf bag. Precision engineered in aeroplane
dural and aluminium, it is rust-proof and extremely light. It looks
right on every course.

Track extended 25″, folded 9″, with 12″ × 1¼″ Dunlop
tyres. Weight 13 lbs. Ball-bearing wheels.

THE XMAS GIFT WHICH
LASTS A LIFETIME, £7·10·0

Bag Boy plus £1·13·4 Purchase
Tax. Order through
your Club profes-
sional. Also from
Sports Stores.

GUARANTEED   SIX MONTHS

U.K. MANUFACTURERS & EXPORTERS • A.C. CARS LTD. THAMES DITTON, SURREY

huge contract from the Ministry of Pensions to build a glass-fibre-bodied three-wheel 'invalid carriage'. Eventually, such vehicles would be rightly regarded as a wholly inappropriate approach to mobility, from the points of view of both safety and dignity, but in their day (and that lasted into the mid-1970s) the ugly, pale-blue single-seaters became a familiar if sadly derided sight on Britain's roads.

With even less excuse, AC also made an 'able-bodied' two-seat version of the 250cc Villiers two-stroke-engined three-wheeler, the Petite, and (helped by tax and licence concessions) managed to sell some 2,000 risible examples up to the late 1950s.

Even more esoteric, but all keeping the wolf from the AC door, the Bag Boy was an electric golf trolley made under licence from the USA, while AC also built four small electric trains that stayed in service on Southend Pier right up

LEFT: **Probably the furthest flung of the AC's 1950s fringes, the Bag Boy, 'The World's Finest Golf Cart', manufactured and marketed under licence from the USA – a useful commercial bridge.**

BELOW: **Another piece of non-motoring opportunism, one of the four electric railcars that AC built for Southend Pier, and which stayed in service until 1979.**

to 1979. Invalid cars, Petite, Southend trains and Bag Boys were all made at a factory called Taggs Island (a small island in the River Thames, near Hampton Court, and nowadays a base for the river's most upmarket houseboating community), which AC had acquired in 1940, for war work.

So, their sporting reputation had slipped, but under the Hurlocks, turning out vehicles that probably even made them shudder just a bit, AC were doing well in financial terms. Since the war, profits had been averaging over £50,000 a year, and in October 1951 AC became a public company, increasing capital by a £50,000 issue of one-shilling shares.

On the other side of the Atlantic, Carroll Shelby was just emerging from the chicken-farmer episode. And the car that changed the image, changed AC's direction, and ultimately became the final link to the Cobra was about to play its crucial part.

PLAYING THE ACE

The Ace had itself grown out of another happy series of coincidences, starting at Buntingford, in Hertfordshire, where the aluminium bodies for the Buckland were made by the Buckland Body Works, run by the aforementioned Ernie Bailey.

Close to Bailey's works was another small-scale sports car maker, John Tojeiro – who, as previously remarked, became in effect the 'grandfather' of the Cobra. Alongside building his own well-regarded but essentially made-to-order specials, Tojeiro helped pay the bills by painting some of Bailey's newly bodied AC Bucklands, in a barn that he rented from another local garage owner, Vin Davison.

Primarily for racing, Tojeiro had developed a strong, lightweight tubular chassis with all-round independent suspension, and sold several examples into which customers fitted a variety of engines and onto which they grafted an equally catholic variety of bodies.

One of the nicest of these Tojeiro specials was built for well-known racer Cliff Davis early in 1953, and registered LOY 500. It had a Bristol 6-cylinder engine and an elegantly simple open two-seater body

that was virtually a straight copy of the Ferrari 166 Barchetta – as well as of a previous Davis car, JOY 500.

Davis had an enormous amount of racing success with LOY 500 and suggested to Tojeiro that they might, together, put it into some sort of production. They never got as far as that, but a very similar Tojeiro owned by garage owner Vin Davison (whose barn Tojeiro used as his AC Buckland paint-shop) was eventually shown to AC, via Ernie Bailey (whose Buckland Body Works made the bodies, some of which Tojeiro painted).

AC bought the rights to build their own version, modifying the shape just enough to avoid shouts of plagiarism, not from Tojeiro or Davis but from Ferrari in Maranello. They launched it at the 1953 Earls Court Motor Show as the new AC Ace – inevitably with its own version of the ubiquitous Weller 6-cylinder engine.

The Ace was an instant success. It was quick, sharp-handling and beautiful. Production started slowly but racing successes came thick and fast, and thanks to the Ace, AC became known as a sports car maker again. The Ace would stay in production until 1964 (*after* the Cobra had gone into production), going through AC, Bristol and Ford engine generations. But it was the fact that the Ace was looking for another engine at the very moment that Shelby was looking for a car that made the Cobra happen.

The key link to the next sporting generation, and ultimately to the Cobra: LOY 500 was Cliff Davis' Bristol-engined Tojeiro, and the direct catalyst for the AC Ace.

CHAPTER THREE

THE ACE

The London Earls Court Motor Show, in October 1953, was dubbed by the British press as 'The 100mph Motor Show'. At least twenty exhibits would better the magic 'ton', including the new drophead version of the Jaguar XK120, the Triumph TR2, Austin-Healey 100-4, Alfa Romeo 1900, the new Aston Martin DB2/4 and Allard J2X – the kind of Anglo-American hybrid that Shelby would race on the other side of the Atlantic. Alongside them, attracting as much admiration as any, was the new AC, the Ace.

Outside the declining ranks of the brand-faithful (which had never been large), it was some time since the launch of a new AC had caused real excitement among ordinary folk. The marque's image had long ago slipped from modestly sporting to pedestrian. Few people expected that to change now, but how wrong they were.

There were two Ace exhibits on the AC stand, a complete car and a rolling chassis, showing what was new under the pretty body. The car was undeniably handsome; the slickly presented bare chassis appeared simple but was cleverly engineered. Other than the far more expensive 3-litre Lagonda, the new Ace was the only British car (XK120 and DB2/4 included) in the show to feature all-round independent suspension.

What no one could know was that a little over eight years later, in April 1962, essentially the same chassis layout (with a few tweaks appropriate to increased power) and the same lovely shape (again differing only in a couple of new swoops) would be back on another show stand. This one would be in New York, the car would have a new lightweight 260cu in Ford V8 engine, and a new name, Shelby AC/Cobra.

LAYING FOUNDATIONS

The line was that direct. In those eight years, the Ace had gone from its Weller-generation 6-cylinder AC engine to the 6-cylinder Bristol and finally a 6-cylinder Ford engine.

The 1953 London Motor show was a truly international affair, and notable as 'The 100mph Motor Show', with a list of new sports cars that included the brilliant new AC Ace.

JOHN TOJEIRO – THE 'GRANDFATHER'

The man who designed the chassis that led to the Ace, and ultimately the Cobra, reckoned his success was partly down to his unusual name: 'I well remember Roy Salvadori coming up to me at a race meeting in 1953 and saying "you'll be alright, nobody will forget that name!"'

John Tojeiro was born in Estoril, Portugal, in 1923. His English mother had met his Portuguese banker father while she was on holiday. In the 1930s, after his father died, she brought John to England, where he developed a mechanical interest through the traditional mediums of model cars and Meccano. After school and before the war, he started an engineering apprenticeship with a commercial vehicle builder in Hertfordshire.

He bought his first motorcycle in his teens, followed by his first car, moving back to a 'bike while he was working on flying boats in his Fleet Air Arm training squadron on the south coast during World War II.

Demobbed in 1946, he returned to his engineering training and married in 1947, while trying to think of a way of earning a living connected with cars. His first venture was buying, refurbishing and selling second-hand cars, learning as he went along. Having discovered motor racing, he bought a fire-damaged MG TA and gave it a lightweight body. Well-known local tuner Harry Leicester helped give it more power, but not yet having worked out how to improve the notoriously flexible chassis, Tojeiro spent a lot of time frightening himself.

So he set out to build a new chassis of his own design that would be simple and relatively inexpensive to build and maintain, easily adapted to other engines, but with fine handling to make up for lack of power pending more funds. Like several others, he followed the simple layout of the Cooper 500 racer, which in turn borrowed its transverse leaf-spring suspension from the tiny Fiat Topolino saloon. Tojeiro had one other advantage – a Cooper to copy from: because he rented a workshop from local garage owner Vin Davison, and Davison looked after a racing Cooper for Eric Winterbottom.

Tojeiro eventually gas-welded a frame that he was happy with, and that chassis, via Davison, Cliff Davis and Ernie Bailey, was the start of AC's path to the Ace. Years later, Tojeiro said that of all the cars he built, LOY 500 (Davis's

ultra-successful Bristol-engined Tojeiro that caught the eye of the Hurlock brothers at AC) was his favourite.

Through his handful of early ladder-frame chassis, Tojeiro made many racing contacts, and a reputation as a successful chassis builder even before talking to AC. His later wishbone suspension chassis became even more successful. His first spaceframe was given the Lea Francis engine from the Davison Tojeiro that became the prototype Ace, and was driven by Davis – whose LOY 500 and JOY 500 race cars inspired the Ace's bodywork.

His next chassis, in 1956, was a Jaguar-powered car for John Ogier, and became one of the lightest and quickest of Jaguar-engined cars. It was even lighter than Jaguar's own monocoque D-Type. In 1956, in *Autosport*, John Bolster reported that it was the quickest car he had tested to date, with a top speed of 152mph (245km/h) and a 0–100mph time of 12.6 seconds. In their day, future world champions Jim Clark, Graham Hill and Jack Brabham all drove Tojeiros.

Tojeiro was now machining parts he previously had to buy in, and his precision-engineering operation began to supply parts to customers. He even built a Coventry-Climax 1100 engined chassis for one Major Hope of the US Air Force, as the basis of a proposed production sports car. One chassis was delivered, but nothing more came of it.

Alongside the brilliant Jaguar-engined cars, Tojeiro built several smaller-engined racers. His last was a small mid-engined coupé for Ecurie Ecosse in 1962 – beating the Lola Mk 6 by almost a year to the distinction of being the world's first mid-engined GT. After that he concentrated on his engineering business until 1970, when he bought a well-established plastics moulding company, which he ran until the early 1980s.

He had one later Cobra connection, as engineering director for DJ Cars, one of the better British Cobra 'replica' manufacturers, with the properly engineered Dax. He planned to celebrate forty years in motor racing by hand-building five Jaguar-engined cars, each a replica of one of his most successful chassis, to original specifications. At the projected £250,000 per car they would have represented a large step from the initial £500 he was paid for the Ace chassis. John Tojeiro died in March 2005.

At that point, Carroll Shelby entered the picture, brokered the move from English 6-cylinder Ford to American V8 Ford, and triggered the evolution from Ace to Cobra.

But back to the birth of the Ace. As the Cobra would be in its turn, it was a fine piece of opportunism on AC's part, and had evolved in a matter of weeks, not even months. AC in effect bought the Ace off the shelf from Tojeiro, the sports car builder and amateur racing driver, who happened to have come into the AC picture through his links with Ernie Bailey, the Buckland Body Works, and Vin Davison.

At first, Tojeiro had been respected in his peer group but little known outside of it. With his first chassis, people began to take notice. He started by building a couple of box-frames along the lines of contemporary Coopers he'd studied, then progressed to that tubular chassis; not an exotic and expensive multi-tubular spaceframe, but something more basic, easier to build, and (given the inevitability of picking up occasional damage in racing) easier to repair.

Having acquired (as Tojeiro put it) 'a couple of lengths of pipe', he designed a simple ladder frame of three 3in-diameter alloy-steel tubes – two parallel longitudinal tubes about a foot and a half apart, with a third, transverse tube linking them roughly across the centre. The resulting H-shape was bridged at its open ends by steel box sections fabricated from twelve-gauge sheet – giving the frame its rigidity and providing mounting points for suspension, steering, and final-drive unit.

Satisfying one of the most important design requirements, the suspension was all-independent, with tubular wishbones as lower links and transverse leaf springs as upper links. It was a simple but effective layout, very similar to those of both the original Fiat 500 Topolino and one of the Cooper sports racers that Tojeiro had studied.

That was another MG-powered car, built by Lionel Leonard, a successful club racer in the late 1940s and early 1950s, notably with the car registered JOY 500. This reportedly began life in 1949 as a rear-engined single-seat Cooper with JAP 1100 engine. By 1951 Leonard had somehow reconfigured it as a front-engined two-seater sports car with 1250 MG TD engine. He also gave it a body unashamedly copying the Carrozzeria Touring shape of the Ferrari 166 Barchettas that finished first and second at Le Mans in 1949.

Cliff Davis at the wheel, and most of the ingredients in place in LOY 500 at Goodwood early in 1953: Tojeiro chassis, Bristol engine, and 'Barchetta-style' body by Eric Gray.

Imitation and flattery? You don't have to look too hard to see the inspiration for the Ace's lines in the chasing Ferrari Barchetta (or 'little boat').

RIGHT: **Against the old-school open-wheel lines of the chasing Frazer-Nash, the beautiful simplicity of Cliff Davis' Bristol-engined Tojeiro LOY 500 looks very modern indeed.**

BOTTOM: **As well as being a hugely successful driver, Davis was a popular and flamboyant character, whose checked shirts were almost as much a trademark as Shelby's striped dungarees.**

Tojeiro's tubular ladder chassis, on the other hand, while incorporating some familiar elements, wasn't, overall, a copy of anything; it was simple, clever, original, and designed to make up through minimal weight and fine handling for any lack of power. It also made clever use of readily available low-cost running gear, including rack and pinion steering derived from the Morris Minor, Morris hubs, an ENV/Jaguar rear axle, Girling dampers, proprietary Alfin cast-alloy drum brakes, and Turner alloy wheels.

'Toj' sold his first tubular chassis even before he'd finished building it, let alone tested it, to Chris Threlfall, a young Cambridge student who subsequently raced it with an MG engine. Threlfall had enough success with his car to attract the attention of several other potential customers. One of those was Brian Lister (later a respected racing car manufacturer in his own right, with a later Shelby link) who fitted his with a JAP V-twin engine; another was Chris Sears, who fitted his with a Lea-Francis engine from a Frazer-Nash.

THE KEY LINK

Most salient to the Cobra story is the chassis Tojeiro sold to Cliff Davis in 1952. Davis was already an experienced and successful club racer who had previously bought an MG Magnette-based special from Lionel Leonard, then bought Leonard's well-known Cooper-MG, JOY 500 – which Leonard apparently sold in frustration, after the latest in a string

A familiar figure at all British circuits, CLIFF DAVIS first made his motor racing mark with a Cooper-M.G. with which he dominated the 1½-litre sports car class in 1952. From there was but a step to the 2-litre class with a Bristol engine in a Tojeiro designed chassis. Cliff today drives a Lotus-Bristol much less frequently than of old but just as successfully.

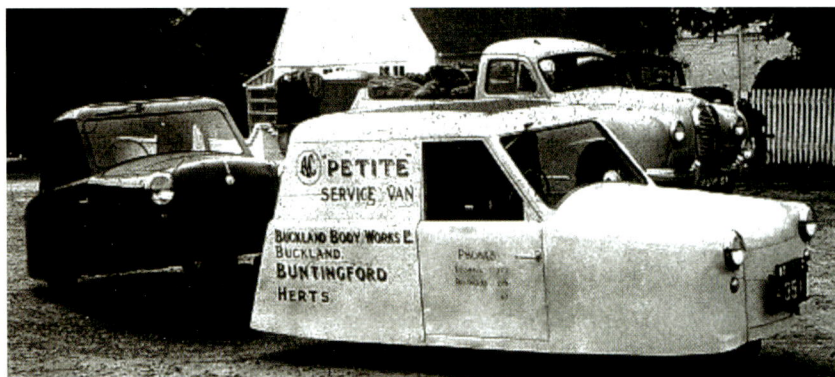

Ernie Bailey's Buckland Body Works made the aluminium bodies for AC's rather dowdy Buckland tourer, but was another key link in the Ace chain – with interesting workhorses.

of engine failures. By the Easter 1953 Goodwood race meeting, Davis had turned his own Tojeiro chassis into a stablemate for JOY 500, appropriately registered LOY 500.

Davis had the new car bodied by Eric Gray in Hammersmith, west London, in hand-formed aluminium over a lightweight tubular superstructure – Superleggera-style. It looked virtually identical to the ex-Leonard JOY 500 (and hence the Ferrari 166) but Davis gave it a more powerful and hopefully more reliable 2-litre 6-cylinder Bristol engine.

Chris Davis was an almost stereotypical amateur racing driver of his day, a larger-than-life London car dealer with a reputation for wild parties and an equally wild driving style. But he was rather good at it, won first time out with his new Tojeiro-Bristol, and kept winning quite regularly throughout 1953 using both JOY and LOY.

With his car dealer's radar tuned to anything potentially saleable, Davis suggested to Tojeiro that the two of them might go into partnership to build and market copies of the car on a bigger scale. He even jumped the gun slightly by announcing up-coming availability of the car, in *Autosport* magazine. Tojeiro, however, was either less ambitious or more realistic, and for the moment was content to carry on building one-off examples to order as he always had. Then came another of those twists in this tale where coincidence shaped the future.

Tojeiro's small workshop was at Buntingford, midway between London and Cambridge and just down the road from Ernie Bailey's Buckland coachworks – which built the bodies for the AC Buckland. Tojeiro painted some of those Buckland bodies for Bailey in the old barn he rented from local garage owner Vin Davison.

Again as we've seen, Tojeiro sold another example of his chassis to Davison, who (like Chris Sears) fitted it with a Lea-Francis engine, and a slightly different body shape, with the familiar Ferrari Barchetta-style 'egg-crate' grille, but a slightly swoopier profile, with the upper wing line dipping a little through the door line before sweeping up again over the rear wheels. It was another clear step towards the lines of the Ace and Cobra.

Davis having failed to convince Tojeiro to turn manufacturer, Ernie Bailey had another try, and put him in touch with AC, whose management were, of course, occasional visitors to Bailey's Buckland works, and therefore at least vaguely aware of Tojeiro's offerings.

Contrary to the rather staid appearance of AC's current range, the Hurlocks hadn't lost interest in more sporty cars. The drawback at the time was more that they had neither the time nor the funds to build a new car from scratch, as they would really have had to do, given the age of their own designs, if they were to create something truly modern and exciting.

Conflicting with that, they were well aware that the market for genuinely sporting cars was growing enormously (especially in the USA) in tandem with returning postwar prosperity and freedom of spirit. If the right design happened along from an outside source and at the right price, they would be happy to take it on.

Which was how Charles Hurlock and his nephew Derek (son of William) came, via Ernie Bailey, to be shown Vin Davison's Tojeiro Lea-Francis. That in turn, in the simplest of terms, was how the Ace was conceived and the Cobra made possible.

CONVINCING THE SCEPTICS

AC started by studying Tojeiro's design with a view to adapting it for production, while the Hurlocks also started discussing financial terms with the designer, who eventually agreed to receive a small lump sum for the chassis and body designs plus a royalty of £5 for each car subsequently built by AC, up to the first 100 cars. In return, he would help AC turn the racing chassis into a production chassis.

Sometime in the middle of 1953, only months before the approaching Motor Show, the Hurlocks and their Polish-born designer, Z.T. Marcewski, had the chance to try Davison's car on the road. The Hurlocks were already tempted, Marcewski initially less so, until Tojeiro himself took him for a ride in the car. Tojeiro later recalled the occasion:

I motored down to Thames Ditton and showed the car to their management, including the chief designer, Charles Hurlock, a dry character who said 'we couldn't build this here; you'd need all sorts of special machinery and modern welding equipment and so on'.

To which Ernie Bailey replied, 'I can tell you that that car was built in a place that probably isn't as big as your toilets!'

Anyway, they had a good look at it and I think they were a bit impressed, but the designer, a very clever man without a doubt, had his own ideas on such things. I think he looked at it and thought 'what a flimsy little thing this is'. Anyhow, they said 'take him for a ride', so I whipped him up the Kingston by-pass and we had a bit of fun.

The welcoming committee was outside the works when we got back and Charles Hurlock said to Marcewski, 'Well, what did you think of it?' 'It was an experience', he replied. That's all he said, I shall never forget it...

So Marcewski may have been shaken by his first encounter with what was to become the Ace, but he came back prepared to concede that in the Tojeiro chassis the Hurlocks had found a viable basis for their new car. It was already well sorted through racing, and had proved reliable in long-distance races as well as being quick in sprints. It should be easier and cheaper for AC to build than their existing offerings, and would be readily adaptable to accept other power units – though he mightn't have thought 'V8' at the time.

Having made their commitment, with virtually no time to spare before the planned reveal in late October, the work that followed was almost all based on Davison's car, originally registered LER 371. Davison was also given a job at AC, as development engineer, to work on turning his own car into the car for AC's 1953 Earls Court Motor Show stand – and then, even more importantly, turning the show car into a production car.

John Tojeiro built LER 371 for Vin Davison, and it sold the Ace concept to AC. The lines are already closer to the future Ace than to the Ferrari Barchetta, and as developed by Tojeiro, Davison and AC, this became the first Ace prototype, and ultimately the first Ace show car.

Re-registered as TPL 792, the original Ace prototype (formerly LER 371), worked hard for its living after the launch, including this appearance in the Daily Express-sponsored RAC Rally.

The transformation would involve both mechanical and cosmetic surgery. In becoming the AC Ace show car, LER 371 changed its cast-alloy wheels for the knock-off, chromed wire ones that road-going sports car enthusiasts still preferred in the early 1950s, and which better showed off the prototype's polished and drilled Alfin brake drums. In place of Davison's frameless curved Plexiglas windshield it gained a fully framed flat-glass screen, shielding a fully trimmed two-seater cockpit with split-bench seat, folding hood, and sliding Perspex sidescreens, not dissimilar to the ones that would still be offered when the Cobra arrived. It was re-registered to AC with the new number TPL 792.

The most predictable change in evolving from Tojeiro to AC was in fitting the familiar AC 6-cylinder engine – already thirty-four years old even by 1953, but still respected for its light weight, outstanding smoothness and decent power in a lightweight chassis.

THE FIRST TRUE ACE

Alongside the Tojeiro-built, AC-modified Ace at the 1953 Show was that rolling chassis, numbered AE01, registered UPJ 75, also with the AC engine – and this was the first chassis built by AC themselves, with a number of modifications from the original Tojeiro specification appropriate to production needs.

At this point, however, neither the complete car nor the bare chassis were in final production form, simply because there hadn't been anything like time for that since the project was given the nod – but they had taken the most important step.

Aiming for road-going durability, the chassis had been beefed up, retaining the same 3in-diameter main tubes but in heavier-gauge steel. There was a stronger suspension-carrying box-section front cross-member, and modified AC 2-litre saloon radiator – ahead of the suspension assembly. At this stage the steering gear was rack and pinion, mounted on the back of the front suspension cross-member.

Initially, both front and rear suspension used wishbones for the lower link and the ends of the transverse leaf springs for the upper links. For now, the lower wishbones were simple tubular fabrications just as on the Tojeiro, with no added bracing; later Aces gained reinforcing webs inside the wishbones. All the uprights were fabricated units, and the dampers were Armstrong telescopic type, angled inwards and top-mounted directly onto the box-member at the front, and onto a high-mounted cross-tube at the rear.

The gearbox was a four-speed Moss unit, which didn't need a remote linkage as the engine and gearbox were mounted so far back in the chassis that the shift-lever emerged in almost the ideal position for the driver's hand. That also meant the car only needed a very short propshaft between the gearbox output and the nose of the differential, with Hardy Spicer universal joints at each end. The ENV hypoid-bevel differential was rigidly housed in the box-section rear cross-member, driving the rear wheels through short, heavy-duty sliding-spline driveshafts, again with Hardy Spic-er type joints inboard and outboard. The all-drum brakes had Girling hydraulics inside the Alfin finned drums. The flat, rectangular petrol tank was located low down, immediately behind the rear axle.

Dressed with a good number of polished and chrome-plated components, and carrying a number plate that simply read AC-ACE, it was an eye-catching addition to the show-stand, impressively compact and purposeful. It was also already close to the first generation, transverse leaf-spring Cobra chassis of almost a decade later.

The naked Ace chassis was an impressive complement to the fully bodied ace on the 1953 Motor Show stand, clearly showing the twin-tube ladder and transverse leaf springs.

The earliest advertising showed the Ace with its original shape, almost exactly as LER 371, with its longer nose and droopier tail – which wasn't nearly as pretty as the definitive version.

There would be early changes for production purposes. The steering was changed from rack and pinion to worm and sector, with a control arm to an idler arm behind the front box-member, and further links from idler to steering arms. That was a more complicated arrangement than they might have liked, but necessary to accommodate the unavoidably large suspension geometry variations inherent in the simple transverse-leaf top-link layout – as can be seen in pictures of the chassis with body off, and the unloaded suspension adopting quite dramatic angles of droop that even the brochure copy noted.

That steering layout, compromise or not, survived right through to the second series Cobra, when, with revised geometry, they finally made a rack-and-pinion system work.

Evolving from Tojeiro to Ace, AC also improved the hubs and kingpins, and adopted 16in wire wheels with offset rims to improve straightline stability. In a big step forward (after starting with narrow-section Dunlop crossply tyres on early cars), AC began fitting wider Michelin X radial tyres – a first for a genuine sports car. Ironically perhaps, the Michelin X was adopted because its relatively soft sidewalls worked especially well with the marked geometry changes of the original suspension that had caused the steering issues.

The body, too, changed as production approached, initially and most visibly around the nose, where the headlights were raised by some 6in (15cm) in deference to US rules (and because, of course, exports were the Ace's prime *raison d'être*). That made room to reposition the sidelights below the headlights and above rather than below the prominent downward sweep of the styling line from the bonnet into the wings. The grille was toned down a little, slightly

recessed and given a subtle forward rather than rearward slant.

Overall, it made the whole front end look shorter and chunkier, with the convenient bonus of looking less Ferrari-like. By general consensus it looked even better. On the downside, it definitely spoiled the original visual balance between nose and steeply raked tail, but they modified that too, with a taller, squarer profile that restored the balance and gave the definitive Ace a look that many people thought could hardly be bettered. As a bonus for a road car, the

Technical Excellence

Designed by enthusiasts for enthusiasts. Independent suspension on all four wheels by transverse leaf springs and wishbones. Hand-built to a tight specification. Correct weight distribution. Ideal sought and attained.

The chassis illustration will be of interest, as it clearly shows the layout of the rear axle. It should, however, be pointed out that this is not the normal angle of drive, when loaded the halfshafts are practically level.

Tubular construction of the chassis and body framing provides tremendous strength, from the robust 3″ tubing of the main chassis frame to the 1½″ scuttle anti roll bar and the ¾″ body assembly tube, the whole welded to provide a simple yet robust structure.

The full flow exhaust manifolds will be observed, two branches of three pipes finally merge into two, proceeding through the silencer in dual form and continuing to atmosphere. The weight distribution is such that there is 18% more on the rear wheels than on the front. This is another feature which has assisted in providing the stability for which this Ace chassis is now well renowned. Centre lock wire wheels and Al-Fin brakedrums are included in the standard specification.

The Aceca specification from the chassis point of view differs only in the fact that the differential is rubber mounted.

The all weather equipment can be viewed in this illustration. Use is made of plastic hooding which has the advantages of remaining impervious to the sun, and is also easily cleaned, the whole being stretched over two steel detachable uprights. Rigid perspex sidescreens 3/16″ thick provide their own support, and the rear portion swivels forward from a fulcrum in the centre middle corner. This produces an easy means of entry, and also allows simple and unobstructed hand signalling.

The changes between prototype and full production versions were subtle, but changed the look of the car out of all proportion, and very much for the better. The headlamps are higher, the nose shorter and less droopy, the tail is squarer, but the prototype's expensive Alfin drums have gone. This later brochure also shows the robust simplicity of the chassis.

new rear-end shape gave the production-ready Ace usefully more boot space.

It's also to AC's credit that they didn't spoil the pure shape with unnecessary add-ons. They kept the furniture to nothing more than vertical overriders front and rear, but no conventional bumper blades (except for the US market, where they satisfied the regulations, if not the aesthetic effect, with unattractive tubular bars in addition to the overriders). The rear lights were simple small round lenses, there were no external door handles (you reached over the door to inside door-pulls) and virtually the only punctuation mark in the beautifully clean lines was the flip-up fuel-filler on top of the left rear wing.

All those modifications were made in the winter of 1953–54, between the prototype's appearance at the October 1953 Show and an on-sale date in March 1954. The numbering started with chassis AE22, where AE stood for AC engine. AEX denoted an AC engine plus left-hand drive, so the X suffix subsequently always identified an export car. Later, BE would mean a Bristol-engined car, and later still RS meant Rudd-tuned Ford.

When the prototype was shown in 1953, quoted output for the standard 2-litre 6-cylinder AC engine with three SU carburettors and 6.5:1 compression ratio (as in the saloon or the Buckland tourer) was 75bhp; or with 7.0:1 compression (optional since 1951) 85bhp. In both cases, maximum safe revs in the long-stroke engine were limited to a modest 4,500rpm. The long stroke, on the other hand, helped towards a useful peak torque figure of 105lb ft, right down to 2,750rpm, which represented very impressive flexibility.

The show car introduced the UMR CR series engine, with compression raised again, to 7.5:1, but it still claimed the same 85bhp and unchanged peak torque figures, and that's how the engine went into production and into the Ace.

AN ENDURING PHILOSOPHY

By 1953, in the wider sports car world those were only modest peaks, but that was where Tojeiro's philosophy of

building as light as possible (and AC's resistance to changing that) paid off. As it went into production, the Ace was still as simple and therefore as light as was practicable. There was no unnecessary internal trim or equipment, just two well-shaped and comfortable leather-covered bucket seats (rather than the split bench), the inside door pulls were simple leather cords, and the folding top and side screens (which would carry over virtually unchanged into the Cobra) were easily detachable to stow in the boot.

With nothing that didn't need to be there, the production Ace weighed little more than the racing Tojeiro on which it had been based: 1,685lb (764kg) according to AC. Even with only 85bhp that gave a perfectly respectable power-to-weight ratio of 113bhp per ton.

Top gear pushed the Ace along at 21.4mph (34.4km/h) per 1,000rpm. With both peak power and safe maximum engine speed at 4,500rpm that wouldn't quite have delivered the psychologically important 100mph (161km/h) top speed, but early testers were told they could use 5,000rpm in small doses, which did the trick so far as published results were concerned.

The best reported two-way maximum came from *Motor* magazine's first test, with the first wholly-AC car, UPJ 75 built on the 1953 Show chassis. Driving it early in 1954 they recorded an average of 103mph (166km/h), with 0–60mph in 11.4 seconds.

It was good, but it was only the start, as a familiar factor quickly came back into the equation. With an eye to both development and publicity, AC still had motor sport in mind. Even before production started they entered the mainly-Tojeiro show car, TPL 792, into the 1953 RAC Rally (traditionally a winter event) for Cliff Davis and David Blakeley, then continued to use it extensively for developing improvements.

UPJ75, built up from the bare show chassis AE01, became the first definitive production Ace, and the first magazine road test car, with Weller's 6-cylinder AC engine.

In particular they confirmed that to guarantee a genuine 100mph (without which it wouldn't look nearly so attractive) they would need a bit more than the original 85bhp and 4,500rpm limit. In that respect they were well aware that they were in a competitive part of the market (remember that 1953 Show line-up). The Ace wasn't going to win on price, either. It was launched at £1,439, against only £1,064 for the BMC-backed Austin-Healey 100-4 (with very similar top speed), or £1,616 for Jaguar's much quicker XK120 drophead coupé, which had silenced at least some cynics by showing it really could beat 120mph (193km/h), if maybe taking a few liberties with how they did it.

What the Ace driver was getting, though, to an even greater degree than any of those excellent mass-produced rivals, was a delicacy of handling and degree of individuality that genuinely set the race-bred, hand-built Ace apart.

AC'S ENGINE DILEMMA

The Ace's development continued through competition, especially in rallying, as well as on the road, and at the 1954 Motor Show AC unveiled the Aceca, a beautiful-looking coupé based on the Ace. It was one variant that wouldn't carry on into the Cobra generation, but it was highly regarded; over the years a total of 349 Acecas were built, alongside 694 Aces.

When design ideas came on paper rather than a CAD screen: an early styling rendering of what AC referred to in 1954 as the 'Ace Coupé', and which went into production as the Aceca.

Ace production started slowly. Through the remaining nine months of 1954 after the March launch, AC built just twenty-two Aces, plus one more that became the basis of the first Aceca. It sold in increasing numbers over the next three years: sixty-two in 1955, 110 in 1956, and 176 in 1957 – the most it ever reached in a single year, even though it stayed in production until 1964. In total, AC built some 260 AC-engined Aces, 466 Bristol-engined ones, and just thirty-seven with the Ford engine: in all, fewer than 800 cars over a period of ten years. Given the tiny production numbers, and in spite of the car's success in small-volume manufacturer terms, AC (perhaps not surprisingly) made no profits from 'proper' car-building during the Ace era. They did, however, remain profitable overall, thanks to outside contracts such as those for the invalid carriages and aero industry parts.

Throughout the early life of the Ace, AC did what they could to squeeze more power out of the elderly 6-cylinder, but were always fundamentally constrained by its inability (mainly limited by the valve gear) to rev beyond an occasional 5,000rpm. That said, in 1955 with improved bearings and lubrication and compression ratio raised again to 8.0:1, the CL series took quoted power to 90bhp (still at 4,500rpm) with 110lb ft of torque at only 2,500rpm.

Its final power hike came with the CLB series in 1958, as compression ratio reached 9.0:1 (possibly not least because petrol quality was steadily improving) and 102bhp at the previously rationed (and still slightly nerve-testing) crankshaft speed of 5,000rpm. A nitrided crankshaft in the CLBN series made those revs a bit less scary, but it was becoming clear that this was as far as the old engine could reliably go in production form.

Fortunately, although the final AC-engined Aces weren't built until the 1960s (meaning it had been built during six decades), since 1956 AC had actually had a rather fine, easily adaptable alternative, the 6-cylinder Bristol engine.

Like the AC engine, it had been around for a remarkably long time, dating back to a BMW design of 1936, but it had been reborn after World War II, when the design had been passed to Bristol (principally an aircraft manufacturer) as war reparations. They substantially updated it, especially in terms of improved metallurgy and build quality, used it them-

The 6-cylinder Bristol engine that became the Ace's staple power unit was based on Fritz Fiedler's pre-war BMW 6-cylinder design, acquired by aircraft builder Bristol as wartime reparations, and considerably improved on – particularly in terms of metallurgy.

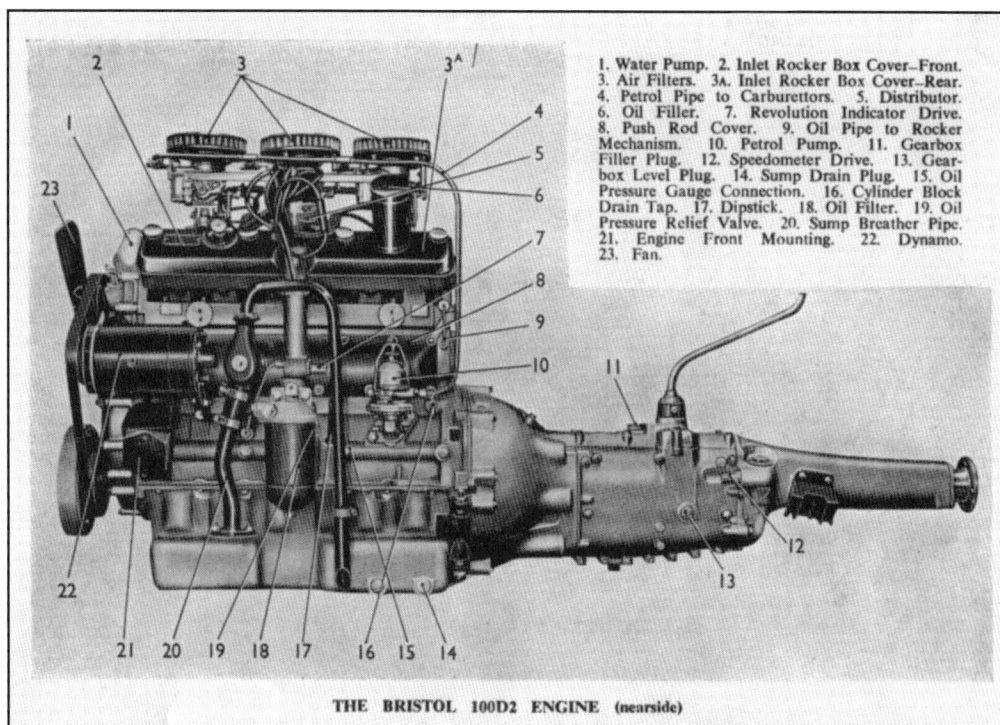

1. Water Pump. 2. Inlet Rocker Box Cover–Front. 3. Air Filters. 3A. Inlet Rocker Box Cover–Rear. 4. Petrol Pipe to Carburettors. 5. Distributor. 6. Oil Filler. 7. Revolution Indicator Drive. 8. Push Rod Cover. 9. Oil Pipe to Rocker Mechanism. 10. Petrol Pump. 11. Gearbox Filler Plug. 12. Speedometer Drive. 13. Gearbox Level Plug. 14. Sump Drain Plug. 15. Oil Pressure Gauge Connection. 16. Cylinder Block Drain Tap. 17. Dipstick. 18. Oil Filter. 19. Oil Pressure Relief Valve. 20. Sump Breather Pipe. 21. Engine Front Mounting. 22. Dynamo. 23. Fan.

THE BRISTOL 100D2 ENGINE (nearside)

selves, and gave specialist car makers one of the best engines of its generation.

It had much the same capacity as the AC six (at 1971cc compared to 1991cc), and its bore-to-stroke ratio was barely any better than the old long-stroke AC's, with the same implications. But its brilliantly effective valvegear far exceeded the AC's in its ability to rev freely without breaking, so it could produce substantially more power, and do it reliably.

In one way it seemed, on the face of it, inferior, with an iron block and aluminium head rather than the AC's lighter aluminium block and iron head. But where the AC had reached its production peak at 102bhp, the Bristol had proved good for as much as 150bhp in racing spec. By the mid-1950s, even standard production versions in Bristol's own 404 offered between 105 and 125bhp at 4,500rpm, depending on specification.

Again, the catalyst for the AC-Bristol link, promising brilliant handling with reliable power, had come through motor sport. Ken Rudd was a racing driver and AC dealer, with a garage at Worthing on the English south coast. He had done well in racing with his 1954 AC-powered Ace, VPL 422, but as with many others, more by virtue of its chassis than its power – even when wrung right out to a reliable 105bhp.

At the 1956 Goodwood Easter Meeting, Rudd appeared with a race-tuned version of the Bristol engine in his Ace,

The definitive Ace-Bristol was still every inch an Ace, but given a new lease of life by the more modern engine after Weller's brilliant but ancient AC six finally ran out of developments.

In 1956, AC were still offering both AC and
Bristol engine options, in Ace and Aceca.

AC initially offered the engine in what Bristol themselves
labelled 100B tune. That meant 105bhp at 5,000rpm on an
8.5:1 compression ratio with three downdraught Solex carburettors. AC mated the engine with Bristol's own 4-speed
close-ratio gearbox (rather than the Moss gearbox that
came with the AC engine), and added Laycock overdrive,
which operated on the top three gears and gave the Ace
particularly good cruising ability. AC also changed Bristol's
'freewheel'-type first gear for a fixed first gear, and many
Bristol customers formed a queue for the modification at
AC's stores. In 1961, after the Bristol engine went out of
production at their own Filton factory, Bristol customers
were queuing at Thames Ditton for AC versions of the Bristol 100D2 engine, too.

The D2 was the highest specification Bristol engine
offered by AC for the Ace. The 100D, introduced in 1957,
was unique to AC, and virtually all Aces produced that year
used it in preference to the milder, base-option 100B. The
100D gave 120bhp at 5,750rpm; the 100D2, as used by Ken
Rudd in 170 DPC at Le Mans in 1957, was introduced in the
production Ace for 1958. With 9.0:1 compression, modified
triple Solex carburettors and 'big-nose' crankshaft with a
Holset viscous damper, it gave 128bhp at 5,750rpm.

Rudd's performance at Le Mans was impressive. With
cowled air-intake, partly faired undertray, and small wind-

and won the production sports car race. By the end of the
year they had won the *Autosport* Production Sports Car
Championship, and AC were quick to spot the potential of
the race-winning Bristol engine for the production Ace.

The only obvious drawback was that it would be markedly more expensive than the home-grown AC six, and that
was already expensive compared to a real mass-produced
engine. But AC began to offer the Bristol engine as an option
(primarily for competition as they originally saw it), and
launched the Ace-Bristol at the 1956 Earls Court Motor
Show, alongside a Bristol-engined version of the Aceca
coupé. It was a popular move, and soon AC were using more
Bristol engines than Bristol themselves – eventually building
465 Bristol-powered Aces between 1956 and 1963, plus 170
Aceca-Bristols.

The Bristol engine was a good-looking affair, but
what appeared at first glance to be a twin ohc
layout actually used a single side-mounted camshaft
operating inclined valves (in hemispherical combustion
chambers) via ingenious crossover pushrods.

Three variations on the mid-1950s sports car racing theme – Ace leads Morgan leads Lotus at Silverstone. All three, in their ways, have proved to be very enduring shapes.

screen, it reached almost 130mph (209km/h) on the Mulsanne Straight, lapped at over 100mph (161km/h), and averaged 97mph (156km/h) for the 24 hours.

As a road car, the Ace-Bristol was predictably a good deal quicker than the standard, AC-powered Ace, with a top speed of as much as 117mph (188km/h) and a 0–60mph time of less than 10 seconds even in standard production trim. From 1957 it offered another option first tried on Rudd's Le Mans car – front disc brakes. From 1959 there was a new gearbox option with Triumph TR2 gears in a lightweight AC case, operated by a short, remote shift instead of the original cranked, direct lever.

Racing was always in the picture. The Ace-Bristol quickly made a name for itself both in Europe, from club level to Le Mans, and (crucially) in the USA, in the prestigious SCCA Production Championships. There, Ace-Bristols won Class E in 1957, 1958 and 1959, before the authorities reassigned them to Class D for 1960. They won there as well, and in 1961 when they were obliged to move up again, to Class C, they kept on winning – in a class previously won by Mercedes, Ferrari and Porsche.

It's hard to ignore the likelihood that among the interested parties watching that string of 1950s SCCA successes would have been Carroll Shelby – nearing the end of his racing career and starting to think about his own sports car project. Not least, in 1959 – the year when Shelby won

Le Mans outright for Aston Martin with Roy Salvadori – a near-standard Ace-Bristol entered by Rudd, driven to and from the circuit, and driven in the race by Jack Turner and Ted Whiteaway, outlasted far faster opposition in a race decimated by heat to win the 2-litre class and finish a creditable seventh overall. Shelby must have noticed.

The Ace, though, was already moving into its final phase, and towards the hiatus in engine supply that would give AC such headaches – but open the door for Shelby, Ford and AC to co-operate on turning the Ace into the Cobra.

ENGINE BY FORD

Before that happened, there was one more twist in the Ace story, using a 6-cylinder Ford engine built by Ford in Britain. Again, Rudd was the catalyst.

AC's need to find another engine was triggered by struggling Bristol announcing in 1961 that, for their new 407 model, they were about to switch from their own engine to off-the-shelf Chrysler V8 power – signalling the end of their 6-cylinder production. As it worked out, AC would be able to continue fulfilling orders from existing Bristol inventory right up to 1963 (albeit in tiny numbers by that stage). In fact when they finally did stop using them in Ace production, they were still able to sell off 100 engines from stock.

This time, Rudd's racing alternative was less exotic than the complex BMW-based Bristol, but bigger, cheaper, easily tuned, and capable of giving ample, uncomplicated power. On the downside it didn't have anything like the thoroughbred pedigree of the Bristol engine (or even the AC), but power was more useful in racing than heritage, and in their pursuit of performance, even those earlier sixes had lost much of their refinement.

The new engine was the 2.6-litre straight-six Ford Zephyr unit. With simple pushrod overhead valves it had considerably less sophisticated valvegear than either Weller's ancient ohc engine or Bristol's unique hemi-head/inclined-valve layout. On the upside, it had far more modern 'oversquare' cylinder dimensions, with larger bore than stroke, giving it the advantages of larger piston and valve areas than the long-stroke/small-bore AC and Bristol engines, implying a better capability for high revs.

THE MOTOR August 30 1961

Ruddspeed

still more about the

RUDDSPEED ACE—

AUTOSPORT—reports (J. Bolster)
"judged on a basis of performance for your money, must be well ahead of anything else."

MOTOR SPORT—reports (M. Twite)
"a performance far in excess of that provided by the Bristol engine can be obtained for a considerable lower expenditure."

CAR & DRIVER U.S.A.—reports (Dennis May)
"as a true blooded sports car should be—the Ruddspeeder is a constant incitement to pleasurable violence."

* ARRANGE A PERSONAL DEMONSTRATION AND JUDGE FOR YOURSELF!

K. N. RUDD (Engineers) LTD. AUTOMOBILE DISTRIBUTORS
41 High Street, Worthing 7773/4
Manufacturers of RUDDSPEED Equipment

Ken Rudd was instrumental in introducing AC to the possibilities of adopting the Bristol engine, which he'd discovered through racing, and later to the Ruddspeed Ford 6-cylinder.

Being all-iron it was heavier than either of its iron/alloy forerunners, but AC accommodated that by adding an extra leaf to the transverse front spring. Again, there was a balancing advantage: it wasn't as tall as either of the older engines, which allowed a smoother restyling of the bonnet area and a more efficient, handsomely smaller grille.

In the big Zephyr saloon its standard output was only 85bhp, but like most Ford engines of the time it was highly tuneable, and under his Ruddspeed banner Ken Rudd offered several stages, with up to 170bhp available to special order.

AC didn't need that much, but offered a 155bhp version in an Ace around March 1961, and decided almost immediately to adopt the engine for production, from mid-year.

Rudd's 'Stage 1' option had a modified cylinder head with larger valves, and three 1.75in SU carburettors. Stage 2 added lightweight pistons. Stage 3 used a light-alloy six-port Raymond Mays head, lightweight pistons and three SU carbs. Stage 4 was as Stage 3 but with three twin-choke Weber DCOE carburettors – a choke for each cylinder. These options gave 90, 125, 150 and that range-topping 170bhp respectively. AC sensibly also binned the three-speed Ford gearbox and used their own four-speed box, while front disc brakes now became standard in line with the increased performance.

In its higher states of tune, the Rudd-Ford-powered Ace was significantly faster and more flexible than the AC and Bristol cars, but even in its highest stages of tune it was considerably cheaper to build than the Bristol-engined car – which continued in production.

Unfortunately for overall Ace sales, it was still more expensive than most of the mainstream opposition, and the Ford engine did have its faults – notably with the bottom end, which became increasingly prone to failure as power output increased, especially if owners chose to abuse Rudd's carefully calculated rev limits. In 1962 Ford did produce a much improved version for the Zephyr MkIV, with a stronger crankshaft and better bearings, but they became available too late for all but one or two end-of-production Ace 2.6s.

Only thirty-seven Ford-powered Aces and just eight Acecas were built, and that really was hard to ignore as evidence that the AC had finally reached the end of the road.

But not quite. In September 1961, just as supplies of the Bristol engine were drying up and before the Ford 2.6 had proved what it could do, a letter arrived on Charles Hurlock's desk. It was from Carroll Shelby, and it outlined his idea for putting a compact but potent US V8 engine into the Ace and creating a rather special kind of sports car.

CHAPTER FOUR

FROM ACE TO COBRA

To recap: by 1961, Bristol had decided to stop production of their 6-cylinder engine, leaving AC Cars (among others) with holes under their bonnets that needed filling. On the other side of the Atlantic, 1959 Le Mans winner Carroll Shelby had retired from motor racing and was looking for a home for a project he'd had in mind for a while now.

Bristol had triggered AC's problem via solving their own. They had dropped the ageing BMW-based 6-cylinder engine for their new 407 model because they had already found a replacement – an off-the-shelf American V8 (and Torqueflite automatic transmission), from Chrysler. Not exactly sophisticated or thoroughbred, but pragmatic: ample, affordable power that they could buy in whatever numbers they might need, with no manufacturing complications or massive financial risks for complicated new tooling.

Shelby probably wouldn't have touched the far from sporty three-speed Torqueflite with a long bargepole, but Bristol's 407 was much more GT, or gentleman's tourer,

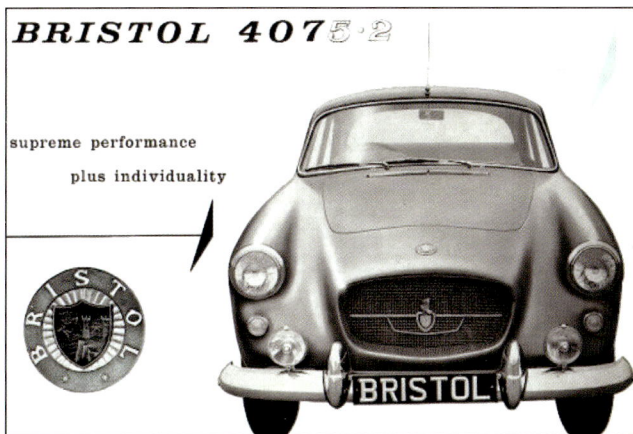

The Bristol 407 helped pave the way for the Cobra in two ways, showing the viability of a large, affordable US V8, and triggering the end of Bristol's own 6-cylinder engine supply.

than Shelby's idea of a sports car, so in that respect it wasn't such an odd choice.

By his own admission, Shelby had already told himself (if not the outside world) that his racing career was ending, and his final European trips were as much about forging contacts and picking up ideas on European-style sports cars as about racing.

There were two other factors. Le Mans 1959 had been a big pay-day, and briefly brought 'celebrity endorsement' income, but that spike apart, even as a successful racer, Shelby wasn't getting rich. Around May 1960 he also started to have serious recurrences of the childhood illnesses eventually diagnosed as his long-term heart problem. He had driven with nitroglycerine capsules under his tongue 'just in case', and his later life would be dominated by heart issues, ultimately including a transplant. In a relatively rare moment of grasping the real world, Shelby knew he had to change his lifestyle.

SHELBY'S LIFE CHANGES

In February 1960, he moved to southern California, initially to La Mirada, a small town near Disneyland in the southeast Los Angeles area, but soon after that to Santa Fe Springs. He moved mainly to be close to the motor racing community, but more, now, for the specialized car-building talents that abounded all around where he settled. He left Jeanne and their three children in Dallas, as they continued their drift towards eventual divorce.

It wasn't immediately obvious that he was making his life easier. He was still racing when he opened his Goodyear race-tyre dealership and planned his racing drivers' school – perhaps as his way of staying as close as he could to the sport, and especially to a particular coterie of racing people, without actually racing himself.

The Shelby School of High Performance Driving would be running by 1961, based on the relatively new Riverside

Having retired as a racing driver in 1960, Carroll Shelby carefully kept his racing links open, including launching the Carroll Shelby School of High Performance Driving at Riverside.

circuit, in Moreno Valley, California. Shelby started promoting it with a $90 advertisement in the motoring press, which brought 1,400 requests for information, at a dollar each – $1,400 before Shelby ever put a pupil on the track.

Unlike with the chicken farming, the early promise held, and this time, he minimized his capital risk. The school worked on the basis of renting track time on one or other of the circuit layouts, at favourable rates, on a week-by-week 'as needed' basis. Shelby tailored tuition packages to customer needs – in effect, individual tuition, in a school car (for a fee) or the pupil's own, often for maybe a week at a time. And he charged proper, commercial rates.

ENTER PETE BROCK

Aside from a telephonist/secretary, Shelby's first employee was Pete Brock, whose name will recur throughout the

Cobra story. In 1961, Brock was only twenty-three, but with experience (and ability) beyond his years. He had studied automobile styling and had already spent a year with General Motors, where he had been involved in styling what would become the Sting Ray. He left GM because he couldn't cope with big-industry slowness in making decisions. So he went back to California, where he had grown up, and was introduced to Shelby by a mutual acquaintance in motor sport, Max Balchowski – one of those specialists Shelby had come to California to be near. Brock was an amateur racing driver, too, latterly running a Lotus 19. He was very much in the Shelby mould, although in later years they would have massive conflicts – though that wasn't unique to Brock.

Brock was involved with the school from day one, mainly as an instructor, but also in keeping the cars running and improving them where possible, and as a capable administrator, running the school day to day and organizing Shelby's growing accessories business.

Soon he would be responsible for all the Cobra graphics, including the iconic snake's-head, and for many early press ads. Most famously, he would design the Daytona coupé that beat Ferrari to the World Sports Car Championship. For now, Brock was exactly what Shelby needed, someone he could trust with most of the everyday workload while he concentrated on his business commitments and sports car plans.

In Shelby's mind, those now revolved around building a minimum of 100 cars – not coincidentally, the magic number to satisfy 'homologation' rules on what constituted a 'production' model. As with most homologation cars, most of those would be sold as road cars to finance the small proportion of actual race cars. Shelby had neither the facilities nor the funds to build a hundred chassis himself (or anything like that number), so by 1961 he was actively looking for an outside partner.

The whole idea had become more realistic (and more pressing) after 4 December 1960, when Shelby finished fifth in the third Annual *Los Angeles Times Mirror* Grand Prix for Sports Cars, in a T61 'Birdcage' Maserati, at Riverside. It helped him win the 1960 USAC Drivers' Championship, but it was also his final race.

After the telephonist/secretary, Shelby's first employee in 1961 was multi-talented Pete Brock, engineer, designer, graphic artist, driving instructor and administrator: a very important man.

AN IDEA TO SELL

The nuts and bolts of his sports car project were already taking shape in Shelby's mind. The key element was to use an American V8, which meant finding a chassis strong enough to deal with its weight, power and torque, and wide enough to accommodate it. While he was still racing he had spoken (of course) to Aston Martin, and to De Tomaso and Jensen. Both the latter would eventually build American V8-powered 'European' sports cars (but not until after the Cobra); and through Ford, Shelby would later be linked with De Tomaso's Pantera, but in 1960 and 1961, none of these was the answer to Shelby's problem.

One man who nearly was the answer was Shelby's old friend Donald Healey, who might have been happy to supply the chassis Shelby discussed with him – except that his new benefactors at Austin and the British Motor Corporation wouldn't let him.

Then John Christy, a journalist at *Sports Car Graphic* magazine and long-time friend, told Shelby of AC's impending loss of the 6-cylinder Bristol engine, and Shelby borrowed an Ace-Bristol to see what it was about the little Ace that had

In the early days of the Cobra, Brock did almost all the graphic designs, including many of the early press ads, and most notably, the definitive Cobra 'snake's-head' emblem.

After their 1950s record-breaking exploits, Shelby became good friends with Donald Healey, and but for his partnership with Austin, Healey might have been the man to build Shelby's car.

When Shelby started to push the Cobra idea, he didn't have a specific engine in mind, but the all-aluminium Buick V8 (which later became the Rover V8) was undoubtedly among the options.

made it such a difficult car to beat in SCCA racing and elsewhere in recent years. It didn't take him long to realize the latent potential, and he now had another firm target.

Almost immediately, Shelby telephoned AC and spoke to works director Harry Sidney, who confirmed the situation regarding the Bristol engine, and maybe added that AC had already started looking at other possibilities. These included the 6-cylinder Ford 2.6 Zephyr engine they actually used, but also engines as diverse as Jaguar's superb 6-cylinder XK, Daimler's all-alloy V8, and another all-alloy V8, from Buick in the USA – which would eventually have an entirely different niche in the Cobra story, via its reincarnation as the Rover V8, engine of choice for many a Cobra replica.

AC hadn't tried it themselves, but a couple of other US racers had beaten Shelby to putting V8s into Ace chassis. As early as 1957, east-coast racer Roger Wing had put a small-block Chevy V8 into his Ace-Bristol and had a reasonable amount of racing success with it. Sometime later, Jerry Scheberies, helped by Walter Petersen, put an Oldsmobile F85 V8 (sister to the all-alloy Buick) into his 1958 Ace, mated to a Corvette transmission. He called it the Mongoose, because a mongoose kills snakes, but he could only make the joke because he built it after the real Cobra appeared.

Pre-Shelby, politics as well as engineering compounded AC's dilemma. Rudd had championed the lightweight Buick V8, and AC clearly saw its potential but ruled it out as it was still in production and too expensive (Rover made the formula work a few years later by buying rights to manufacture the engine rather than having to buy ready-built ones from GM). The Daimler V8 might have worked but was ruled out because Daimler's own V8-powered SP250 Dart was uncomfortably close to the Ace's marketplace. And Jaguar's XK six, brilliant as it was, was really too big and too heavy to keep the Ace's all-important balance and fine handing – although a good few people tried it.

So although AC didn't know much about Shelby at the time, and although Shelby still didn't yet have a specific engine nailed down, Charles Hurlock was quite receptive to the outline ideas in Shelby's airmail letter of 8 September 1961.

THE VITAL CONNECTIONS

Shelby, too, had thought about both the small-block (all-iron) Chevy and the all-alloy Buick, but his faith in General Motors was badly compromised by earlier approaches. Without knowing it, though, Shelby had actually already made the contact that would deliver.

On 4 July 1961, Independence Day, Shelby had been at the Pikes Peak Hill-climb, wearing his Goodyear race-tyre-supplier's hat. Also in attendance, representing Ford, was one Dave Evans – at the time in charge of Ford's NASCAR stock-car racing programme, and especially involved with the engine development side.

Crucially, this was a time of change for Ford, towards a new, sporty image. In 1960 their range included just a couple of moderately high-performance cars and the company was far better known for conservatism and safety consciousness. But within a couple of years, Ford had tried (and failed) to buy Ferrari, and started a racing division of their own, Ford Advanced Vehicles, to take them on instead. Within a few more years they had done it, winning Le Mans for the first time with the GT40. And that was the tip of the iceberg.

The philosophy of 'Total Performance', encompassing the global motor racing scene from sports cars to rallying to Indianapolis to F1, was masterminded by Lee Iacocca, head of the Ford Division of Ford Motor Co since 1960. Iacocca was the son of Italian immigrants, avid 'car guy', big fan of European sports cars and European racing, and a firm believer in motor sport as a shop window for a new, sportier Ford for a younger generation.

TOP: **In the early 1960s, driven by Henry Ford II and Lee Iacocca, 'Total Performance' became Ford's mantra, courting a younger, sportier market by attacking virtually every discipline in motor sport, from Indianapolis and F1 to rallying and, of course, sports car racing.**

RIGHT: **As well as being prime mover in Total Performance, Iacocca was 'father of the Mustang', Ford's first young-market car, and is seen here with primary Cobra link Don Frey.**

Post World War II, racing in America was a very mixed bag, from straight-line drag races to mainly redundant airfield-based 'road' racing. But what attracted the big manufacturers was NASCAR 'stock car' racing – centred originally on Daytona Beach (actually on the beach).

In fairness, it wasn't only Ford who had a dowdiness issue in the late 1950s, but Ford did carry some of the blame directly. To understand why, you need to look back at the racing culture in America at the time. America, in spite of its end-of-war flirtation with European sports cars, didn't (in general) take much notice of European motor sport. For the vast majority of American enthusiasts, the domestic racing scene had European-style 'road' racing on the fringes, but the mainstream was homegrown US-style oval track racing, and especially with the big NASCAR (and AAA) 'late-model' stock cars.

The NASCAR organization (North American Stock Car Auto Racing), was founded in 1948, to formalize the previously largely ad-hoc races for production-based (or 'stock') saloons on Daytona Beach, Florida, writing technical rules and sanctioning a series of races with an overall championship at the end of it. NASCAR quickly built a massive following, spread nationwide, and inevitably attracted the major manufacturers to promote cars that bore at least a passing resemblance to showroom stock models. In 1954, NASCAR rules were rewritten to say that stock cars must be truly stock, not stock-plus-options. Whereupon the Big Three (Ford, GM and Chrysler), having been beaten by upstart Hudson for most of the early 1950s, took to NASCAR, officially or unofficially, in a big way.

The 1954 ruling changed the face of the industry. Now, the most powerful car a manufacturer could list as a 'stock' model for racing would be the most powerful model actually in production. The horsepower race had begun.

THE ROAD TO TOTAL PERFORMANCE

The same year, Ford openly returned to racing for the first time since the 1930s – with a new ohv V8 for their Lincoln Capri sedan – via the Carrera Panamericana road race, where it had won the Large Stock Car division in 1953. Ford also dominated the NASCAR ranks, but via a bit of a back-door programme: up front, Ford maintained a strong anti-racing lobby and refused to support racing directly with factory cars – while cynically supplying dealers with all the special parts they needed to win by proxy.

It was also because of Ford's disingenuous position that, in 1957, the Automobile Manufacturers' Association (AMA) recommended that none of its members should participate in motor racing any more. This makes it all the more ironic that in 1962, Ford (through Henry Ford II), was first of the major manufacturers to announce that they would no longer abide by the AMA's 1957 ruling, but would return – officially. That was the background against which Carroll Shelby met Dave Evans at Pikes Peak in July 1961.

On that first brief encounter, Shelby didn't specifically mention his sports car plans to Evans, and hadn't spoken to him again before posting his letter to Hurlock in September. But around October, another journalist acquaintance of Shelby's, Ray Brock, editor of *Hot Rod* magazine, put the two of them back in touch. Brock (no relation to Pete) had heard about Shelby's approach to AC, and about an interesting new engine from Ford.

The engine could have been purpose-made for Shelby's ambitions: an all-new lightweight cast-iron unit using new thin-wall casting techniques making extensive use of resin-bonded casting cores, to bring weight down close to that of an alloy unit like the GM V8 but without the costs – which was just as crucial to Shelby's plans. It also had advantages in being both stiffer and quieter than an aluminium block – with fewer vibration-damping and thermal expansion problems – and cast iron with a high graphite content combined good lubrication properties with good resistance to wear, for low friction with a long service life.

Under the radar, it had been around for a while. The

RIGHT: **Henry Ford II (on the right, with Lee Iacocca on the left) was the grandson of Henry the founder, the man who took Ford back into motor sport, sanctioned investment in the Cobra, and steamrollered the GT40 to victory at Le Mans with the words 'Henry expects you to win'.**

BELOW: **Mercury was a division of Ford, and a slightly 'soft' way back into mainstream motor sport at a time when participation was a grey area. Billy Myers was one of Mercury's NASCAR stars.**

By 1962 it was once again OK to feature engineering and performance in advertising, and the campaign for the 1962 Fairlane 'compact' showcased the new lightweight, small-block V8.

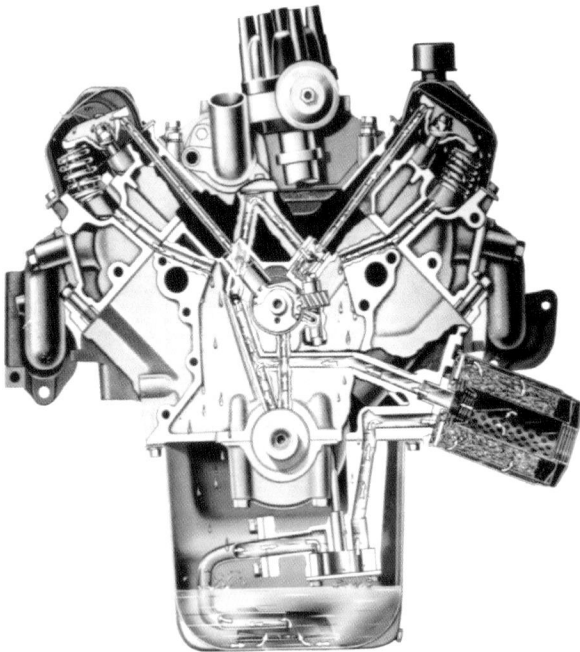

project dated back to 1958, in the Challenger 221 V8, under the guidance of Ford engineer Robert F. Stirrat as an engine for future cars and small trucks. It was launched into production in 1961 for the Fairlane, a new mid-sized car positioned between compact Falcon and 'full-size' Galaxie.

It was offered initially in two versions: the 221cu in was the smallest V8 Ford had ever produced, with the shortest stroke of any engine in its class, and a short, five-bearing crankshaft that gave plenty of potential for high revs and future tuning. Even in its smaller 221cu in (3621cc) form, with bore and stroke of 3.5 × 2.875in (88.8 × 73.0mm) and an 8.7:1 compression ratio, it produced a respectable 145bhp at 4,400rpm.

The new generation small-block V8, which started with the 260 and progressed to the 289, was a seminal engine, introducing new 'thin-wall' casting techniques to give most of the weight advantages of an aluminium engine with the costs of a cast-iron type.

Even more attractively for Shelby's ambitions, at about 450lb (204kg) bare or 490lb (222kg) with all ancillaries, it was exceptionally light – almost 200lb (90.5kg) lighter than Ford's old 'Y-block' V8s, and little heavier than the Ace's 6-cylinder Bristol.

The second variant, available by the time the Fairlane was launched, was 260cu in (4260cc) with the same, short 2.875in (73mm) stroke but larger 3.8in (96.5mm) bore, good for piston area and potentially for valve size. With the same 8.7:1 compression and two-barrel Holley on a cast-iron manifold, the larger engine gave 164bhp at 4,400rpm and an impressive 258lb ft of torque – the area where the lazy but large-capacity US V8 scored most over a smaller displacement but more highly tuned European engine of similar peak power.

TAKING THE BAIT

By the time Shelby resumed contact with Evans (by letter) he knew nothing more about the engine than the fact that it existed. But Evans must already have seen something in Shelby's ideas, because almost as soon as he read the letter, he phoned Shelby from his office in Dearborn to say that he was sending two engines to California for him to look at.

With Ford's new interest in motor sport, Evans was already working on the 260cu in V8 for competition, specifically for the 1963 model year Falcon Sprint, in which Ford saw a possible answer to arch-rival GM's Chevy Monza. In fact one of the earliest manifestations of Total Performance was a Falcon Sprint, prepared in England by Alan Mann Racing for the Monte Carlo Rally, where it did a lot better than most people expected.

For now, Evans held off mentioning the 260 to Shelby and sent two basic 221s to the Santa Fe Springs workshop that Shelby shared with legendary drag racer and bolt-on tuning specialist Dean Moon (of the famous 'Moon-Eyes' logo). By the time the engines arrived in California, Shelby had already sent another letter to AC, telling the Hurlocks of his progress. He now included key weights and dimensions and suggested chassis modifications they could start working on pending delivery of an actual engine; and he asked them to suggest any other changes they thought might be appropriate. That letter was sent in November 1961.

Having examined the 221 engine in detail, Shelby and Moon quickly agreed that it looked both rugged and highly tunable. Keeping one in Santa Fe Springs, they crated and shipped the other to Thames Ditton, with an equally important four-speed manual gearbox. When it arrived at AC, more or less out of the blue, the storeman saw Ford's 'FoMoCo' logo stencilled on the crate and told his boss that something appeared to have arrived from Japan.

Consistent with the UK's notion of 221cu in being 3621cc in real money, all AC's early drawings for the Cobra project had references to 'AC 3.6' – but it may not have been what it seemed. Much later, and after many intervening years sitting

A key reason for Carroll Shelby locating his operation in southern California was to have access to competition-bred specialists – like Dean Moon, equipment-supplier extraordinaire.

UNIVERSAL JOINTS
WHEEL DRIVE SHAFTS [4]

REAR HUBS
BOTH SIDES

BRAKE MASTER
CYLINDERS[2]

VERTICAL LINK
SWIVEL PIN BEARINGS
BOTH WHEELS

SPRING ENDS
REAR SUSPENSION
BOTH SIDES

ACCELERATOR
PEDAL SHAFT

SPRING ENDS
FRONT SUSPENSION
BOTH SIDES

STEERING
PINION BEARING

DIFFERENTIAL

GREASE NIPPLES
PARKING BRAKE CABLES [2]

BATTERY

FRONT HUB BEARINGS
BOTH SIDES

SPLINES ON
DRIVE SHAFTS
ONE EACH SIDE

UNIVERSAL JOINTS
PROPELLER SHAFT [2]

CLUTCH MASTER
CYLINDER

STEERING RACK

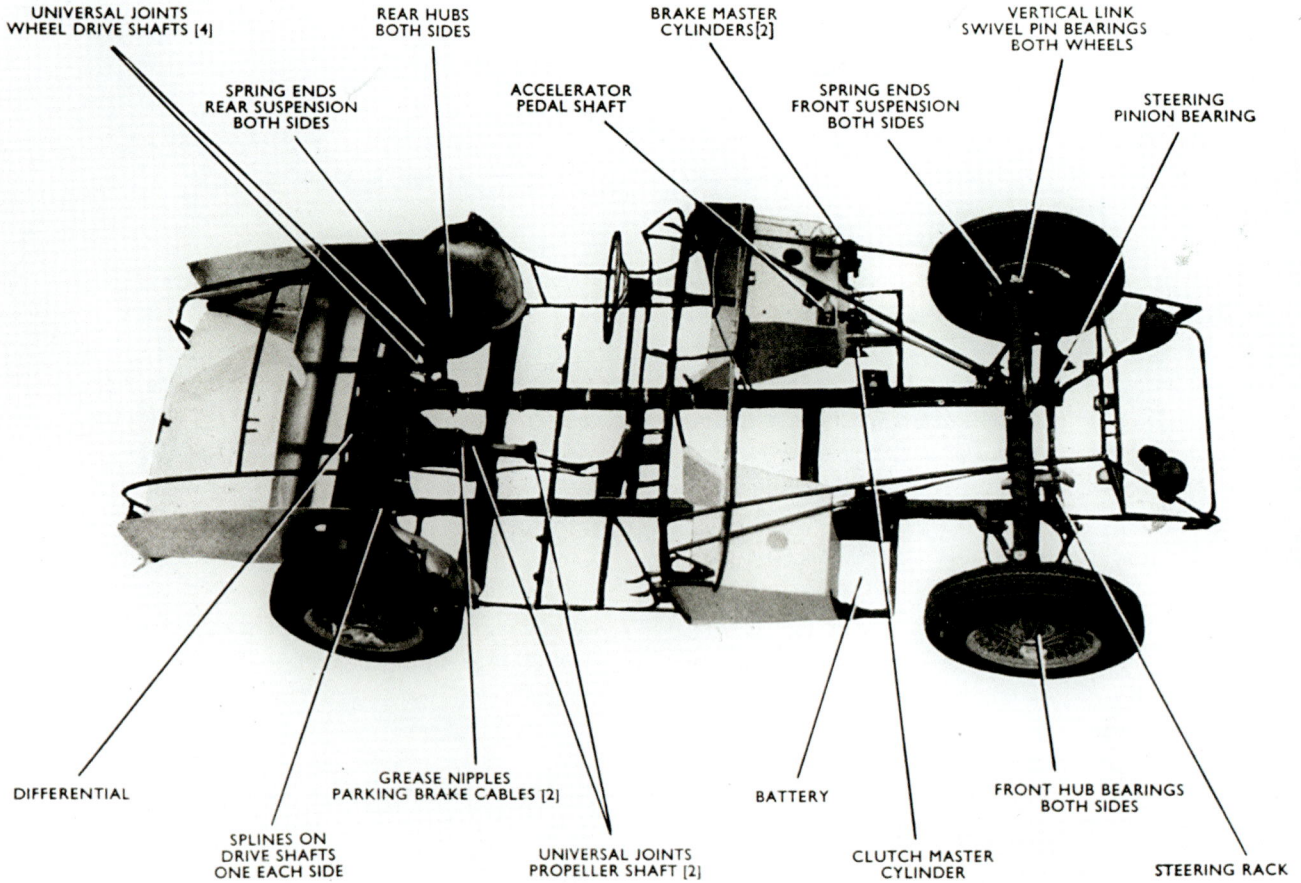

The starting point for the Cobra was as simple and effective as Shelby could have dreamed
of: the classic Ace ladder chassis with transverse leaf suspension, easy to build in flexible
numbers with very little expensive tooling, and already well understood by AC.

unused in the AC stores, the first engine was bought by AC Owners' Club stalwart Barrie Bird, and on dismantling apparently proved to be a 260, outwardly identical to a 221.

Whatever its true capacity, when the 'Japanese' engine arrived at AC, Vin Davison, original owner of the Tojeiro-Ace and as such a crucial early link in the chain, was still with the company, and set to work with chief engineering designer Alan Turner and engineer Desmond Stratton to persuade it to fit into the modified chassis.

Shelby, meanwhile, had another message from Evans, belatedly telling him about the 260cu in development (making the 221/260 anomaly of the first engine even more odd). The message also said that two more engines, of that size, were headed to California. Shelby immediately passed that

intelligence on to the Hurlocks, and from this point on the project was progressing in leaps and bounds. Shelby even scraped together the time and air fare to go to Thames Ditton over the winter of 1961–62, to help finalize details on the prototype.

PUTTING IT ALL TOGETHER

All of this, it's worth remembering, was barely four months after Shelby's first letter to the Hurlocks, in September. Without a specific engine to offer, he had persuaded them that his idea was sound; he had actually found his engine (probably a more suitable engine than he'd ever thought possible); he had persuaded Ford to supply the first engines on credit; he had persuaded AC to do the same with the chassis; and he had got engine and chassis from different sides of the Atlantic into the same building.

But Shelby made a point of sharing the credit. He generously praised the Hurlocks themselves and their small staff at Thames Ditton, for being helpful and enthusiastic even when the necessary modifications proved more complicated than originally envisaged, and he praised the people at Ford without whom he also knew the Cobra couldn't have happened.

Foremost among those were Don Frey and Ray Geddes – management men, who at first glance would hardly seem to be Shelby-type people, but who crucially turned out to be the sort of hands-off collaborators that he could happily work with.

The project continued to thrive on serendipity. The ever-enthusiastic Dave Evans put Shelby in touch with Frey, a bespectacled, academic-looking type in his late thirties who was a Ford Division general manager and also a genuinely knowledgeable sports car enthusiast. While Frey had been in the army in the early 1950s, he had even driven an Allard. He was one of the team Ford sent to Maranello in the hope of buying out Ferrari as a short-cut into international racing. That might have seen Ford-Ferrari road cars and Ferrari-Ford racing cars, and it reportedly almost happened, before Frey's team came up against the Ferrari stubbornness that Shelby had already experienced during his visit with Paravano in 1955.

Frey wasn't the kind of corporate bean-counter Shelby had developed such a dislike for in his earlier dealings with GM. He was in charge of engineering planning in the Ford Division, but liked quick decisions. It was Frey, after minimal discussion with higher powers at Ford, who gave Shelby an almost immediate green light, and even suggested to Ford that they provide the line of credit for the first hundred engines. Little wonder Shelby later described Frey as 'probably the most knowledgeable racing executive in the world'.

Of course, Ford wanted appropriate financial control over the Shelby set-up, but again, Shelby struck lucky with another desk-based intermediary. Ray Geddes was a young lawyer from the Ford financial office, with a master's degree in business management; just as importantly, Shelby respected him as someone else who got things done without ever making him feel stifled by bureaucracy.

While Ford did supply both credit and financial management, they didn't pay for the cars: ultimately, Shelby did that.

And while Ford provided vital access to many design, engineering and distribution facilities, they didn't build the cars. Shelby and AC did.

INTO THE METAL

AC's hands-on efforts started with that first prototype over the winter of 1961–62. They had been essentially correct in anticipating few problems at the first hurdle, fitting engine into chassis. The V8 was very compact, at less than 21in (535mm) long and only 16.5in (420mm) wide (which could have been the troublesome part with a V8). It fitted quite easily into the Ace's spacious engine bay. It was also light, barely 15lb (6.5kg) heavier than the Bristol six, so it didn't demand lots of strengthening, just suitably reshaped and repositioned engine mounts, sitting it as far back as possible for optimum weight distribution.

Choosing to retain the four-speed Ford/Borg-Warner T10 manual gearbox meant the assembly was a known quantity with no need for adaptor plates or linkages. It was perfect for the job, all-synchromesh, capable of handling many times the torque limits of the old Bristol box, but again compact and weighing only 10lb (4.5kg) more than the existing unit. It was also readily available alongside the engine, which meant it was cheap by previous standards.

There was a bit of juggling required to get a suitably efficient tubular exhaust system in, with twin tailpipes to provide adequate cooling and neat plumbing, and to tailor things like wiring loom and throttle and clutch linkages to suit the new engine layout. Amazingly, they had it close to right first time, which gave them a flying start. But only a start: next, the Ace chassis would need to deal with markedly more power – and around twice as much torque as it had originally been designed for (almost a decade earlier). It would also have to handle the increased cornering forces and brake loads associated with a much quicker car.

At the same time, both Shelby and AC were committed to maintaining the underlying simplicity that defined the concept, and that included the basic layout, even in one area where it looked a bit primitive – the transverse leaf springs.

They did have a choice. Tojeiro had built a streamlined, space-framed, coil-and-wishbone 2-litre Bristol-engined car for AC for Le Mans in 1958 (where it finished eighth overall), and could have done a similar chassis for the new road car, but they resisted. So the first prototype chassis was basically identical, in layout at least, to the ladder-framed, leaf-sprung

The leaf-spring Ace chassis wasn't the only option, just the best one at the time. As long ago as 1958, John Tojeiro had developed a Bristol-engined car for Le Mans with a full spaceframe chassis and coil-spring suspension in a streamlined body, but simple won the day for Shelby.

Ace, with parallel main tubes of the same large diameter, separated by the same 17in (430mm), albeit with a heavier gauge again.

The differences were in the detail, much of it unique. Most obvious was the change from drum to disc brakes at the rear, with Girling callipers. That would improve braking and benefit handling by reducing unsprung weight, but there was a downside for racing use in that the brakes were harder to access for quick pad changes. It meant, however, that AC could use existing calliper mounts on the substantially strengthened final-drive assembly, based on a Salisbury limited-slip diff from the new, independent rear-suspension Jaguar E-Type/Mk10.

There would be heavier duty driveshafts and additional bracing from the nose of the differential to a new chassis cross-member. A substantial reinforcing framework of square section tubing was added around the rear suspension mounts and across the full width of the car, with other bracing plates wherever deemed necessary.

Wheels from AC's Greyhound saloon had a bigger offset, and with a slightly longer front transverse spring, which gave a small increase in track. Reacting to stress breakages on early front-suspension test assemblies, they upgraded the front hubs, front kingpins and steering-box to chassis mounts. With that, it was ready to try.

THE FIRST RUN

The first car ran for the first time at Silverstone in January 1962, with Carroll Shelby driving. That was just before Ford had agreed to supply their V8 in quantity.

It was only a brief shakedown and as soon as it was completed the first prototype had engine and gearbox removed (for customs purposes) and on 2 February it was air-freighted to Los Angeles, via New York. It carried chassis number CSX2000. Presaging any number of subsequent differences of opinion (and worse) on chassis nomenclature, AC understood that to mean Carroll Shelby Export, while Shelby went for Carroll Shelby Experimental.

Between Thames Ditton and Los Angeles, it gained its proper name – Cobra. According to Shelby, it came to him in a dream, and he woke up and wrote it down on a notepad. It had previously been used as a trademark in the 1940s by American car-maker Crosley for their 'Copper-Brazed' engines; but as Crosley had gone out of business in 1952, both Ford and AC were happy to go with Shelby's choice.

Again, it wouldn't be the last time that rights to the Cobra name would be cause for discussion, and the doors to that controversy were opened more or less at the beginning. AC always wanted their name on the car, acknowledging who had supplied the chassis. Oddly, it was Ford, not Shelby himself, who most forcefully insisted on having Shelby's name on it – while originally not wanting their own name included. Whatever, the first car was referred to initially as the Shelby Ford AC Cobra; but in line with Ford's preferences, their contribution was almost immediately restated with discreet 'Powered by Ford' badges on the front flanks, while the car itself was redesignated Shelby AC/Cobra, including, in early print ads, the apparently anomalous position of the forward slash.

When it went on sale in Britain (some time later) it was usually just AC Cobra (or subsequently AC 289, or AC MkIV). In America it always had the Shelby label, but Ford eventually came to own the 'Cobra' name, so some later cars were known simply as Ford Cobras, while a very different 'Cobra' was a species of Mustang-based muscle car. At various times, both Shelby and Ford staunchly opposed misuse of the name.

By any name, Shelby's Cobra dream had become reality, and when CSX2000 arrived at Los Angeles airport, Shelby borrowed a trailer from one of his racing school pupils, and Dean Moon's truck to tow it back to base. When it came out of the packing crate it was unpainted and dotted with labels: 'For Export Only'; 'Add Oil Before Driving'; 'No Water in Engine'.

The last two were superfluous as there was no engine in the chassis, or indeed in the crate. There was one in the workshop, though, and within eight hours of the car arriving at 10820 South Norwalk Boulevard, Santa Fe Springs, that and a four-speed Borg-Warner gearbox were installed in the prototype chassis. Whatever the truth about the original engine at AC, 221 or 260, this one was categorically a 260, further modified by Shelby and Moon while it had been with them.

CSX2000: JOB ONE

The definitive details, as listed in the Shelby American Automobile Club's *Shelby American World Registry*, say CSX2000 was completed on 26 February 1962 (obviously the California re-completion date rather than the 'test' completion in Thames Ditton). It had the 260 V8 with single carburettor, worm-and-sector steering, inboard rear discs, 5.5in (140mm) chromed wire centre-lock wheels, and Ace-style bodywork, with standard, long Ace bootlid.

Unpainted, in bare aluminium, it differed from the Ace mainly in its smaller grille, and neat wheelarch extensions, accommodating the larger wheels and wider track. Shelby would have preferred a fibreglass body, for lower cost and ease of production, but AC's supply line from their part-owned subsidiary, the Brownlow Sheet Metal Co. in west London, was well established and reliable, the all-aluminium body weighed barely 50lb (22.5kg) complete, and there were more important things to argue about, so alloy it was.

As soon as it was finished, Shelby and Moon took it onto a makeshift test track around the local oilfields. Shelby would hang on to CSX2000 for the rest of his life, but his first obligation (and given their close relationship, probably his first inclination) was to show it to Dave Evans at Ford. Having seen it, Evans was apparently happy, too.

The first regular test driver, as the original car was refined over endless miles around Riverside, was Pete Brock. An accomplished graphic designer on top of his other talents, Brock would add another detail: it didn't appear even on the prototype until rather later, but Brock had already designed the soon to be famous stylized snake's head badge.

The programme continued at a remarkable pace. The car was shown to the press on 10 April 1962, still unpainted but with its aluminium shell now highly polished, which, according to Moon, took 'a dozen people and at least twenty boxes of steel wool'.

A VERY PUBLIC DEBUT

The next time CSX2000 appeared, under the bright lights of the Ford stand for the opening of the 1962 New York Auto Show on 21 April, it was finished in a striking bright yellow.

If the 1953 London Show where the Ace debuted had been the '100mph Motor Show', the 1962 New York Show was the one that confirmed that the American auto industry (after the hypocritical years of 'non-participation'), had rediscovered performance in a big way, as a marketing tool. GM had their latest Corvettes and Corvairs, Ford had their Corvair-baiting V8 Falcon Sprint compact. Alongside many more flamboyant show cars throughout the halls, the Cobra was simply a stunningly handsome showstopper.

The next steps were to let the outside world actually drive one, and hopefully to start taking orders. First on

There was some confusion over exactly what engine first sat in the first Cobra chassis, but the workshop shot clearly shows the valve covers labelled 'XHP 260-1'.

the invite list would be the key US magazines; and with Shelby's reputation, flamboyant profile and impeccable contacts list, they were falling over themselves to be near the front of the queue. The big problem was that an opportunity to test the Cobra was just that – an opportunity to test what so far was the *only* Cobra.

Understandably, as Shelby was a 'Contributing Editor', the first to drive it was *Sports Car Graphic* – actually before its New York Show reveal, and before its yellow paint, but with hand-painted 'Shelby' scripts on its nose and tail, and small 'Powered by Ford' badges on the front flanks. It was also road-registered, as CL 10303.

It had one of the two original 260 V8s, first of a special series supplied by Ford with a different camshaft, and solid rather than hydraulic cam-followers, high compression pistons, and modified heads with larger ports. It had a single four-barrel Holley carburettor and 9.2:1 compression ratio. The 'test' engine was numbered XHP-260-1, and was quoted as producing 260bhp at 6,500rpm and 269lb ft of torque at 3,600rpm.

Sports Car Graphic's first-ever test was published in May 1962, and they loved it:

> We spent a day playing with the car and can safely say that it is one of the most impressive production sports cars we have ever driven. Its acceleration, even with the much maltreated and dynamometer-thrashed single four-throat engine can only be described as explosive and at least equal to that of the better running hot Corvettes and Berlinettas we've driven…

They didn't include measured figures in that first test, but did so in a follow-up test in the August issue, by which time the car had gained a coat of paint but kept the same 260bhp engine spec – albeit in this case a fresh engine with a slightly larger version of the single four-barrel carburettor. That

The Cobra made its New York Show debut (and its first test drives) unpainted, with its alloy body highly polished – which, according to Dean Moon, involved 'a dozen people and at least twenty boxes of steel wool'.

gave the same peak power and torque figures and a bit less low-down torque, but much better mid- to top-end punch.

PROOF IN THE NUMBERS

The figures are still at the sharp end of the very-quick bracket more than fifty years later, but in 1962, for a road car, they must have been almost unbelievable. They were accurate, too, measured with a calibrated fifth wheel because the Cobra generated too much wheelspin to use the instruments. With a 3.54:1 final-drive ratio, *Sports Car Graphic* recorded 0–60mph in 4.1 seconds, 0–100mph in 10.8, and a standing quarter-mile in 12.9 at 114mph (183km/h). Their two-way average maximum was 152mph (245km/h), reached in less than a mile; first gear ran to 41mph (66km/h), second to 78mph (126km/h), and third to 109mph (175km/h).

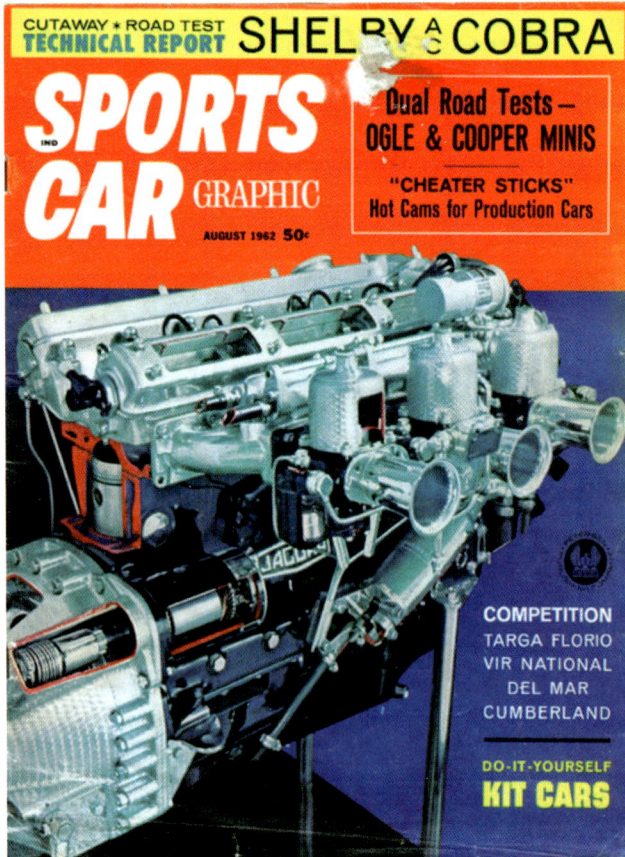

The very first magazine to test drive the 'prototype' Cobra, pre-New York debut, was **Sports Car Graphic**, with a first drive in May 1962 followed by fuller coverage in August.

They tacitly admitted that a degree of restraint was advisable, but praised the handling (on Goodyear SS racing tyres), the brakes, and especially the fact that in their opinion the car was docile and comfortable enough to be perfectly usable every day.

In both tests, *Sports Car Graphic* reported engine options: the top-tune 260 with 11.0:1 compression, reinforced main-bearing caps, and four twin-choke side-draught Weber carburettors on a crossover manifold, claimed 330bhp and could rev to 9,000rpm. In May they also suggested that the homologation process was in hand, to put the Cobra into the FIA's GT category as a standard car, or Improved GTs as a modified one. Shelby was also looking to homologate the Cobra with the SCCA, for the B and A Production classes (standard and modified) respectively.

In quick succession, other leading magazines tested the Cobra, with consistent results (*Car Life* and *Road & Track* both recorded 4.2 seconds to 60mph and top speeds over 150mph or 240km/h), with much the same awestruck enthusiasm. On the face of it, there was a real test 'fleet' – a red car for one magazine, a yellow one for another, or a blue one, alongside *Sports Car Graphic*'s first, unpainted one. In reality, all the tests were with the same car, because it was still the only car. Shelby simply kept repainting it between bookings to make it look as though production had already started.

It hadn't, but starting in the UK and finished in the USA, it was about to.

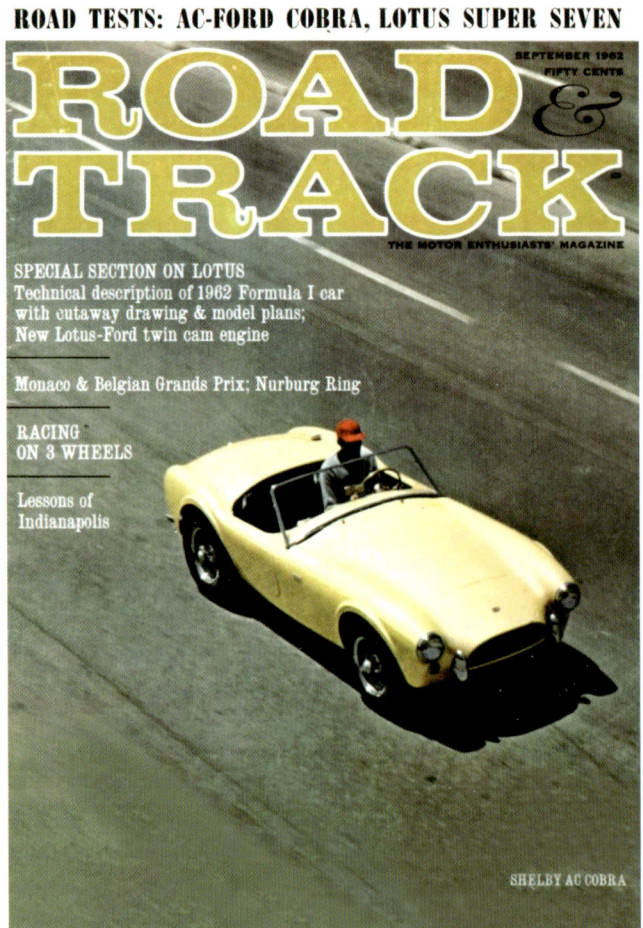

Road & Track was also near the top of the test-drive rota, and announced its first full test with the cover shots of the car in its yellow livery – the first actual 'colour'.

CHAPTER FIVE

THE LEAF-SPRING COBRA

The first Cobra, the uniquely inboard-rear-braked CSX2000, with 260 Hi-Performance V8 and four-speed Borg-Warner manual transmission, was completed by Shelby and Dean Moon within hours of it arriving in Santa Fe Springs in February 1962. It was quickly shaken down by Shelby, declared finished on 26 February, and introduced to the specialist press in early April, initially with unpainted, but laboriously polished, aluminium bodywork.

By the time it appeared on the Ford stand at the New York Auto Show on 21 April, it had been painted bright yellow, and proved to be a showstopper. As quickly as he could turn the one and only running car around between bookings (usually including repainting, so at least it didn't look like the only one) Shelby passed it to the next magazine on the rota. Like the show-goers, they loved it, and the orders started to flow.

At this point it's worth remembering that the Cobra had come from conception, through development, to 'job one' in barely five months; it was built almost entirely by hand, partly in Britain, partly in America; and it was already in the spotlight. Virtually every early car had minor differences as they learned how to build it and racked up the testing miles. On top of that, virtually every customer wanted (and could have) slightly different detail specifications – as there were already a considerable number of factory options for the road (and many more for racing); and with almost every delivery, there was a stream of user feedback.

HANDS-ON DEVELOPMENT

So in effect Shelby and AC approached the reality of turn-

The first car, CSX2000, led a very busy life, between shakedown tests, the show circuit, the magazine test schedule, and general demonstrations. Here, at Riverside, it's a course car.

ing the Cobra from first prototype into genuine production car by resolving any issues and preferences as and when they emerged, using each early customer car as an additional prototype.

Fortunately, it became a positive process rather than a negative one, as it might have been from a manufacturer with less flexibility and willingness to react. The Cobra had been so close to right first time that it needed few major changes. In fact, in the lifetime of the Cobra only two were big enough to merit an 'official' model-number change. Changes happened as and when appropriate, and not necessarily in strict chassis order, simply because AC and Shelby didn't complete the cars in strict chassis order. That said, there were running changes to improve performance, reliability, and occasionally to accommodate variations from different suppliers. None of these necessarily implied faults or shortcomings, it was just how the process worked – and it did work.

After CSX2000, the next cars to be delivered actually were CSX2001 and CSX2002 (with the CSX prefix now officially meaning Carroll Shelby Export). In the longer term, the first '2' signified a leaf-spring chassis, a '3' would later signify coil-spring. Additionally, COB would indicate 'Cobra Britain' (for AC's home market), while COX meant 'Cobra Export' (for markets other than Britain and the USA, predominantly mainland Europe). The numerical part of the COB and COX identification always began with a '6', whatever the chassis configuration.

Very late in the programme, eight 427-type chassis were built with EFX prefixes, for a run of experimental electric-powered cars built by Electric Fuel Propulsion Inc. of Ferndale, Michigan – described in Chapter 9. There were other numbering anomalies, also described later, such as HEM-6 and A-98. There were 'in-series' chassis numbers that were never originally Cobras in the true sense (like the Paramount Studios film chassis). Most controversially of all, there were chassis numbers that were never originally completed, but emerged at various later dates with a range of justifications, again detailed later.

The story of CSX2001 and CSX2002, by comparison, is reasonably straightforward. Like CSX2000, both were airfreighted to the USA to be completed by Shelby. CSX2001 arrived in New York on 19 May 1962 to be completed by Shelby's east-coast distributor, Ed Hugus, in Pittsburgh, PA, and as CSX2000 stayed with Shelby, this became the first customer Cobra.

THE FIRST RACER – CORVETTES BEWARE

CSX2002 went direct to Shelby in California and became the first Cobra racer. It made its competition debut in an SCCA three-hour race supporting the Riverside GP (right on Shelby's doorstep) in October 1962. It was driven by Billy Krause, in what turned out to be an encouraging day for the Cobra and a worrying one for anyone racing a Corvette.

The Cobra, still clearly a prototype, was eligible within an SCCA 'experimental' class, ironically created mainly to accommodate the still to be homologated 327 Corvette. The Corvette raced with number 00, Krause's Cobra carried XP98. From the start, Krause ran away from the opposition, Corvette included, at an impressive rate.

Within an hour he had a lead of around one-and-a-half miles, until a rear hub failed.

The story of the Cobra's racing development begins in

It would be fair to say that the kind of people represented by the artist in this early US advertising material probably weren't the typical Cobra customer.

The Cobra's first competition outing was at Riverside in the supporting race for the Riverside GP. Like the Corvette that it's chasing, it was accepted as a prototype, bearing the race number XP98 and driven by Billy Krause. It immediately showed the Corvette what to expect.

Chapter 7, but in a nutshell it quickly became a regular sports car contender, and habitual race winner.

As well as transforming the Cobra's image and sales prospects, racing experience played a huge part in developing the road cars (especially for reliability) as they started to arrive from Thames Ditton in a small but growing trickle. CSX2003 and the next four in line had been delivered (like CSX2001) via Ed Hugus. CSX2003 was promptly sent to Ford, in Dearborn, Michigan, so the people who had largely financed the car could have a proper look at it. By this point, in spite of Ford's support, Shelby reckoned he had spent around $40,000 of his own money on the project, so with cash in short supply he sent it on a stand-by flight.

FORD'S SIDESHOWS

A couple of other cars from the first half-dozen followed it to Dearborn, where Ford were still examining the option of getting more deeply involved, perhaps even to the extent of moving production in-house. That never happened, of course, or the Cobra story would surely have been very

different. For instance, they did commission a couple of styling exercises for an 'Americanized' body shape – perhaps the last thing the Cobra needed. The first was by Ford's director of styling, Gene Bordinat, and became known variously as the Cobra III, XD Cobra or Bordinat Cobra. By 1960s US styling standards, it was quite restrained, but very different from the softly muscular original – a two-seat roadster, with squarer, sharper-edged lines, a hint of the first Thunderbird in its bullet-nose profile, retractable headlights and lots of louvres set into the bonnet. What it had lost was the Cobra's handsome simplicity, and while it didn't look bad, it soon looked dated, where the 'real' Cobra remained impressively timeless.

In the Bordinat Cobra, Ford also dabbled with new materials and production processes. Its body used a high-impact-resistance composite called Royalex, which was vacuum-moulded in a single piece then bonded onto the Cobra chassis. Adopting that rather than hand-formed aluminium would clearly have allowed much bigger production numbers with lower unit costs, but would surely have lost another Cobra unique selling point.

Dearborn's second exercise, the Cougar II, had more technical extravagances, more like a 1960s dream car than a

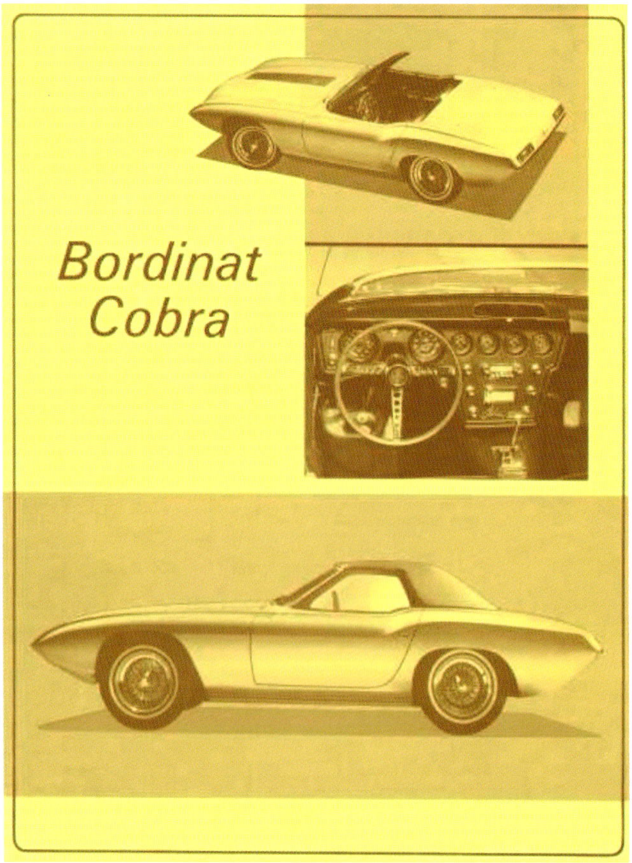

Ford did entertain early thoughts of 'Americanizing' the consciously European Cobra, and their thoughts included these alternative treatments by director of styling Gene Bordinat.

reinterpretation of something so inherently simple. It was a fastback coupé version of the Bordinat roadster, with candy-apple-red paintwork and brushed stainless steel roof panel. It had 'gullwing' doors, pop-up headlamps and trick aerodynamics, with a panel between the rear light clusters that opened automatically at higher speeds to relieve interior cabin pressure that might otherwise have blown the rear window out – as it did on the Cobra hardtops at Le Mans in 1963. As in the Bordinat roadster, the 260 V8 was set back in the chassis to allow a lower bonnet line. Aside from its cheesy grin, it was a clean looking car for its day, and probably aimed as much at Ferrari and Lamborghini as at obvious rival, the Corvette – and it appeared before the classic Stingray, with its Pete Brock connections. But that was as far as it went, and it certainly wasn't a Cobra.

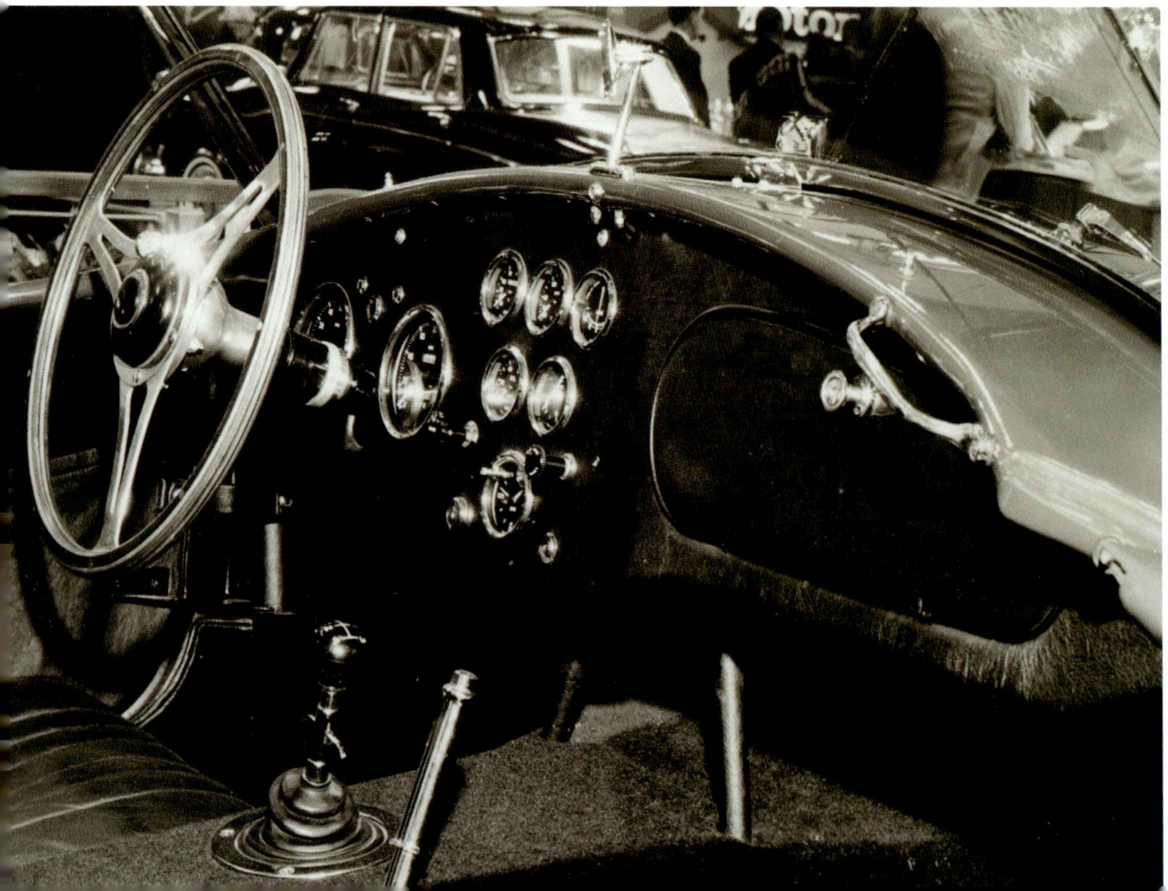

The Cobra really was a fairly simple car, with very few frills, but great functionality. The cockpit layout was logical rather than stylish, and nothing was there that didn't need to be.

A Ford team led by Dan Jones continued the process of tidying up development glitches on the production car, always keeping Shelby and AC in the loop, and underlining the effectiveness of a working relationship built on mutual respect. Ford resolved the detail problems a small company like AC couldn't really afford to do – like cooling issues (especially cockpit cooling), steering, electrical system and instruments. Getting the details right meant Ford could back the Cobra with confidence, and Shelby acknowledged that they 'did a pretty thorough job'.

SPREADING THE WORD

They did put their name on it, albeit rather modestly. Shelby's earliest advertising was headed 'Shelby AC/Cobra Powered by Ford'. It showed the car as prepared for its 1962 New York Auto Show debut, with chromed wire wheels and vibrant yellow paintwork. For a car with the Cobra's performance, the first advertising image was pretty corny: photographed in open countryside with a young model ill-attired in evening dress, long white gloves and a tiara! The information inside was a bit more in keeping with the car, showing a bare chassis and a car in the course of construction; but the words were classic 1960s American ad-speak:

> Racing, touring, everyday enjoyment of a thoroughbred car, they're all yours in the new Shelby AC/Cobra. Here is a true sports-touring automobile which can actually be raced, with every expectation of success, in its normal street trim.
>
> Yet in the city or cross-country, it remains a docile and extremely comfortable means of transportation. The Shelby AC/Cobra achieves this often-promised-seldom-delivered ideal for one simple reason; it was designed that way. In no respect is it a compromise.
>
> Representing the fusing of two tried and proven engineering programmes and backed by the manufacturing experience of two of the most respected automotive firms on either side of the Atlantic, the Shelby AC/Cobra has a faultless background. It has an equally exciting future.

The main copy line in the early brochure read 'BUY IT! . . . OR WATCH IT GO BY!' It went on to paint a vivid picture, albeit one that the Cobra could probably live up to:

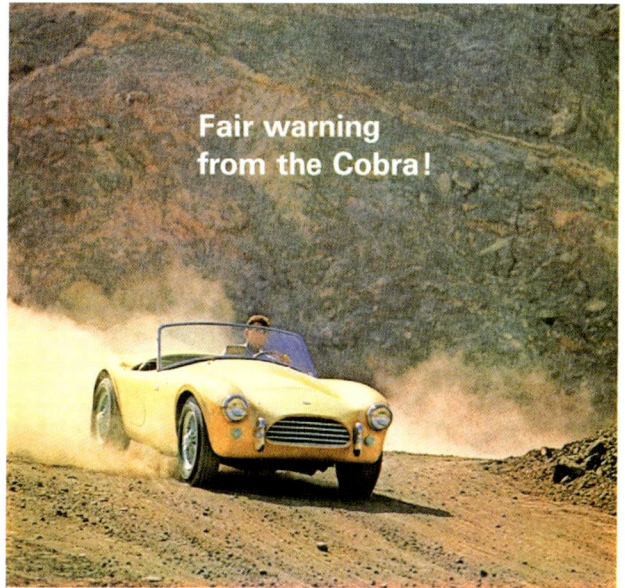

Fair warning from the Cobra!

From this day on, drivers of the world's proudest sports cars are advised to stick to the right-hand side of the road. For at any moment an AC/Cobra can come storming past, belly low to the road with twin pipes ripping out a curt "good-by!"

There's not much point trying to argue with this potent new combination of super-hot Ford Fairlane V-8 and super-light AC chassis—260 solid American horsepower on tap all day long in a car that weighs 2,020 pounds curbside. The AC/Cobra roadtests zero to 100 in a breath-stopping 10.8 seconds . . . and comes smoking down to zero again in the grip of disc brakes big enough for a Diesel truck. The seats are deep glove-soft leather, the suspension is supple four-wheel independent, and the way it claws around corners rewrites all the laws of centrifugal force. The V-8 is a real piece of magic. Product of Ford's research in precision-molded "thin wall" cast iron, it is short, narrow, light—and ready to look at the other side of 150 mph (and 7,200 rpm) any time your foot slips. But even whispering around town it doesn't know what "temperament" means and that, coupled with the generous cockpit room, the civilized ride, the reasonable luggage space and the sleek Italianate lines of the hand-formed aluminum body, make the AC/Cobra a touring sports car of the very first rank.

Unhappily, the production is severely limited and, since the price is only $5,995 p.o.e., only those who drop a line right now to Carroll Shelby Enterprises, 1042 Princeton Drive, Venice, California, will be able to know what it feels like to drive the most explosively exciting car you can own.

COBRA
Buy it . . . or watch it go by

'Unhappily, the production is severely limited, and since the price is only $5,995, only those who drop a line right now to Carroll Shelby Enterprises ... will be able to know what it's like to drive the most explosively exciting car you can own.' Or, as the punchline said, 'Buy it ... or watch it go by'.

> Arrowing through a warm desert evening at one hundred fifty plus miles per hour [it didn't say where you could do that], or snarling up pine and snow-covered mountain switchbacks, the Cobra's precision steering and supple four-wheel independent suspension retain the perfection of 'line' required of a thoroughbred racing car. Conventional stopping distances become obsolete with a slight pressure on the four-wheel Girling disc brake system. (A firm pressure defies the laws of inertia!).

The copy ended boldly: 'Demand for this unique automobile is already beyond expectation. Production is limited. Order your Shelby AC/Cobra now'.

People did. Carroll Shelby, on the back of the brochure in sharp suit and tie, a million miles from the laconic Texan/

chicken farmer image, certainly looked like the sort of man you could trust to buy a sports car from. But some people would have smiled knowingly at this particular, squeaky-clean corporate version of Shelby. In his excellent book *Shelby's Wildlife*, author Wallace A. Wyss sums the man up beautifully in a single sentence:

> *Shelby's glamorous image — tall, gentlemanly, white teeth, California tan, cowboy hat — seemed bright and promising in the drab Detroit atmosphere, and Ford executives were surprised later when they asked* Hot Rod *editor Ray Brock about the extensive holdings of Mr Shelby, the Texas cattle baron, and found that Mr Shelby owned little more than his smile and his hat…*

The hat and the smile … Sidelined by end-of-previous-season injuries at Sebring.

Writing many years later in *Car and Driver*, Pete Brock also hinted at the other side of Shelby:

> *… the Cobra prototype was a rocket, and it really opened the eyes of Ford's engineering staff. That summer, Shelby returned to Dearborn and asked for $25,000 to build a racing version of the Cobra, which would debut at Riverside in October 1962. Iacocca was so impressed with the car, and the Texan's swagger, that when Shelby stepped out of the room for a moment, he told the execs gathered there, 'Give him the money and get him outta here before he bites somebody!'*

HOMOLOGATION AND PRODUCTION

The first batch of 100 cars was ordered from AC during 1962 for completion by early 1963, the vital agenda being to qualify for 'production' racing homologation. The first thirty or so were finished by June, seventy-five or eighty were complete by the end of the year, and the initial run was completed by April 1963. Some were completed by dealers (notably Hugus in Pittsburgh and long-time racing supporters Tasca Ford in East Providence, Rhode Island), while many of the cars Shelby completed had competition connections themselves. It was soon apparent, however, that Shelby needed more assembly space than he had at Santa Fe Springs, where he'd completed his first thirty cars at the rate of only around two a week.

The process was labour and space intensive. At the AC end, in Thames Ditton, most chassis parts were made in-house, almost entirely by hand, including seat and hood frames. The chassis and body frame tubes were all cut, bent and assembled (using both gas and arc welding) in the works, starting with the large-diameter main tubes and smaller cross-members, then building upwards with suspension and final-drive mountings, and the superstructure to carry the body, in both round- and square-section tubing. Suspension, steering and brake assemblies were fitted, then inner panels, bulkhead firewalls and foot-boxes riveted to the framework, and electrical equipment fitted.

The aluminium bodies were hand-made, and riveted to the lightweight superstructure. That was more or less it so far as AC was concerned; a Cobra really was a simple car. Each chassis, though, took about four weeks to complete,

A far cry from a Ford production line, chassis building by AC at Thames Ditton. Drum and disc brake options say Ace and Cobra, leaf springs say 289, with Aceca coupés in background.

The other side of the Atlantic, in Santa Fe Springs, and final touches in the engine bay on CSX2000, the first chassis shipped – again, not exactly a production-line environment.

and AC's maximum capacity was no better than about ten to fifteen cars a week, which was marginal for demand.

Rolling chassis then sat in the AC showroom waiting to be transferred, a few at a time, by road to London's Victoria Docks (without engines and gearboxes, of course, but also without driveshafts, because incomplete cars were subject to significantly reduced import duty than complete ones would have been). On the same basis, they were often shipped on old Ace 'slave' wheels, reversed if necessary to give clearance for the bigger brakes. The correct wheels were fitted by Shelby, with the slave wheels returned for the next batch.

Shipping by sea was also about cost: only urgently needed chassis (which usually meant either racing or development ones) had the luxury of going by air.

On the other side of the Atlantic, the cars arrived at the port of entry with the bodies protected by wax, but not always painted, with windscreens stored under the tonneau, ready to be fitted. Bare engines arrived with Shelby (or the relevant dealer) direct from Ford, in crates, and had ancillaries fitted on receipt. At that point they were also mated to alloy-cased versions of the four-speed Ford/Borg-Warner manual transmission, modified with stronger input shafts and carefully calculated, closer internal ratios.

However well the cars were packed for shipping, the vulnerable aluminium bodies were often damaged in transit, so that they needed tidying up. Standard preparation work included de-waxing the cars, removing the bonnets for easier access to the engine bay, fitting water, oil temperature and fuel lines, then lifting the car onto stands so that three or four mechanics at a time could work on fitting the engine and transmission assembly.

As it was completed, each car was put through a seventy-five-point checklist, the engine was run gently, and finally every car was tested for about 30 miles (48km) on a mixed road route near the factory – much of it around a convenient new commercial site at Marina del Rey, often with Shelby driving and the local police apparently choosing to ignore any minor infringements of local speed limits and so on.

The final jobs were paint and trim, which always included leather-trimmed bucket seats and full carpeting. The body originally offered just two colour options (only one more

Dropping in the engine at Shelby's workshop, with basic equipment and plenty of hands-on involvement. Other parts shipped in cardboard boxes in the car for finishing touches.

It became fashionable for customers to go to the Shelby workshops to see their cars finished and take delivery. Some customers were better known than others. This is Steve McQueen.

than Henry Ford's Model T boast 'any colour you like so long as it's black'). But the original choice of red or white was soon extended to include blue, black, green or maroon.

Plenty of customers (many of them converts from Corvette or Jaguar XK) took up the offer of visiting the works to see their own car being completed, which was one more complication for Shelby alongside the ongoing process of developing the early cars as they went along, and offering an extensive list of options.

A COBRA FOR EVERY PURPOSE

Enough to mean that every car was near enough unique, but that was what the market expected. The options list was at its most complicated, of course, for the competition cars. Typically it began with mandatory safety features like roll hoops, competition seats and seatbelts, plus bodywork modifications like additional vents, drag-reducing underbody tray, small competition windscreen, supplementary driving lights (especially for endurance racing cars) and even a radiator stoneguard.

Chassis modifications offered for racing included additional brake-cooling scoops, alloy brake callipers, dual master cylinder, competition-spec springs and dampers, various specifications of front and rear anti-roll bars, uprated wire or alloy wheels, and larger fuel tanks, up to a massive 37gal (168ltr) alloy tank, again for endurance racing.

As for engine and gearbox, you could specify pretty much anything you could think of and afford; the small-block V8 already had a massive choice of tuning options, including carburation and inlet layouts, various competition exhausts

From the start, the relationship between street and competition was crucial, and
Shelby never missed an opportunity to underline it. Spot the differences?

Typical 'street-spec' 289 underbonnet, with
single four-barrel carb and pancake air-filter.

High-end 'competition' 289, with most exotic (and
expensive) quad-Weber carburettor option.

(including a side-pipe option), and uprated ignition systems. There were also more fundamental, bigger-buck options like the alloy block and cylinder heads from the Ford 'Indy' engine, and a full range of high-performance internal component and machining options.

The performance, trim and accessories list for roads cars was shorter than for the race cars, but still extensive. It featured mainly bolt-on cosmetic and comfort options, like aluminium rocker covers, chromed air-cleaners, aluminium intake manifold, chromed exhaust pipe finishers, luggage rack, front grille and rear bumper guards, adjustable wind deflectors, tinted visors, whitewall tyres, exterior driving mirrors, and AM radio. Just because it was a sports car didn't mean you couldn't pile on the 1960s bling.

More usefully, you could soon order a lift-off glass-fibre hardtop and a Smiths heater if you lived somewhere cooler than California. Even if you weren't actually going racing but wanted to look the part you could specify competition seat harnesses.

The fact that the heater was only an option was an interesting one. Apparently nobody had thought of including one in the original spec, but depending on where a car was delivered, north or south, and depending on time of year, a Cobra could equally easily roast or freeze its occupants. With a heater, at least you didn't have to freeze. It would be a bit longer before you could have the air-conditioning option.

As well as for driver and passenger, there were early cooling issues with the cars themselves. The first chassis supplied by AC were delivered with the Zephyr-type radiator used by the last of the Ford-engined Aces. While that had been fine for the 6-cylinder engine in the home counties, it couldn't cope with the V8 in California. Shelby's first palliative was to fit aluminium Corvette radiators, bought anonymously at Chevrolet dealers, because sourcing them openly could have been embarrassing for Ford. He soon found a better solution in a custom-built brass-cored radiator manufactured by the McCord Radiator Co. to Ford/Shelby specifications. While this issue was being resolved, AC supplied several more chassis with brackets for the old Zephyr radiator, which made assembly difficult.

Early cars were also fitted with the mechanical cooling fan from Ford's compact Falcon, but only intended for the car's first 6,000 road miles (10,000km) while the engine loosened up, then to be replaced by a more efficient electric fan.

The COBRA Hard Top

The A.C. Cobra fitted with a Fibre Glass Hard Top, designed and manufactured by A.C. Cars.

A large plastic wrap round rear view light, provides excellent all round visibility.

A.C. CARS LIMITED, THAMES DITTON, SURREY, ENGLAND
Telegraphic Address: Autocarrier, Thames Ditton   Telephone: EMBerbrook 5621

Weather protection wasn't a big feature on the basic car, and the standard soft-top was a crude affair, but you could soon specify a glass-fibre hardtop with wraparound rear window.

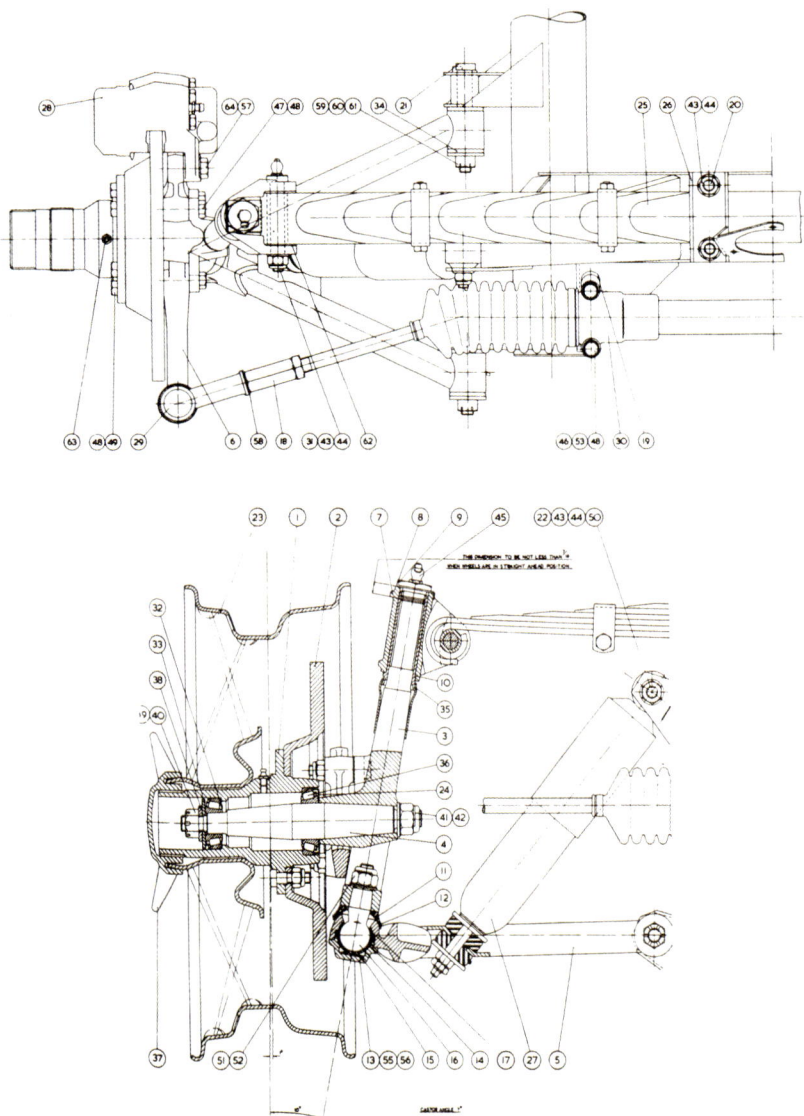

The original leaf-spring suspension layout was simple but quite effective, using the ends of the transverse leaf spring as the upper mounts to the hub carriers, over lower wishbones.

the time-saving compromise of inboard rear discs on the first car, all subsequent cars had all-outboard brakes, with 12in (305mm) front discs and 11in (280mm) rear discs, all by Girling. Even the later Ace only ever had discs at the front, sticking to drums on the rear. The Cobra had worm-and-sector steering, with less than two turns from lock to lock, but no power assistance – you just had to be strong.

As on the prototype, the production final drive was the proven Salisbury unit, and the gearbox was the Ford/Borg Warner four-speed manual, with direct ratio top gear, and a short lever operating through a remote linkage. The clutch was a hydraulically operated single dry plate type and, like the steering, it gave the muscles a work-out.

The first standard engine specification was the 260cu in (4261cc) all-iron Challenger V8, with single camshaft in the block and two pushrod-operated overhead valves per cylinder, using solid cam-followers. The camshaft was a Shelby special, and the key to a good part of the power increase over the basic engine. Other improvements came from a single four-barrel Holley carburettor (slightly larger on subsequent cars than on the first prototype) on a fairly ordinary cast-iron manifold, and four-into-two tubular exhaust headers.

The oversquare bore and stroke dimensions were 3.80 × 2.87in (96.5 × 72.9mm) and with a 9.2:1 compression ratio, it claimed 260bhp at 5,800rpm (one bhp/cu in, or 61bhp per litre in European money, was a top-end specific output for a US V8, first achieved by Chevrolet in 1957). Arguably more important in terms of character, maximum torque was

There were visible variations, too. On early cars the exhausts emerged in front of the rear wheels, on later ones they came out, much more neatly, below the rear bumper.

THE FIXED POINTS

Notwithstanding detail variations on individual cars, the basic specifications were quite firmly set by now. The chassis was the classic Ace-type ladder, uprated as described, but retaining the 'classic' transverse leaf-spring upper-link, wishbone lower-link layout, with telescopic dampers all round. After

269lb ft at 4,500rpm. Maximum permissible engine speed was 7,200rpm, which was some way above peak power speed, but magazine testers reported that the Cobra would reach those revs even in top gear, which said something about the overall gearing.

THE PERFORMANCE SECRET

Good as it was, power was only half the secret of the Cobra's performance. By the standards of muscle car-mad early 1960s America, 260bhp wasn't exceptional. But the Cobra was also exceptionally small and light, and big power-to-weight figures meant performance way beyond almost anything else on the road.

The Cobra was very compact – only 151.5in (3,845mm) long, and 61in (1,549mm) wide, on a 90in (2,286mm) wheel-base. In 2014 terms, that's almost 7in (175mm) shorter over-all than a Mazda MX5, the epitome of compact sports cars, more than 6.5in (171mm) narrower, and on a 1.7in (44mm) shorter wheelbase. A 2014 Porsche Carrera is no less than 25.4in (646mm) longer, 10.2in (259mm) wider, on a 6.5in (164mm) longer wheelbase.

The early Cobra had front and rear tracks of 51.5in (1,308mm) and 52.5in (1,333mm), and usually sat on 6.40 × 15in front and 6.70 × 15in rear Goodyear SS high-performance tyres.

It weighed just 2,020lb (916kg). That equates to 288bhp/ton, almost identical to a 2014 Carrera GTS. That is some way, admittedly, from the most extreme 'modern' supercar

One of the great beauties of the Cobra (especially the 289) was its wonderfully compact size.

Moving to Lance Reventlow's old Scarab workshop was a brilliant move for Shelby, giving the operation essential space and facilities, and, not least, engineer and ace test-driver Ken Miles – who had worked on the Scarab sports cars and F1 car.

with far more outright power, but impressive even today and astonishing for 1962. And that was only entry level for the Cobra. Given the available tuning options, a customer didn't have to break the bank to have 325bhp for the road (that's 360bhp/ton, a bit more than a 2014 Carrera GT3), while for racing you could ultimately have a reliable 380bhp, and even less weight. That's better than 400bhp/ton, more than a 911 Turbo, or a Nissan GT-R.

Once it had passed from AC to Shelby, each Cobra required about eight hours work to complete the build. Not a great deal of time, but it did have an impact, in that Shelby's original premises were only big enough to deal with a couple of cars a week – which didn't stand up to the original ambition to build as many as 1,000 Cobras a year.

That would never happen, but in June 1962, still with similar expectations, Shelby (with a little help from Ford),

found bigger premises. While the geographical move from Santa Fe Springs to 1042 Princeton Drive, Venice, California, wasn't far, the change was enormous. The new premises, at about 10,000sq ft (929sq m), still weren't huge (in fact about the same size as AC's premises in Thames Ditton), but they were on a scale much more suited to the operation. They were also already set up for just this kind of project: previously this had been the Scarab workshop, where Woolworths heir Lance Reventlow had built his Scarab sports cars and ultimately Scarab Grand Prix cars.

When Shelby moved into the leased premises in Venice in 1962, a useful amount of Reventlow's old machinery remained, while the bigger premises gave scope to build up to five cars a week, and equally importantly, space to store incoming engines and other parts. It accommodated a bigger staff, quickly growing to around thirty-five people, including his race mechanics. A couple of those, Ken Miles and Phil Remington, had worked as engineers on the Scarab project, and now became pivotal parts of the Cobra story.

RACING PEOPLE

English-born Miles was a racing driver, and one of the finest development drivers in the business. He had designed the chassis for the Scarab sports car, would turn the Cobra into a race winner, and would go on (with Shelby) to do the same for the GT40.

Remington, too, had been around racing cars for most of his life, starting as a pioneer Californian hot-rodder in the 1930s. Like Shelby, Remington had flown bombers during the war, but in Remington's case, on active service in the Pacific. Back in peacetime America he worked for well-

known race-engine builders Traco, and from the late 1940s became involved in an earlier 'American sports car' project, with a wealthy Californian by the name of Stirling Edwards – another clear precursor of the Cobra philosophy.

Edwards was an industrialist and sportsman, and at the St Moritz Winter Olympics in February 1948 he saw a Cisitalia sports car that set him thinking about an American-built car that could combine the best of European looks and handling with an affordable and accessible American powertrain. Sound familiar?

Edwards revealed his first car, the R26, right at the end of 1949 – a 2+2 sports roadster with removable hardtop and split windscreen. It had a tube frame, all-independent coil-spring suspension, a 125bhp 153cu in (2507cc) Ford 'flat-head' V8, and automatic transmission. It had a hand-formed aluminium body and was built by racing specialists Diedt & Lesovsky in Culver City, California – with Phil Remington working on the chassis.

LANCE REVENTLOW – AN INSPIRATION

Alongside the likes of Briggs Cunningham, Dan Gurney and Carroll Shelby, Lawrence Graf von Haugwitz-Hardenberg Reventlow was an American racing icon. His mother was Barbara Hutton, of the Woolworths dynasty; his father was a Danish count, Kurt von etc, one of seven husbands that Barbara collected over the years. Lance was born in England in 1936, briefly had Cary Grant as one stepfather, and, from 1947 to 1951, Prince Igor Troubetzkoy as another. Reventlow was always A-list: he was married (briefly) to actress Jill St John (Bond girl Tiffany Case in *Diamonds are Forever*) and drank coffee at a roadside café with James Dean half an hour before Dean was killed on his way to the same motor race as Reventlow. So far as our story is concerned, though, Troubetzkoy was the key character. In 1948, while he was married to Barbara Hutton, Troubetzkoy became the first man to drive a Ferrari in a Grand Prix (in Monaco), and also won the Targa Florio that year. So twelve-year-old stepson Lance discovered motor sport via the deep end.

Like Shelby, he raced in the USA then went to race in Europe; and like Shelby, when he retired from racing he wanted to build cars. So he moved into the premises in Venice, initially to build Chevrolet-powered 'Scarab' sports racing cars that were technically quite sophisticated, and very successful in SCCA racing – a major rival to Cunningham in the USA.

One of them won a fairly important race at Continental Divide Raceway, Colorado, in 1959 – driven by 1959 Le Mans winner Carroll Shelby.

Unlike Shelby, Reventlow didn't have any dream of building road cars, and only built three of his first front-engined sports racers. He then built America's first modern Grand Prix car, which raced very briefly in Europe in 1960. Patriotically, it was powered by derivatives of the 4-cylinder Offenhauser Indy engine; but beautifully built as it was (in a small facility in the UK), having the engine in the front put it out of its depth in a world now dominated by mid-engines. It narrowly beat the Aston Martin that Shelby drove to become the last front-engined car to race in a Grand Prix, in the 1960 season-ending US GP.

Reventlow did build a mid-engined sports car and a mid-engined Grand Prix car, both powered by race-prepared Buick V8s, but by that stage the tax man had decided that his motor racing was more than a hobby and prompted him to give up; the later Grand Prix car never raced. Reventlow himself died as he'd lived, in the headlines. Scouting locations for a ski resort he planned to build near Aspen, Colorado, he was in the passenger seat rather than his usual pilot's seat when his plane crashed in the mountains in 1972.

ROAD and TRACK

DEC. 1949 35¢

THE NEW EDWARDS
SPORTS CAR P. 10

The Motor Enthusiasts' Magazine

Shelby's R&D director Phil Remington was previously involved in another foray into the dual-purpose sports car world, Stirling Edwards' glass-fibre bodied R26, with detachable hardtop and notional street/ competition options, but it never went into production.

The US specialist press thought it was wonderful, and as a 'dual-purpose' road race car (familiar again?) it had half a dozen reasonably successful races. But that was as far as it went, and just one car was built. With Remington's help, Edwards rethought the basics and (via another one-off prototype) created another car that appeared at the end of 1953, the Edwards America. This had a glass-fibre body on a production Henry J chassis, and after one Oldsmobile Rocket V8-powered example it adopted the mighty Chrysler Hemi V8, beloved of racers like Cunningham and Allard. It was a good-looking car, and very much in the Cobra mould, but they only built five (two convertibles, three hardtops) over the next couple of years. When the Edwards project ended, in 1955, Remington went off to work for the Hilborn fuel injection company, and then to Scarab.

When Shelby moved to Venice, Remington joined him as Director of Research and Development, charged with translating the comments of testers like Miles (and to a lesser degree, those of the early customers) into the metal. Shelby respected him both for that engineering ability, and as an administrator.

The other key administrator in the Shelby line-up would be Al Dowd, who was introduced to Shelby by a journalist contact, late in 1963 when he had just left the US Coastguard after a twenty-year career. Dowd had another big asset, in that he'd raced Aces. At Shelby he became the main organizational link between Ford, AC, Shelby, key Cobra race teams, suppliers, and anyone else who mattered.

NEVER STAND STILL

In this phase, the development people at Ford and Shelby were never short of something to do on the Cobra. Even the first production cars differed in many details from the inboard-braked prototype. As well as relocating the brakes, the fuel tank was soon moved from the old Ace-style horizontal position under the boot floor to a new, better-protected vertical position behind the cockpit, over the rear axle. That improved chassis balance (although the Cobra was still tail-heavy) and made the handling more consistent whether the

Silver-finished wire wheels were standard equipment for the early 289, with the option of chromed wires, or alloys – all a bit bigger and stronger than they had been on the Ace.

tank was empty or full. It also created space for a spare-wheel well under a flat boot floor, and the bootlid itself was smaller than on the Ace (and CSX2000), to improve rear body stiffness. New tubular bars between the usual over-riders were both neater than the Ace's old US-style bumpers and gave better protection from minor nudges.

Standard wheel and tyre wear for the early Cobra was silver-painted, 72-spoke, 15.5 × 5.5in wire wheels with Goodyear Blue Streak tyres (not only because they were good tyres for a car with the Cobra's performance but because Shelby was still a Goodyear distributor). Chromed wire wheels were always an option, and alloy wheels were always another for racing, but most early customers chose standard wires.

The soft-top was a typically crude British affair, comprising a detachable tubular frame and separate fabric piece to cover it, all held down with clips and pop-studs. The story goes that when Shelby received the first car from AC he didn't have the vaguest idea how to put the top up, and there were no instructions to help him.

But the Cobra was virtually all positives, and not just for performance and looks. As launched, at $5,995 plus taxes, the first Cobra cost less than the last of the Ace-Bristols. Early invoices suggest that the dealer mark-up on a basic car was typically around $1,000. Then you could have a mid-range street/competition version from $6,150, or an off-the-shelf full-race car for around $9,900.

To put those prices into 1962 perspective, the only real alternatives that could deliver anything approaching Cobra performance were either high-end European exotics like the Ferrari 250GT and 400 SuperAmerica, the Aston Martin DB4GT, or the two fastest volume-production sports cars, the new British Jaguar E-Type or classic US Corvette. The Ferraris and Aston were in a price bracket way above the Cobra, and even then (and even in their most aerodynamic coupé forms) couldn't touch the Cobra's top speed. In mass-market terms, the Cobra obviously wasn't such a bargain-basement prospect (no AC, with its very small production numbers, ever had been), so both the E-Type (by a whisker) and the Corvette (by a long way) undercut the Cobra on

This is a few years down the line from the early 289s, but the principle is the same – Cobras in the showroom alongside the more mundane metal, to pull in the enthusiasts.

price. The remarkable E-Type could also give it a run for top speed, but by the time the Jaguar got anywhere near that, the massively more accelerative Cobra would have been long gone.

That, in a nutshell, was the Cobra's long suit. The Ferraris, Aston, Corvette, even the first E-Type could beat its standard 260bhp from the original 260cu in V8; but the Cobra was the lightest of the group, by far, which meant the highest power-to-weight ratio, by far. This was why, in 1962, nothing else on the road, at any price, could remotely approach the Cobra's acceleration figures. It wasn't really until best part of thirty years later that figures like the first Cobra's appeared again, with exotic supercars like the Ferrari F40 and Porsche 959 just about beating it, while 'real-world' cars still only dreamed.

A HALO FOR THE BLUE OVAL

Another part of the marketing secret was that Shelby's arrangement with Ford allowed him to sell the Cobra through Ford dealerships. That halo effect had been a major reason for Ford committing to the project in the first place, and as far as Shelby was concerned the only drawback was

By the time they finally started offering it on the right-hand side, the Cobra's steering wheel had been improved from the original version after the additional stresses of racing showed a tendency for the Ace-type wheel to break. Right-hand drive implied an AC badge, too.

that he had to find the dealers himself. After the first few magazine road tests appeared, they were finding him.

By 1964 he had 175 of them but was planning to cut back to around 100 of the 'right' type. That turned out to be an issue, with Ford having a big say. Ford never wanted the Cobra to be available through just any dealer; they wanted to target areas where Corvette sales were strongest (there being little doubt which rival was the primary target), and they also wanted a say in how many cars were allocated to particular areas.

It wasn't difficult to find showroom space for a Cobra to draw in customers who wouldn't ever buy one but would look at 'lesser' Fords. It was reasonably easy to find staff who could talk about the Cobra in the dealership. It was something else to find a salesman who could demonstrate a Cobra on the road without frightening himself and/or his customer half to death, or without bending the car. Sadly, at least one salesman is reported to have killed himself (it invariably was a 'he' in the early 1960s) and his potential customer during a demo drive. Another Cobra on the early chassis list was reportedly badly damaged by its new owner just two-and-a-half miles after taking delivery. That was with the 289; when the even more fearsome 427 came along, the problem of finding salesmen who could offer a meaningful demonstration in complete safety became even more serious.

The first year of Cobra production saw several significant specification changes prompted by experience in service. The first came with car number seventy, when the 3.54:1 final-drive ratio was changed to 3.77:1. The original ratio had been a bit too tall for the original engines; the lower (numerically higher) ratio gave even better low-speed flexibility (and standing-start performance) while retaining a top speed, of over 140mph (225km/h), that very few US customers would ever use. When the 289 Cobra went on sale in Europe, however, it kept the more long-legged 3.54:1 – on the basis that, in theory at least, there were more places (in pre-limit days) where a customer could use the maximum speed.

Those first seventy cars also used wholly Lucas electrics; from car seventy-one the system adopted a higher-output Ford dynamo and from car number 201 an entirely new electrical system by Ford – including wiring looms and a change from dynamo to alternator. Officially, the change was as much for cost as for reliability, but failure-prone Lucas did have an unfortunate reputation in the USA as 'The Prince of Darkness'. The instrument supplier also changed from car 201, from British Smiths to American Stewart Warner.

Under racing conditions, a small number of cars had suffered steering wheel breakages, so the original Ace wheel was soon replaced by a stronger one made specifically for the higher loads associated with the Cobra, even on the road.

THE DEFINITIVE 289

By far the biggest early change came at car number seventy-six, during 1963, with the availability of a new, larger-capacity version of the small-block V8 from Ford. This was the Challenger 289, evolved from the 260 as part of the normal Ford updating process, and offered as the base V8 engine for the mainstream Ford 'full-size' range for 1964 model year. As before, the Shelby version had solid cam-followers rather than the hydraulic ones that were one of the few weak points on the standard engine – eliminating a tendency to valve-float at the higher revs the Cobra owner was more likely to explore.

That did highlight one other issue, but one more about the driver than the car: owners who respected the quoted redline for the engine rarely had any reliability problems; ones who broke the recommended rev limit just as frequently broke their engines.

SHELBY AC COBRA 289 (1962–1965)

Layout and Chassis

Body type — Two-seater sports roadster, all aluminium

Chassis — Twin-tube ladder frame with tubular cross-beams, box-section suspension mountings and body-carrying tubular superstructure

Engine

Type — Ford small-block V8
Block material — Thin-wall cast iron
Head material — Cast iron
Cylinders — 8 in 90-degree V, five main bearings
Cooling — Water
Bore and stroke — 101.6 × 96.5mm (4.00 × 3.86in)
Capacity — 4736cc (289cu in). NB: 4261cc (260cu in) up to chassis no CSX2074
Valves — 2 valves per cylinder, operated by pushrods from single central camshaft in block
Compression ratio — 11.6:1
Carburettor — Single four-barrel Holley carburettor; four twin-choke downdraught Weber carburettors optional
Max. power (DIN) — 271bhp at 6,000rpm (260bhp at 5,800rpm for 260cu in)
Max. torque — 314lb ft at 3,400rpm (269lb ft @ 4,800rpm for 260cu in)
Fuel capacity — 15.0gal (18.0 US gal/68ltr)

Transmission

Clutch — Single dry plate, hydraulic operation
Gearbox — Borg-Warner 4-speed manual, all-synchromesh

Internal Gearbox Ratios

First — 2.36:1
Second — 1.78:1
Third — 1.41:1
Fourth — 1.00:1
Reverse — 2.36:1
Final drive ratio — 3.77:1 (numerous options)

Suspension and Steering

Front — Independent, by lower wishbones and transverse leaf-spring upper links, telescopic dampers, anti-roll bar
Rear — Independent, by lower wishbones and transverse leaf-spring upper links, telescopic dampers, anti-roll bar
Steering — Rack and pinion; worm and sector up to chassis no. CSX2125
Tyres — 7.35 × 15in cross-ply or 185 × 15in radial
Wheels — 15in centre-lock wire wheels
Rim width — 6.0in J section

Brakes

Type — Solid discs front and rear

Dimensions

Track, front — 51.5in (1,308mm)
Track, rear — 52.5in (1,333mm)
Wheelbase — 90.0in (2,286mm)
Overall length — 151.5in (3,848mm)
Overall width — 61.0in (1,549mm)
Overall height — 49.0in (1,244mm)
Ground clearance — 5.0in (127mm)
Unladen weight — 2,170lb (984kg)
Power to weight ratio — 279.7bhp per ton

Performance

Top speed — 138mph (222km/h)
0–60mph — 5.5sec
0–100mph — 13.0sec
Standing quarter — 13.9sec
Fuel consumption — 15.1mpg (18.7ltr/100km)

The larger capacity was achieved with the same 2.87in (72.9mm) stroke with bore increased to an even more over-square 4.0in (101.6mm). That equated to 289cu in (4736cc) while leaving the short-stroke's ability to rev freely, and adding even more piston area – a proven route to improved power and torque. Shelby's basic 289 for the Cobra used an 11.0:1 compression (which was pretty high for its day) and a single four-barrel carburettor. In that form it promised 271bhp (not quite the 1bhp per cu in specific output of the 260, but a useful overall increase) and a much bigger maximum torque increase, to 312lb ft at 3,400rpm.

Oddly, according to later magazine tests, none of this made the 289 any quicker than the early 260s. In fact no later magazine test bettered the figures for the original 260 cars. That might have begged the question of how standard were the original 'standard' road-test cars; but the big advantage for the 289 was that it made the Cobra more flexible for the road, and even more tuneable for competition.

Another big plus was that increasing power didn't increase the price. Even in 1964, by which time the Cobra (with 289 V8 and numerous other refinements) could justify becoming known as the MkII, the basic price was still listed as $5,995, exactly as it had been at launch in 1962. In truth, that wasn't a realistic selling price for the people who built the car, not least because of volume issues. The Cobra simply hadn't sold in anything like the numbers Ford or Shelby had initially hoped, and although it continued to go out of dealers' doors at a fairly steady rate, it had long ago become more important to Ford for its 'halo' value and more important to Shelby for its racing abilities than it was to either of them purely for income. Something similar could obviously be said for AC – the Cobra was keeping then busy rather than making them wealthy.

NOT JUST COBRAS

Still, in financial terms, Shelby wasn't doing badly by this stage. By late 1964 he had grown out of the Venice premises, too. Having become involved with the GT40 programme and creating hotter versions of Ford's new Mustang, by 1964 his turnover had grown to around $7.5 million – around $5 million of which represented Shelby-badged car sales and tuning equipment. The positive image of Total Performance, and not least the Cobra, had taken Ford sales to new levels; and if only a few hundred of those sales were actually Cobras, that wasn't the point – the car had done its image-building job well.

The production numbers speak for themselves. By the time of the switch from 260 to 289, Shelby and AC had built just seventy-five cars. Sixty-two were purely road-going examples; four were 'works' racers (later updated, as were many customer cars, with the 289 engine); one was a racer prepared by the factory for a private entrant; seven were sold as competition cars to be prepared entirely independently; the other was a single Cobra which became the first of a handful of 'Dragonsnakes', designed specifically for drag-racing (also later updated with a 289).

After the big jump from 260 to 289, the next change may have sounded less fundamental but in a way was even more significant. It came with chassis number CSX2126, completed on 31 January 1963, the car with the first major chassis as opposed to engine change, from the Ace's old worm-and-sector steering to more precise rack-and-pinion.

Chassis records refer to CSX2126 as a prototype, sent to Ford in Dearborn for evaluation. They presumably approved the changes, as CSX2127, completed on 7 March (specifically to race at the 12 Hours of Sebring that month) was the first 'production' Cobra with rack-and-pinion steering. The Sebring link is interesting, as the change was largely prompted by racing customers wanting better steering precision, without the worm-and-sector layout's susceptibility to toe-in/toe-out changes as the suspension rose and fell.

It wasn't as simple as swapping the steering box, or Shelby would have done it from the start – they used the worm-and-sector because it was already used on the Ace. To fit rack-and-pinion they also had to make slightly shorter wishbones with more widely spaced pivots, plus revised uprights and spring mountings. The rack came from nowhere more exotic than the MG Midget parts bin, and the changes were engineered in Thames Ditton by AC's Alan Turner and Shelby's Phil Remington, who had flown out specially for this job. It certainly worked; everyone preferred the new feel, and when it went back to Shelby for testing, the car proved to be a full two seconds a lap faster around Riverside.

They continued developing the chassis, and from car 160, road-car handling was further improved by switching from 5.5in (140mm) to 6.0in (152mm) rim widths, which allowed the Cobra to use the newer and wider Goodyear G8 tyre. That required subtly wider arches to cover the new rubber; there were also new louvres in the front wings to improve cockpit cooling (as tried on the 1963 Le Mans cars), and a return to a slightly larger grille opening, for better under-bonnet cooling with the bigger V8. From car 164, brake performance was improved by adopting a dual (rather than single) master-cylinder, and from 187 the manually adjustable handbrake linkage was changed for an automatically adjustable one.

RECROSSING THE ATLANTIC

All the detail changes together meant a steadily improving car; by this time, too, the specifications were becoming more standardized. The Cobra, though, still hadn't gone on sale in Europe. During 1962 it had made European motor show appearances in both Paris and London, alongside the Ace and Aceca, which were still in production. The grey European show car, with blue leather interior, was chassis number CSX2025, and being European rather than specifically British, it had left-hand drive.

The first right-hand-drive Cobra wasn't far away, and was distinguished by a new chassis designation, CS2030 – dropping 'X' from the prefix because it wasn't intended for export from the UK, either to the USA or Europe. It was retained by AC themselves, with a '4.5-litre' engine, in best UK tradition. Shelby American credited AC for the car to keep the books in order, and it was registered 300 PK, on 1 November 1962, to become the first Thames Ditton demonstrator. One of the people it was demonstrated to was Stirling Moss, who was pictured sitting in it in London, chatting to Charles and Derek Hurlock.

The first British magazine test of a Cobra appeared in *Autosport* in June 1963, when doyen of road testers John Bolster (famous for his handlebar moustache, deerstalker hat, and GP and Le Mans pit-lane commentaries) spent a long day on British roads with

Even the extremely specialized Dragonsnake could find its way onto the dealership forecourt.

The Dragonsnake also had some extras that didn't appear on other Cobras …

By 1963, one of the earliest brochures for the right-hand-drive specification 289 showed the original wheelarch style for 5.5in wheels, and simple overriders.

By the time the later European/British 289 appeared, it had the more curvaceous wheelarches, front wing vents and the shorter bootlid to make way for the new filler cap.

Shelby's own early left-hand-drive 289, temporarily registered QQ 907. Bolster was also well-known as a former racer in his own right, so, of course, he loved it.

The next right-hand-drive cars were CSX2130 (the unraced 1963 Le Mans prototype that fell foul of the FIA's homologation requirement) and CS2131. The latter dropped the X again because it was never intended for export, but, adding another twist to the numbering scheme, there was also a CSX2131 – an AC coupé along the lines of the later Daytona, described in Chapter 8. CS2131 (as opposed to CSX2131) was one of two cars entered for Le Mans 1963, prepared by John Willment (later a key part of the GT40 programme, with John Wyer) and driven by Ninian Sanderson and Peter Bolton. Eligible for the production GT class where CSX2130 hadn't yet qualified for the GT Prototype class, it finished third in class and seventh overall, which wasn't a bad result.

Aside from those cars, it must be said, you couldn't actually buy a right-hand-drive Cobra in the UK (or anywhere else in Europe) until 1963. Then it was AC who introduced the 'European' cars, built entirely in Thames Ditton with no transatlantic excursions for engines or running gear as with the Shelby cars. They introduced another chassis nomenclature, with COX6- numbers for European 'export' cars and COB6- for British domestic market cars (which also, by definition, meant right-hand drive).

The first three European Cobras went to France, the fourth was sold in Britain in November 1963, to Lord Cross, who raced it extensively and successfully. The next car in the chassis sequence, and the second right-hand-drive 'production' car, became AC's first right-hand-drive works demonstrator. AC had originally only intended a run of a dozen right-hand-drive cars, not because they didn't think they could have been sold, but because they were fully stretched in building chassis for Shelby. So right-hand-drive Cobras weren't properly available in the UK until around September 1964, which was quite a long wait.

As launched in the UK, the Cobra wasn't quite such a bargain as it had been in the US. At a starting price of £2,030, the 289 was expensive compared to the opposition, and two years on from the big splash of the US launch, it had probably lost a lot of the 'new-car' impact, impressive as it still was in terms of numbers. What's more, as a European/UK car it didn't enjoy the US benefits of easy mechanical parts availability, and even more significantly, of dirt-cheap US fuel prices for big, thirsty V8 power.

Against those disadvantages, only sixty-one European-spec leaf-spring Cobras were built, the last of them in mid-1965. By then, a new and even more spectacular breed of Cobra was emerging from Shelby's workshops. This one had undergone a dramatic metamorphosis from the old Ace-based transverse-leaf-spring chassis to a far more modern coil-spring layout. It also signalled the start of a new and even more attention-grabbing phase in the Cobra legend, with a mighty new engine option – the 427.

Chassis number COX6011 had an interesting early history, starting life as a left-hand-drive show car in Geneva, then switching to right-hand drive (and registration number 47 COB) when it returned to the UK in 1970 – as a superb example of the classic 289 shape.

CHAPTER SIX

COIL SPRINGS AND THE 427

By March 1964, Ken Miles, who Shelby had inherited when moving into the old Reventlow-Scarab workshops in 1962, had spent more time than anyone racing and testing Cobras of every variety. The Cobra owed much of its effectiveness to Miles' skills as engineer and test driver. Miles was also a formidable race driver, especially with sports cars.

The 12 Hours of Sebring, in Florida, was (and is) widely regarded as second only to Le Mans in the world of endurance racing. The old airfield-based circuit is fast, and its mainly concrete surface is notoriously bumpy, making Sebring a searching test of both performance and durability for any team serious about surviving 24 hours at Le Mans in June.

Sebring takes place in early March, starting on Saturday morning and running into darkness, with the 1964 race (second round of the FIA World Sports Car Championship)

finishing at 10pm. Miles arrived with a new car co-driven by Shelby American mechanic/driver John Morton. But even the experienced Miles was having problems coming to terms with car number 1. During practice he spun off going through the Esses, and managed to hit more or less the only

Ken Miles, on the right, with Bruce McLaren on the left, conceived the notion of shoehorning Ford's 427 'big-block' V8 into the Cobra, and eventually made it work.

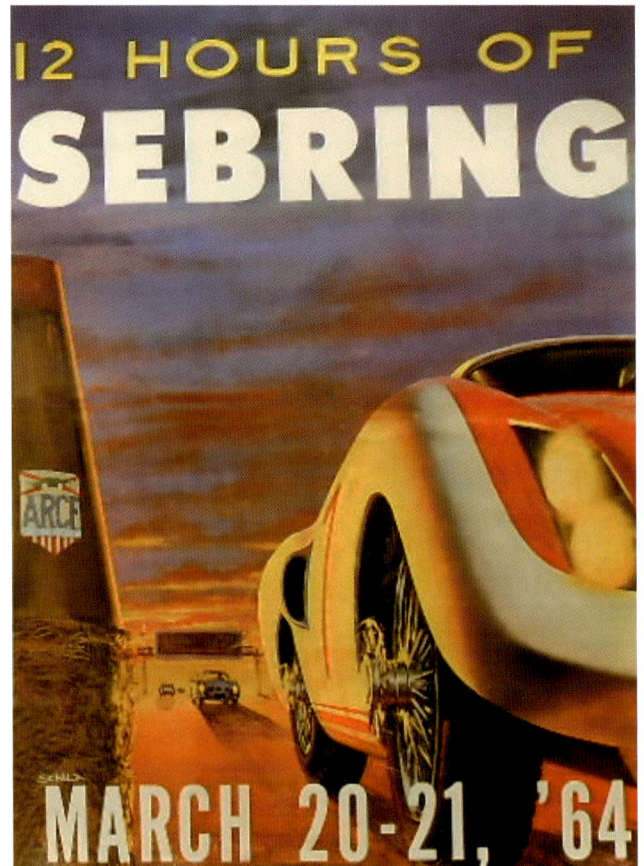

The 12 Hours of Sebring in March 1964 was where Miles first showed up with his big-engined Cobra, crashed it even before practice ended, blew the engine in the race, but showed that there was something worth persevering with.

96

KEN MILES – TESTER SUPREME

Ken Miles was one of the biggest assets Shelby and the Cobra project could ever have had. Competition manager-cum-development engineer, Miles was widely acknowledged as one of the finest test drivers in the business, with the engineering knowledge and design skills to translate what he learned on track into the metal. And as the icing on the cake, he had the ability to communicate both problems and solutions to those he worked with.

Like the Cobra, Miles was Anglo-American, born in Sutton Coalfield near Birmingham on 1 November 1918. Between the wars he started competing on two wheels, then became a tank sergeant in the army. After World War II he switched from two-wheel competition to four, going vintage racing with an Alfa Romeo, an Alvis and a Bugatti, before starting to make a name for himself in a 'modern' Ford V8-powered Frazer-Nash. With its usual Bristol engine the Frazer-Nash was second cousin to the Ace; with the Ford V8 it echoed the Cobra.

Miles moved to California in 1952, and almost immediately started racing again. Like many, he restarted with a standard MG TD, but was disqualified from his first US race, at Pebble Beach, for 'reckless driving'. In truth the brakes on the MG had failed but Miles had carried on regardless, at barely reduced lap times.

Back at Pebble Beach, in 1953, he started a run of fourteen consecutive wins with a tube-framed MG special, much as was paving the way to the Ace in the UK. Now nicknamed 'Mr MG', from 1954 he drove an MG TF while he was building another MG special that came to be known as the 'Flying Shingle'. In 1955 he also drove a Triumph TR3, and from 1956 a series of Porsches, including another 'hybrid', a Porsche-engined Cooper, the 'Pooper'.

He drove Porsches, winning even against works cars, right into the 1960s. In 1961 he had a leaner interlude with a Maserati, but started working as a test driver for Sunbeam, developing the Alpine. At Shelby he also worked on the Alpine-based Ford V8 powered Tiger.

Miles joined Lance Reventlow's Scarab project, and transferred to Shelby when Reventlow called time and Shelby moved into the Scarab workshops. Miles had worked as a consultant for Reventlow and designed the Scarab chassis, which were far more complex than the Cobra's but shared the philosophy of tubular frame, big V8 and alloy skin.

The lean, hawk-nosed Miles wasn't an easy man to know: he spoke his mind, often quite forcibly, with a strong British accent and often out of the side of his mouth. He didn't think much of people who didn't listen, but so long as he was around racing cars, he usually had a smile on his face. And, of course, he was hugely respected, and fitted well into Shelby's small, tightly-knit organization, with capable, like-minded people and minimal red tape.

With Shelby, Miles worked on the 289, effectively conceived the 427, was a massive influence on the Daytona, and worked on the Tiger, the Shelby Mustangs, the GT40, then Ford MkII and the mighty J-Car descendant of the GT40 programme. He was also one of the more successful GT40 drivers, wining a lot of major races in various versions.

In the end, his job (and his passion) cost him his life. Testing the GT40 J-Car at Riverside on 17 August 1966 he lost control, crashed heavily and was killed.

tree on Sebring's flat, bare expanses. The car was repaired overnight, and made it into the race, but only to lap 81, when the engine threw a connecting rod.

It wasn't the usual 289 engine. CSX2166, race car number 1, had started life as a 289 (a fairly ordinary red street car with black leather interior) in July 1963. By March 1964 the 289 engine had gone, and in its place was a 427cu in (6997cc) Ford NASCAR racing engine, plus 'top-loader' racing transmission. It was, for now, a one-off car, a long way from a production possibility, or even from racing homologation; but it revealed a new direction.

DRIVEN BY MOTOR SPORT

The reason for building a more powerful Cobra was simple: motor sport. Or rather, the next step in motor sport. From the start, the Cobra had been a quick racing car; as it added reliability to speed it became a hugely successful one. By mid-1963, against strong opposition, 289 Cobras had won everything worth winning in US racing, and were virtually unbeatable in SCCA and USRRC Production racing. Shelby had ambitions beyond that, however. After his run-in with Enzo Ferrari during his time in Europe, Shelby harboured a burning ambition to beat Ferrari on the big stage, in the Sports Car Manufacturers Championship.

The 289 Cobra had been homologated for international racing by the start of the 1963 season, as production numbers satisfied the regulatory requirement for the GT category of the FIA World Manufacturers Championship. By the end of its first season (enthusiastically backed by Ford), the Cobra had notched up a few reasonable international results, including its first FIA race win. But it hadn't done nearly enough to satisfy Shelby's far from secret aim of 'whipping Ferrari's ass'.

Quick as they were, and with reliability improving, once they made the leap from mainly small US tracks to very different European venues, it became clear they had one major shortcoming. On Europe's longer, faster circuits, aerodynamics started to be a bigger part of the equation. On European-style tracks, for all their light weight and ample power (even with the upgrade from 260 to 289), the brick-like Cobra roadster simply wasn't quick enough in a straight line to beat Ferrari's more slippery coupés.

As detailed in Chapter 8, Shelby attacked the maximum speed issue, in 1964, via the far more efficient aerodynamics of the Daytona coupé – and some rule interpretation that Ferrari himself would have admired. The Daytona came within a whisker of winning the 1964 GT Championship, but was beaten at the last gasp not by lack of performance but by another piece of Ferrari rule-stretching. The ass-kicking would have to wait one more year.

Shelby knew that 1965's opposition would, if anything, be even stronger. Ferrari appeared ready to homologate the 275LM; Ford's support for the Cobra and Daytona would inevitably be diluted by the focus on their own GT40; on the home front, Chevrolet expected to have a new 396cu in (6494cc) racing engine for their lightweight Grand Sport Corvettes – definitely levelling the playing field against the Cobras.

Even the best full-race 289s couldn't quite get to 400bhp with real reliability, and that wasn't enough. Hence the monstrous 427, giving even Miles a hard time.

What science, as opposed to brute force, looked like at the time, in Ferrari's mid-engined 275LM, which was as slippery as the Cobra roadster was bluff (even with the body damage).

RAISING THE BAR

In a way, he only had himself to blame. The 427 was largely his own idea, towards the end of the 1963 season, when it was already clear that the main opposition (Ferrari in Europe, GM at home) would soon move the goalposts with bigger engines and potentially a lot more power. For a man like Miles, virtually brought up on parts-bin engineering, Ford's 427 NASCAR engine was a flashing light.

His first attempt at making it work wasn't terribly sophisticated. CSX2166's leaf-spring chassis (originally designed for 289 power) was given some modest strengthening but no major re-engineering beyond rejigging the engine mounts. It wore a hastily chopped-about shell, with crudely cut holes and scoops to help keep the bigger engine cool, and tack-on arch extensions to cover the wider rubber on Halibrand pin-drive wheels (as demanded by what would now be around 485bhp).

Before Sebring, Miles had given it only the briefest of shakedowns, at Riverside. In Florida, even the most casual observer could hardly ignore the surplus of power over traction that helped pitch Miles into that lone tree. The car was repairable, though, and even after failing to finish, Miles's determination to make it work also survived its very unpromising start.

A good deal of work now went into moving forwards with the next 427 pre-prototype (as these effectively were), based on another 1963 289 chassis, CSX2196.

Strictly speaking, this was neither 289 nor 427. As pukka 427s were in short supply, Miles initially fitted CSX2196 with a full-race, all-alloy 390cu in (6391cc) 'big-block' Ford V8, on four downdraught Weber carburettors, to give 427 power with 289 weight.

Before beefing the chassis up, first thoughts were to make it lighter, including throwing away all interior body panelling, and, of course, all the trim. Overall weight came down to barely 1,600lb (725kg), and with close to 500bhp (and 700bhp per ton), it was clearly going to have formidable performance. On the downside, on leaf springs, it didn't promise much by way of subtlety or a forgiving nature.

At a glance, it looked to have an almost standard Cobra body; but this being an experimental car, Miles had literally split it across the middle and hinged the complete nose and tail sections to give instant access to engine and chassis. In public, the car was usually referred to as 'the Flip-Top'; in private, Shelby people called it 'the Turd'.

In December 1964 it appeared at the annual Nassau Speed

Miles ready to drop the first big-block into the Cobra. Getting it in was relatively easy; making the car drivable (even as a racer) wasn't so straightforward.

Weeks with a full 427 V8, and simply ran away from the opposition (including the new lightweight Grand Sport Corvettes). Unfortunately it only went two-thirds race distance before the over-stretched chassis broke; but it and the other prototype had done enough to prove the concept's potential, and Shelby decided the 427 route would work.

As with the 289, if the 427 was to be eligible for FIA racing it would have to meet the 100-off homologation requirement to qualify as a production model – which in turn meant that the 427, however rabid, would also have to be a customer car.

You couldn't do this with just any Cobra. Miles had chopped the 427 prototype body into pieces and hinged the nose and tail sections for easier access to the important bits.

By the time Miles took the 427 to Nassau it had started to look a bit less of a box of bits.

That part of the challenge was a little way into the future. The two Miles prototype racers really had been all but undriveable. Even with the road-based 427 rather than the rare and exotic all-alloy race-prep 390, there would clearly be more power than the existing (Ace-based) transverse-leaf 289-type chassis could handle.

TAMING A MONSTER

This is not overstating the issue. The 427 was a monster of an engine, and not only for its capacity – though that played its part in a car that started with 'only' 260cu in (4261cc). It had been conceived as a NASCAR racing engine, NASCAR was all about maximum horsepower, and the 427 was closer to a proper race engine than a street engine.

Ford's 'big-block' V8 family wasn't new; the line started in 1958, with the 352cu in (5768cc) version. For 1960, Ford uprated the 352 with classic performance options: solid rather than hydraulic cam-followers; higher compression; better exhaust manifolds and a four-barrel Holley carburettor on an aluminium inlet manifold that also saved around 50lb (22.5kg) engine weight. It was one of Ford's first no-compromise performance engines, and the first production Ford V8 (before the 260) to deliver more than 1bhp per cu in – 360bhp.

That was only the beginning. For the full-size 1961 model year Galaxie and the sporting Thunderbird, capacity grew to 390cu in (6391cc), by increasing stroke from 3.50 to 3.78in (88.9 to 96.0mm). It became a long-running engine, and a versatile one. The basic version with 'economy' two-barrel carburettor gave 250bhp; by 1961 you could have anything from 300 to 401bhp, the latter with the dealer-installed option of triple two-barrel carbs.

That 401bhp 390 started with the Thunderbird Special V8, factory equipped with a single four-barrel Holley on a cast-iron manifold and with 9.6:1 compression. That gave 300bhp at 4,600rpm and a slogging 427lb ft of torque at only 2,800rpm. The next option was the Thunderbird Special High Performance V8, with larger four-barrel Holley on an aluminium manifold, tubular exhaust manifolds, a different camshaft with solid followers, and 10.6:1 compression. That gave 375bhp at 6,000rpm and 427lb ft of torque at 3,000rpm. The range-topping option started by bolting on the triple two-barrel Holley intake assembly (shipped as 'special order' in the boot), to give 401bhp at 6,000rpm and 430lb ft of torque at 3,500rpm.

Another manifestation of Total Performance came with this engine (again as a dealer-installed option) in the Borg-Warner T10 four-speed manual transmission – a massive improvement over Ford's stodgy Cruise-O-Matic auto or clunky old three-speed-plus-overdrive manual. Attached to the 'small-block' 260, it was also the gearbox of choice for the first Cobras. In the early 1960s, with the advent of Total Performance, Ford's new image could be summed up by the sign that hung over one well-known American engine tuner's door: 'Speed costs money, how fast do you want to go?'

For the 1962 model year, Ford settled into the horsepower race with a vengeance. The 'small-block' 260 (as in the first Cobras) was introduced, while maximum big-block capacity increased again, to 406cu in (6653cc). That was the first Ford Division engine (Ford Division also included Lincoln and Mercury) to go over 400cu in (6560cc). In an era of excess, it was just the thing to keep up with the latest Chevrolet Impala SS, Plymouth Sport Fury, Pontiac Grand Prix and Dodge Polara 500. It wasn't difficult to see what sold cars in America in 1962.

RACING GOES RESPECTABLE

Now that Henry Ford II had announced that Ford would no longer be shy about racing, the 406 Thunderbird Special V8 became the Blue Oval's staple engine in NASCAR (oval-circuit 'stock-car' sedan) racing. It had a stronger bottom end,

started with a 385bhp single four-barrel version, and went up to a triple two-barrel (6V) version, with the usual solid cam-followers, more aggressive camshaft, and high, 11.4:1 compression ratio. With 405bhp at 5,800rpm and 448lb ft at 3,500rpm, it was Ford's most powerful production engine to date. It held that title only until 1963, when Ford made an even bigger push in NASCAR, with aerodynamic body shapes for the Galaxies that the programme was based on, and even more power.

Even more than in sports car racing, optimum aerodynamics were crucial to NASCAR performance, and in 1962 it had mainly been aerodynamics, not power, that had let Ford down. That wouldn't be repeated in 1963, and power went up again, too – as the 352, 390, 406 progression continued to the magic number, 427.

It became almost impossible to read any description of a Ford 427-engined car without finding adjectives like

Donor car: it was Ford's **NASCAR** programme that gave birth to the mighty 427 big-block (and the even more extreme ohc 427 pure race engine), in the 1963 Galaxie.

'awesome', 'fearsome', 'monstrous'. Wedge-shaped com-bustion chambers gave good swirl characteristics, and big, rectangular ports gave excellent breathing. Capacity (nomi-nally at least) had grown to 427cu in (6997cc) with bore and stroke dimensions of 4.24 × 3.78in (101.6 × 96.0mm) – so the engine was still 'oversquare'. With solid followers, 11.5:1 compression and two Holley 780cfm (that's cubic feet per minute of airflow) four-barrel carburettors on an aluminium manifold, this very special engine, in top 'street' configura-tion, gave 425bhp at 6,500rpm and 480lb ft of torque at 3,500rpm. Of course there was plenty more on offer for any racing class that allowed it.

It was also an extremely strong engine, with a forged steel crankshaft, cross-bolted main bearings and high-strength connecting rods all designed to keep it in one piece dur-ing sustained high-load operation. It had unusually large oil galleries that were good for both lubrication and internal cooling; in 'side-oiler' form (the racing preference) the oil-feed to the main bearings came in from the side of the block rather than from below, offering even more reliable lubrica-tion under heavy (racing) cornering forces.

Even in not far short of 2 tons of Galaxie and even in 425bhp 'street' trim it gave astonishing performance. Shelby and Miles were about to put it into a Cobra that weighed barely half as much as the 'full-size' Galaxie sedan, which obviously seemed like a good idea at the time, but to make it work the Cobra had a whole list of problems to be resolved.

The 427 was physically much larger than the compact 289. It was of the old 'Y-block' school in which the crankcase extended below the crankshaft centre line. It was almost 200lb (90.5kg) heavier than the 289, with its innovative 'thin-wall' castings. The 427 needed more cooling and more fuel flow, so needed bigger radiators and bigger carburettors. Most of all, its power (and especially torque) were now more than the old Ace-based chassis could handle, so it was finally time for a significant redesign.

5. Thunderbird 4-V/427 High-Performance V-8—410 hp. Swift acceleration and top range output to please the most exacting performance fan. Responsive 4-barrel carburetion, special high-speed, dual breaker ignition, solid valve lifters and special valve springs . . . a few of many features for high output capability.

6. Thunderbird 8-V/427 High-Performance V-8—425 hp. Spectacular acceleration and top speed with two matched, synchronized 4-barrel carburetors; special manifolding, low-restriction exhaust headers. Extra-high capacity oil and fuel systems. Transistorized ignition and alternator optional with both 427 V-8's.

C. 4-Speed Manual Transmission—A fully synchronized, fast-shifting gear box with floor-mounted shift lever. Close gear ratio spacing with 2.36 to 1 start-up ratio. Positive reverse gear lockout. Shift pattern on knob.

D. Fordomatic Drive—Two-speed smoothness combined with time-proven reliability and good economy. Vacuum-operated control valve matches transmission shifting to engine speed and load. Available with Six and Galaxie 260 and 289 V-8's.

E. Cruise-O-Matic Drive—Versatile dual-range automatic transmission. Three-speed drive starting in low for most normal driving. Two-speed drive starting in intermediate for gentler start-up on ice or snow. Standard with Galaxie 289 V-8 on 500/XL's.

The 427 was a genuine off-the-shelf showroom engine, as shown in this 1963 model year Galaxie brochure – offering two 427 Thunderbird V8 street specs, the 410bhp 4V with single four-barrel carburettor and the 425bhp 8V with a pair of four barrels.

At least as important as adding the power of the 427 V8 was adding the sophistication of all-round coil-spring suspension, finally replacing the transverse leafs inherited from the Ace.

Having adopted the original Ace-based chassis almost as an off-the-shelf proposition (simply to make the Cobra possible), Shelby, for the first time, had an opportunity to start a Cobra chassis from something like a clean sheet. While his budget, as ever, would be tight, having just signed a five-year 'reciprocal technical and marketing assistance agreement' with Ford (which included the Shelby Mustang and GT40), Shelby could at least call on their full technical support. By the time Shelby, Ford and AC had finished with the 427 Cobra, just about the only carry-over was the basic layout.

Shelby's project engineer, Jin Benavides, started with the familiar tubular ladder, but a much more substantial ladder. The main tubes were increased in diameter from 3in (76mm) to 4in (102mm) and made from yet thicker-gauge material (which together made them three times stronger). They were moved about 5in (127mm) further apart, and the old fabricated-sheet suspension towers were replaced with more robust tubular structures.

That was just the start: the bigger, stronger chassis became the platform for a new and much more modern suspension layout. It finally abandoned the old transverse leaf-spring upper links for a conventional double wishbone layout, with classic concentric coil-spring/damper units – classic in racing, still rare on a road car.

TURNING TO SCIENCE

Science was starting to creep into the process by 1964. Where the Ace/Cobra chassis had been designed around chalk marks on John Tojeiro's workshop floor back in the 1950s, a lot of the 427 started life on Ford's new-generation computers.

The basic four-link suspension layout, including the coil-spring/damper units, was worked out at Ford Engineering by Klaus Arning, who had also worked on the GT40. It drew initially on a layout for a Mustang prototype, but became an obvious choice for the 427. The basics were refined by Ford's Bob Negstadt, again using computer power to optimize location of the pick-up points to allow longer, more compliant travel with the correct degrees of anti-dive and anti-squat, and (crucially) to keep the tyres more vertical more often than had ever been possible with the old leaf springs.

In these early days of computer-aided design, there were anomalies: the computer's 'ideal' solution would have located some key rear suspension pickups around the middle of the driver's bottom; but that was quickly sorted out by the hands-on engineers, who knew a bit more about real-world compromises than the computers did.

Remarkably, one component that didn't need changing was the Salisbury differential, which proved quite capable of handling massively increased torque. The driveshafts, on the other hand, had to be substantially upgraded. They had sliding spines, but even with significantly increased suspension travel they underwent virtually no change in length. According to Miles, that was fortunate, as, with any real change, the torque would have caused any readily available

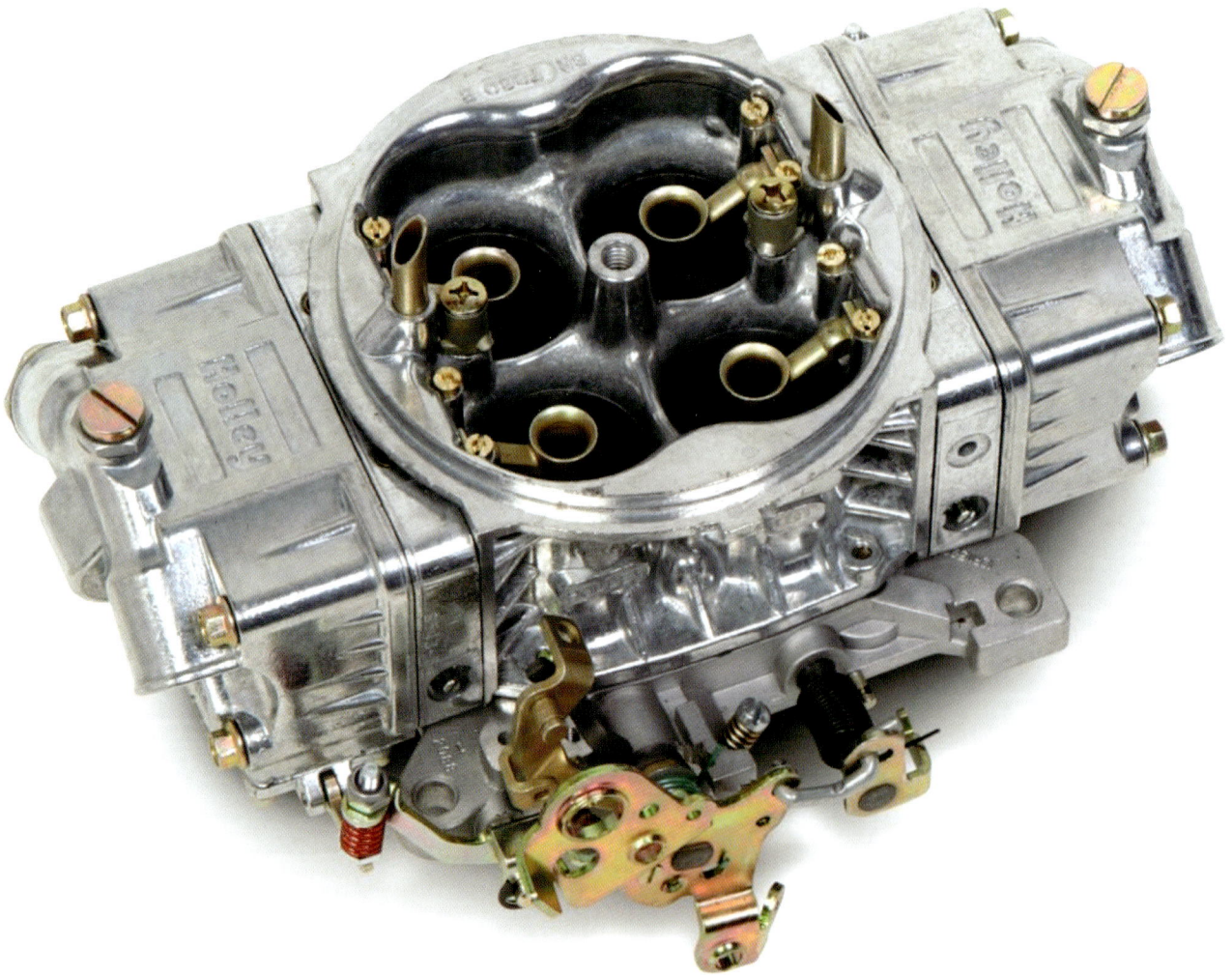

A Holley 'double-pumper' carburettor, nicknamed for its two accelerator pumps, wasn't just a key to power, it was also the key to everyday driveability.

You'd be unlikely to mistake the bigger 427 for a 289 – especially in musclebound S/C spec.

splined drives to bind. Larger, stronger hubs with heavier-duty taper bearings were also specified, and larger brakes were an option on competition cars. The suspension was Rose-jointed (common motor sport practice, to allow easy geometry adjustments), and the links would eventually offer the option of rigid bronze bushes for competition, rather than less harsh, more refined rubber bushes for the road.

Finally, once the computer had had its say and the engineers had done their reality check, Negstadt, Remington (plus much appreciated Ford/Shelby admin man Ray Geddes) went to AC (who would have to build the new chassis)

and put in many hours with AC's chief engineering designer, Alan Turner, in Thames Ditton, to make the new chassis and suspension work in practice as well as on the drawing board.

The car was tested first at Silverstone (a change from Riverside!) while the Ford and Shelby people were still in the UK, and fitted with an 'experimental' engine, supplied by Ford, in quite a high state of tune. That included a Holley 'double-pumper' four-barrel carburettor (with two accelerator pumps rather than one) on a 'medium-riser' manifold – the object being to get the maximum amount of fuel/air mixture into the engine in the shortest time. With a V8

LEFT: **The Halibrand pin-drive magnesium wheels were mainly called for by what happened at the other end of the car, where they had to handle the power through the rear axle, and they were meant to be standard equipment, but Shelby had serious problems with availability.**

BELOW: **Given the 427's thirst, the S/C's huge flip-up filler cap was just the job for quick pit stops.**

engine and carburettors in the centre of the V, the taller the manifold, the straighter the inlet tract can be, and the straighter the tract and better the flow, the better the maximum power – at the expense (generally) of flexibility. For street use, low-rise was standard choice; for NASCAR and drag-racing (where flexibility was a low priority alongside peak power) it was high-rise; at this stage, medium-rise was a suitable compromise for the 427 Cobra.

ADAPTING TO REALITY

So far as complete cars went, Plan A, from August 1964, had been to build four coil-spring prototypes, referred to internally as Cobra IIs. The first three would be roadsters, visibly similar to the 289; the fourth was intended to be a coupé, along the lines of the Daytona. Cars one, three and four were originally schemed around the exotic all-alloy 390 engines, number two (more meaningfully) around the iron-block 427, and the programme was scheduled to be finished by November 1964.

By October, the plan had been revised, extending completion date to December. The last two planned prototypes, including the coupé, never did materialize, as AC built just

two cars designated as AC prototypes – CSX3001 and CSX3002. They had originally been numbered CSX2701 and CSX2702, and completed as far as chassis only, while waiting for new body bucks to be completed. The numbers were changed when it was decided that coil-spring chassis cars would be distinguished by the first '3'.

While the decision-making process was completed, so were the two prototypes, and they were air-freighted (the budget must have improved) to Shelby in October 1964. The first went via Ford in Dearborn, who were obviously keen to have a close look. Both cars were built to racing specs, and 3002 subsequently became the only 'works' 427 racer, campaigned in SCCA events principally as a test-bed. Engine specs for both cars prescribed a 'lightweight' 427 side-oiler with aluminium (as opposed to cast-iron) cylinder heads, water-pump housing, inlet manifold, timing-chain cover, and radiator header-tank – all designed to keep engine weight down to around 565lb (256kg).

Shelby finally resisted any temptation to go for a Daytona-type aerodynamic car, so the 427 looked essentially like the 289 – but on steroids. Only the doors, boot and bonnet lids were the same, everything else was scaled up. It wasn't, however, just overscaled. It still sat on the same, short, 90in (2,286mm) wheelbase, but it was a bit longer overall, and considerably wider, most noticeably in the bulbous wings, to accommodate the necessarily larger wheels and tyres.

It was also heavier, but not by much. The bare chassis put on maybe 50lb (22.5kg) and in its lightest form (with alloy sump, timing chain cover, inlet manifold et al) a 427 V8 was only about 150lb (68kg) heavier than a 289 – but a good 150bhp stronger.

Any cooling issues had been addressed with a re-profiled nose, similar to the 289's but with a bigger main grille opening, and just a simple bar across the middle, rather than the old mesh (not least because SCCA said you had to race with the original grille). There was also a separate scoop below the grille, for the oil-cooler on competition cars.

There were supplementary vertical openings either side of the main aperture, below and inboard of the headlights. On road cars those would be for cockpit cooling (an issue that never went away), or on race cars they could be ducted to provide

additional brake cooling. The king-sized flip-up filler for the big new fuel tank in the boot space was relocated to the centre of the rear deck. With the wider shell, there was more elbow-room, but the bigger transmission tunnel meant the pedals had to be offset to the left (on left-hand-drive cars).

Bigger wheels and tyres were a natural consequence of the power hike, typically to 425bhp and more. Standard wear was now 8.15 × 15in Goodyear Blue Spot tyres on 7.5in (190mm)-wide GT40-style Halibrand wheels – with six-spoke pattern, pin drive, and three-eared knock-off spinners. Those were specially made for the 427, normally finished in black with polished rims and polished edges to the air slots, and they looked terrific. No place for wire wheels any more, of course.

From the wheels up, the 427 looked very muscular indeed, and it could back up the looks, but not before it had overcome a few teething problems.

SEEDS OF CONTROVERSY

Back to the ever-present agenda of racing homologation: to qualify for FIA acceptance into the GT category (alongside the Ferrari 275LM that was now Shelby's main perceived target) the first 100 427s should have been completed by late April. Eager to make that deadline, Shelby commissioned

Even while the Cobra was still very much alive, Shelby had new distractions, in this case handing over the keys when customers came to collect their new street car.

**The classic coil-spring chassis layout – still a simple twin-tube ladder, but beefed up
in every respect to deal with the added power of the big-block engine.**

the first 100 427s as outright competition cars, though he was making life more difficult for himself. He could have bolstered the numbers with road cars from the start; but having been so scathing about Ferrari's political manipulation of the FIA rules in Europe, and particularly in the sports and GT classes, Shelby wasn't about to compromise or take advantage on what he now regarded as a matter of principle.

Unfortunately, that meant that when the FIA inspectors arrived at Shelby's new Los Angeles airport premises on 29 April to inspect the cars, there were only fifty-one completed 427s, not the necessary 100. Homologation was withheld.

Only then did Shelby relent and extend the programme to include road cars, while putting the remainder of the planned run of 100 pure competition cars on hold. As described in Chapter 13, that had far-reaching effects, but Shelby had one small consolation in that Ferrari had also failed to build the requisite number of 275LMs. For now, both would be competing with last year's models. Shelby would have further consolation, as the SCCA proved to be slightly more accommodating than the FIA, and granted the 427 US homologation before the end of 1964 purely on the strength of the prototypes.

Almost simultaneously with refusing the 427's first application, in June 1965 the FIA added another twist by announcing a change in homologation requirements for the following year, when a new category, 'Competition GT', would replace the existing full production GT class. It would require only fifty cars, which would open the door to the 427 in Europe for 1966. Unfortunately it would also put the 427 into the same category as Ford's far more sophisticated GT40, whose sales had been extraordinary.

Ironically, Shelby himself was deeply involved in the GT40 programme, and might have faced an embarrassing dilemma with benefactors Ford – except that the 427, for all its raw power, really wouldn't have had a prayer of competing head-to-head against the mid-engined GT40, or the comparable Ferrari. So Shelby chose not to pursue the one-sided fight,

and that, in effect, was the beginning and end of the 427's possibilities as a works racing car. It was almost the end of the 427 altogether, and by extension, of the Cobra, full-stop.

In the meantime, the first 427 production cars, the first coil-spring production Cobras, were shipped to the USA in January 1965. The last leaf-spring cars for the US market had been completed in November 1964 – although leaf-spring production for Europe (with 289 power, of course, not 427) would continue into mid-1965. Later that year, the coil-spring 427/428-engined 'MkIII' went on sale in Europe.

The skin over the skeleton, reflecting the up-scaling underneath.

Right at the end of the Cobra's original run, when Shelby finally didn't need any more chassis, AC offered the nice combination of coil-spring chassis with 289 engine, but they only ever made twenty-seven of them. On the other side of the Atlantic, in mid-1965, having aborted his original bid for FIA homologation, Shelby had a yard full of around forty unsold 427 Cobras – which wasn't a very satisfactory situation.

About a dozen cars from the original batch of fifty-one had been sold to private owners, mainly to campaign in SCCA production racing. In light of the new fifty-car rule for 1966, Shelby decided to keep back enough of the remaining cars to satisfy the FIA inspectors in November that sufficient 427s had been built to qualify for that new 'GT Production' class.

FAST CARS, SLOW PROGRESS

They were difficult times. Even completing those cars was a slow process, hampered by parts supply delays and pressure of work on Shelby from the GT40 build programme. He was pretty stretched. Even so, the 427s were homologated by the FIA in November, to be eligible for the relevant class from 1 January 1966.

The bigger problem was that the unsold cars represented a significant amount of 'dead' money. By November, Shelby had still only sold around sixteen 427s, and the situation was becoming an embarrassment. Fewer racers could afford a 427 than could have afforded a 289, and even fewer of those were capable of driving one effectively. Without the original FIA homologation (or with the later homologation pitching

The 'ultimate' Cobras were the two 800bhp twin-supercharged Supersnakes, originally owned by Shelby himself and comedian/actor Bill Cosby. This is Shelby's Supersnake about to make $5.5 million (with premiums) at the Barrett-Jackson auction in January 2007.

The secret of 800bhp – two huge Paxton centrifugal superchargers. Hold on very tightly.

the 427 against the GT40), there was no European market at all.

There had to be a solution, and Shelby's management people suggested one. Charles Beidler, Shelby's Eastern Sales Manager, saw the car pool at the works, unpainted and mainly standing on blocks because of a shortage of (expensive) Halibrand pin-drive wheels. They were trickling out of the door one at a time, to individual order.

Beidler suggested completing the rest of the supposed competition cars to an only slightly milder specification and advertising them as the fastest production cars in the world. Thus was born the idea of the 'Semi-Competition'

427 Cobra, the iconic S/C. It worked: three more cars of the original batch were sold as full-house racers, the remaining thirty-one were sold as 427 S/Cs, which had now become an official model designation.

The first car to be called an S/C was CSX3015, which had been completed in January 1965 but had been sitting around at Shelby's premises ever since it was air-freighted to the USA early in the year. In December it was described as '65 per cent complete', and earmarked for shipment back to Britain, to Ford Advanced Vehicles in Slough. Eventually it became one of two 'ultimate' Cobras, this one owned by Shelby himself, the other (CSX3303) originally owned by comedian Bill Cosby. In January 2007 the ex-Shelby CSX3015 'Supersnake' was sold at a Barrett-Jackson auction for $5 million.

Both represented considerable overkill, with 427 engines plus two-stage Paxton supercharging, and Ford T6 super-duty three-speed automatic transmissions. In February 1968, Shelby's car, quoting an output of 800bhp (yes, 800) was presented to *Road & Track* for a road test. It recorded 0–60mph in 3.8 seconds, 0–100mph in 7.9 seconds, and a standing quarter-mile in 11.9 seconds with a terminal speed of 116mph (186.5km/h). The magazine (possibly wisely) didn't attempt a maximum speed run, but suggested that something over 180mph (290km/h) seemed likely.

The 'affordable' S/Cs were not, of course, as manic as that, but easily quick enough to lend credence to that boast of 'fastest production car'. Most magazines tested 'street' 427s and typically quoted 165mph (265.5km/h) and 0–60mph around 4.2 seconds (in one case 4 seconds dead), while 0–100mph was generally claimed in around 9 or 10 seconds, with standing quarter times (a big yardstick in drag-race obsessed America) in the very low 12-second bracket at close to 120mph (193km/h). One of the most impressive and oft-quoted party tricks was Miles' ability to get from 0 to 100mph and back to zero in 13.8 seconds.

THE 427 FAMILY

Most road testers also remarked on how docile the 427 was in 'everyday' use – even alongside a 289. That was mainly because of the carburation on the street cars, set up for flexibility rather than outright power. Their four-barrel Holleys

British race team owner (and later GT40 collaborator) John Willment commissioned two Cobra coupés from Italian coachbuilder Ghia – one for racing, and this one for the road – with some extremely futuristic touches.

SHELBY AC COBRA 427, STREET CAR (1965–1969)

Layout and Chassis

Body type	Two-seater sports roadster, all aluminium
Chassis	Large diameter twin-tube ladder frame with tubular cross-beams, tubular suspension mountings and body-carrying tubular superstructure

Engine

Type	Ford big-block V8. NB: '427' is actually 426cu in (6984cc), '428' is actually 427cu in (6991cc), as described in Chapter 6. Both types were used in the '427' Cobra
Block material	Cast iron
Head material	Cast iron
Cylinders	8 in 90-degree V, five main bearings
Cooling	Water
Bore and stroke	427: 107.7 × 96.0mm (4.24 × 3.78in) 428: 104.9 × 101.1mm (4.13 × 3.98in)
Capacity	427: 6984cc (426cu in); 428: 6991cc (427cu in)
Valves	2 valves per cylinder, operated by pushrods from single central camshaft in block
Compression ratio	427: 10.4:1; 428: 10.5:1
Carburettor	Single four-barrel Holley carburettor; other layouts, including four twin-choke downdraught Weber carburettors, optional
Max. power (DIN)	427: 425bhp at 6,500rpm; 428: 390bhp at 5,200rpm
Max. torque	427: 480lb ft at 3,500rpm ; 428: 475lb ft at 3,700rpm
Fuel capacity	15.0gal (18.0 US gal/68ltr)

Transmission

Gearbox	Ford 4-speed manual, all-synchromesh, 'Top-Loader'
Clutch	Single dry plate, hydraulic operation

Internal Gearbox Ratios

First	2.32:1
Second	1.69:1
Third	1.29:1
Fourth	1.00:1
Reverse	2.32:1
Final drive ratio	3.31:1 (numerous options)

Suspension and Steering

Front	Independent, by unequal-length upper and lower wishbones, with coil springs, telescopic dampers, anti-roll bar
Rear	Independent, by unequal-length upper and lower wishbones, plus additional lower trailing links, with coil springs, telescopic dampers, anti-roll bar
Steering	Rack and pinion
Tyres	8.5 × 15in (later up to 11.4 × 15in at rear)
Wheels	7.5J × 15in cast magnesium, pin-drive, centre-lock, by Halibrand (later up to 9.5J × 15in at rear)
Rim width	7.5 to 9.5in J section (see above)

Brakes

Type	Solid discs front and rear

Dimensions

Track, front	56.0in (1,422mm)
Track, rear	56.0in (1,422mm)
Wheelbase	90.0in (2,286mm)
Overall length	156.0in (3,962mm)
Overall width	68.0in (1,727mm)
Overall height	49.0in (1,244mm)
Ground clearance	5.0in (127mm)
Unladen weight	2,350lb (1,066kg)
Power to weight ratio	405.1bhp per ton

Performance

Top speed	165mph (265km/h)
0–60mph	4.2sec
0–100mph	10.3sec
Standing quarter	12.4sec
Fuel consumption	10.0mpg (28.3ltr/100km)

ABOVE: **In street trim, the 427 underbonnet didn't look very different from the equivalent 289.**

LEFT: **When Halibrand wheel supply became a problem, the ever versatile Pete Brock designed the 'Sunburst' pattern wheel as an alternative – though only Halibrand could make them.**

had relatively small primary chokes for that docile response around town, but enormous secondary chokes gave a huge, instantaneous surge of power and torque if the throttle was snapped open. Several magazines suggested that it was probably wise to have the 427 pointing in a straight line on dead dry tarmac if you intended to try that.

If it was a vice, it was one of very few. The new suspension was seen as an almost miraculous improvement over the near-solid leaf-springs, the uprated brakes (helped by more rubber on the road) were even better than on the 289, and the cockpit was roomier and more comfortable. It did still get unpleasantly hot, though.

Only after AC completed the intended competition cars (including what became S/Cs, plus three additional chassis) did they start building street-spec 427s. Those had another numbering twist, starting at CSX3101, leaving a gap after the last of the competition and S/C cars, CSX3053, plus the three odd chassis – CSX3054, originally intended to be a 427 'Super Coupé' along Daytona lines; CSX3055, which became a Ghia-bodied Willment racing coupé; and CSX3063, which was also given a Ghia body, but as a show car.

The first three street cars were again treated as prototypes, to address any remaining problems – notably under-bonnet and cockpit overheating issues (the latter benefiting from those new apertures near the headlights). AC made the throttle control more progressive, recalibrated the speedometer, added closed-circuit crankcase breathing (an emissions measure), and a new front bumper bar.

That brought the 427 up to three basic specifications, street, semi-competition and competition. There were individual variations, but in general, 'street' cars had two four-barrel Holley carbs on a low-rise manifold, most S/Cs had the medium-riser but otherwise similar engine specs except that the S/C used the full race engine's bigger sump, remote oil filter and oil-cooler. Competition cars had the high-rise manifold as standard, with the medium-riser as an option, usually with a single four-barrel Holley in a cold-air box under the bonnet scoop. Race cars had aluminium heads with 12.4:1 compression (compared to the usual 10.4) and they claimed 485bhp (compared to 425). Street and S/C cars had electric fans ahead of the radiator, full race cars didn't. Street cars had cast-iron exhaust manifolds with pipes emerging under the back of the car; S/Cs and race cars had tuned tubular headers and side-exit pipes – the S/C's with token silencing, the racers' with none at all. S/C and race cars had two electrical fuel pumps to supplement the standard mechanical pump, and had

42gal (191ltr) tanks in place of the street car's 18gal (81.5ltr) one.

S/C and full-race cars sat on 7.5in (190mm) front rims and 9.5in (241mm) rear, rather than the street car's 7.5in all round – with appropriate tyre choice, but still generally from Goodyear (which, as well as coming from Shelby, suited the car).

Street cars listed anti-roll bars as an option; S/C and competition cars had them as standard. S/C and race cars had heavier-duty, quick-change brake callipers, and 3.77:1 final-drive ratios as standard, compared to the normal 3.54 (although there were numerous options for racing, depending on the type of circuit).

Full competition cars had the solid bronze suspension bushes (for control) where the others had rubber bushes (for refinement), while S/C and race cars had even less trim (tending towards zero in racing) than a street car's already fairly minimal fittings – and neither of them had the street car's small but useful glovebox.

Bodywork differed mainly around the wheelarches and cooling and breathing details, like hood scoops and brake/cockpit-cooling ducts – but those varied during the life of the car, anyway. S/C and competition cars had roll hoops and built-in quick-lift jacking points, while full race cars offered a small, low-drag windscreen.

Even with specifications supposedly set, initial production was painfully slow, mainly because Shelby was still suffering component-supply delays, notably with the Halibrand magnesium-alloy wheels. For a while, Shelby got around that by supplying cars on whatever wheels were available, but then had Pete Brock design a wheel specifically for the car – the ten-radial-spoke design that came to be known as the 'Sunburst' pattern. One small irony was that the only people who could make it were Halibrand.

WHAT'S IN A CUBIC INCH?

Early in the life of the 427 there was a far more fundamental change, when it was decided to give the main-production 1966 model year cars Ford's Galaxie 428 (7014cc) engine rather than the original 427. The difference was far more than a cubic inch, the 427 and 428 V8s were entirely different breeds.

Racing, of course, was the key, and specifically NASCAR. Ford sat out most of the 1966 season because their 'ultimate' NASCAR engine, a single-ohc version of the 427, had effectively been outlawed. It was never used in the Cobra, and Ford could have reverted to the well-proven if slightly less powerful pushrod 427 for racing, but also introduced a much less extreme pushrod engine for the road, the 428.

The detail is complicated, but important. The iconic '427' had an actual displacement of 425cu in (6964cc). Oldsmobile already had a 425 engine, and Ford marketing didn't want the conflict, so they used a bit of copywriting licence and labelled their engine '427' – alluding to the NASCAR limit, equating to 7 litres. Which was fine until Ford's milder 428 entered

the picture, because the '428' actually did displace exactly 427cu in (6997cc)!

The marketing men stepped in again, not wanting to draw too much attention to the earlier deception, while still giving the new engine an identity of its own. So those were the labels; the reality was chalk and cheese. Officially, the classic 427 was the '7-litre Cobra High-Performance V8'; the 428 was the 'Thunderbird 7-litre Four-Barrel V8'. But the 'Police Interceptor' 428 (by another name) was much less oversquare than the 427, at 4.13 × 3.98in (104.9 × 101.0mm),

The 427 certainly didn't have the compact subtlety of line that distinguished the original 289.

much more simply built (crucially for ultimate tunability, without main-bearing cross-bolts, for instance), and markedly less powerful.

Simple availability, however, meant the 428 became standard fare, and Shelby-spec 428s in Cobra trim used a single four-barrel Ford carburettor and 10.4:1 compression, to give 390bhp at 5,200rpm and 475lb ft of torque at 3,700rpm. So it was less powerful, and also heavier than the 427, but on the bright side, the Cobra's power-to-weight ratio was still a good deal better than you could find in almost any other street car, anywhere.

It had a different character from the race-bred 427, too, but that was just another nuance. A bigger factor for Shelby was that a 428 cost only $320, where even a basic 427 cost $730. On a 427 street Cobra that still listed at only $7,495, that was a significant element. A basic competition-spec car typically listed at around $9,500, and while nobody would admit it, it's likely that 427 Cobras generally sold at a loss, of about $1,000 per car, to the factory.

Shelby did amend his literature to include the 428 spec but didn't draw attention to the change any more than Ford did. The Cobra kept its '427' tag and even now it's difficult to know which cars were fitted with (425) 427 and which with (427) 428s. Equally confusing, some Cobras were fitted with genuine 427s even post change-over. As to what found its way in to which car in later life, that would be a book in itself.

The engine change would be one of very few production changes in the life of the 427. After the first fifty-one competition (and S/C) cars, most of what followed was officially 'street' spec – but always open to individual interpretation, by option list.

The original street shape had wide rear arch flares, changed to less pronounced flares at chassis CSX3125 –

then back to wider ones at 3158, until the end. At CSX3201 the rear light shape changed from a single rectangular unit to two-piece round lights, while the oil-cooler scoop below the nose was dropped from chassis CSX3301.

That was pretty well all the significant changes. In total, AC and Shelby built 260 coil-spring 427 street cars, two prototype competition roadsters, nineteen 'production' competition roadsters, the aborted Daytona 'Super Coupé', and the three bare chassis. AC subsequently built the thirty-two COB/COX cars for the UK and Europe, and if you add all those together you have a total production of 348 coil-spring Cobras.

A LIFE CUT SHORT?

The final cars were advertised for sale in the USA in August 1968, and the date is a clue to why the Cobra finally disappeared when it did. In the face of growing environmental and safety legislation (especially in the US) it would have had to change beyond recognition. Neither Ford nor Shelby had any interest in that; and while AC briefly dabbled with an evolution in the form of the Frua-bodied 428 (a very different car indeed), whatever they did was about to run head-on into the 'energy crisis' years of the 1970s.

One final nail in the coffin: once the GT40 started winning, Ford and Shelby no longer needed the Cobra in the same way as they had for racing. The Cobra had had its day. But while it went out of production, it never went out of favour. It was a long time indeed before it was overtaken as the fastest full production car ever built, and its straightline performance still raises eyebrows fifty years on. Shelby's dream did work.

CHAPTER SEVEN

THE COMPETITION ROADSTERS

Without racing, the Cobra wouldn't have happened – commercially, *couldn't* have happened. Without racing, even the Ace wouldn't have happened. The vast majority of Cobras were sold as road cars, but it was the racing element that underpinned everything else.

In 1961, Carroll Shelby was a (recently retired) racing driver. His business, based at a race circuit, was running a racing school and selling racing tyres. His second employee, Pete Brock, was a racing driver. Shelby's Ford contacts were racing people. He was no car salesman, not even a sports car salesman, but he knew he could market the Cobra through racing. Not least, he had a burning desire to teach Enzo Ferrari a lesson.

He all but said so when the Cobra was revealed to the press on 10 April 1962, three weeks before it appeared at the New York Show. When cars began to arrive from AC, the first was the show car/demonstrator; the second series-built car became the first 'works' race car.

Shelby's racing ambitions encompassed both America and Europe, and Europe covered the Ferrari issue. In commercial terms the Cobra could satisfy the more modest racing ambitions of a much wider customer base. In rela-

Almost from the beginning, even the advertising material gave the competition cars prominent billing alongside the street versions. The number '98' became a signature race number for the Cobra, starting with the 'prototype' racer XP98, and recurring throughout the car's career.

Even the street car is in a pit setting, with another '98' competition car in the background.

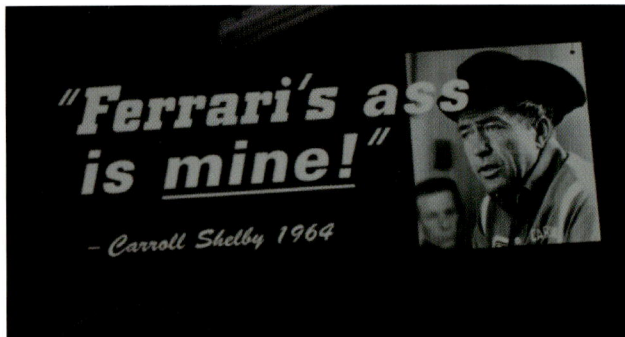

There are plenty of variations on exactly how Shelby phrased his promise, but there was no ambivalence about his intentions.

tion to its performance (and competition potential) it wasn't an expensive car, but offered the genuine possibility, out of the box, of blowing away far more exotic and expensive rivals, even Farraris.

RACING IN PERSPECTIVE

For most of its career, that was the Cobra's unique selling point: not as a top-flight international racer (although it would have its moments) but as one of the most prolific customer racers of all time in such arenas as the SCCA and USRRC (United States Road Racing Club) Production classes, and their European equivalents. Then in 1965,

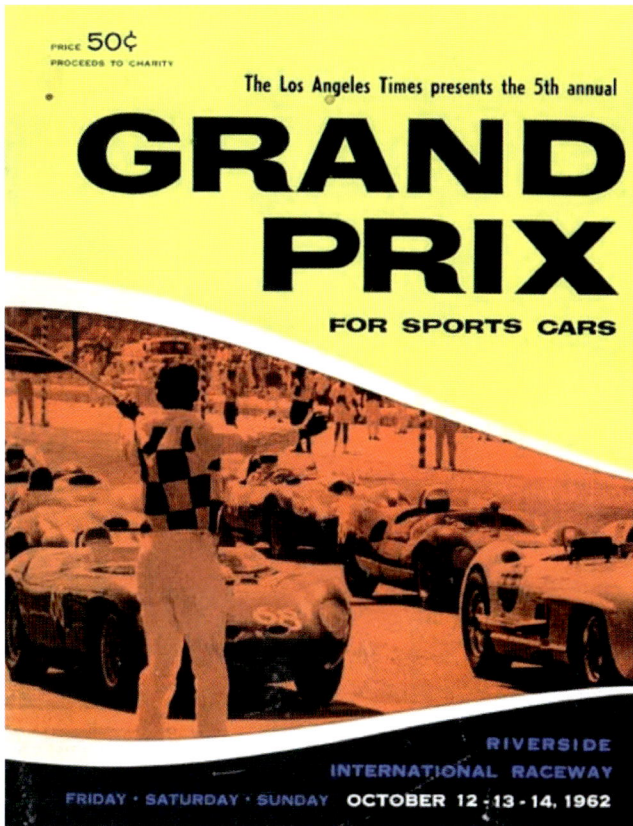

'Grand Prix' was stretching the definition slightly, but the Cobra's debut race outing was at one of Riverside's biggest meetings of the year, so it wasn't a soft option.

Shelby finally beat Ferrari to a World Championship – with the Daytona, a Cobra under its coupé skin (a leaf-spring Cobra at that), skilfully playing Ferrari at his own rule-interpretation game.

Job done, the Daytona only ran to half a dozen cars, but much of what happened in racing at this point has more to do with the timing than the cars. What might have happened if the 427 had been homologated as planned, as a production GT? Or if Shelby hadn't abandoned the 'Super Coupé'? What might have happened if circumstances hadn't brought the Cobra head to head with the GT40 – or even if Ford hadn't felt the need to build the GT40, but backed some other Shelby initiative? All we know is that with little more exotic than a pretty basic chassis and lots of Detroit horses, the Cobras and Daytonas established a 1960s racing record way beyond the sum of its parts.

The story began in October 1962, outside Shelby's office door, at Riverside. CSX2002 was the second production Cobra; the event, sanctioned by the SCCA, was a supporting race for the Riverside GP. Quite late, the SCCA added an 'experimental' class, not for the Cobra but largely to give Chevrolet's not-yet-homologated 327 Corvette a chance to appear in public without taking points off the properly eligible racers; the Corvette, being America's sports car icon, would also bring fans through the turnstiles. Shelby was quick to spot an opportunity for his also non-homologated Cobra.

The Cobra ran with the XP number because as far as the organizers were concerned it was an experimental car rather than a production one – but they were keen to find a space for it.

Billy Krause was a west-coast driver of some repute, having raced serious sports cars like the Jaguar D-Type and Maserati Birdcage, and was a former winner of the Riverside GP. He was about to become the first man to race the Cobra.

The car was virtually standard (as standard as the second of two in existence can be); it had the 260cu in (4261cc) V8, and in terms of modifications, little more than wider wheels and tyres, a long-range fuel tank, racing windscreen and tacked-on bonnet air-scoop. The 327 Corvette would carry the symbolic race number 00, the Cobra would run as XP98.

CORVETTE'S NIGHTMARE

Chevrolet (who had turned down the opportunity to share Shelby's dream, remember) had a shock in store. From the start, the Cobra waltzed away from everything else, Corvette included. After an hour it was a mile and a half (2.5km) clear of the next car, until a rear hub broke, a wheel disappeared, and Krause spun into retirement. The hubs had already been uprated, but racing reveals issues that no amount of road testing can. That hour was enough to tell Shelby that he had a potential winner, and Chevrolet that they had trouble ahead.

The Cobra's next appearance was at the Nassau Speed Week in December 1962, an annual outing with a festive atmosphere, but serious racing. Three Cobras were entered: a 'works' car for Krause, a works-built car prepared by super-tuners Holman & Moody for Augie Pabst, and a works-built but privately owned car for John Everly.

Developments post-Riverside included 12.0:1 compression ratio (with different pistons), roller camshaft-followers, special exhaust manifolds with straight-through side-pipes, electric fuel pumps, special ignition systems, bigger sump capacity and an oil-cooler. The chassis had stiffer springs and Koni dampers, a 38gal (173ltr) fuel tank, alloy brake callipers and brake-cooling ducts, front and rear anti-roll bars, and a forward-braced roll hoop. The top of the driver's door was cut away to provide a bit more elbow room, and that became a regular modification where it was allowed.

Krause retired again, with a broken steering mount (leading Remington to design a strengthening bracket for next time out, and prompting early thoughts of a change from worm-and-sector steering to rack and pinion). Everly had the best results, winning his five-lap heat but managing only sixteenth in the final. Not such a great start to a major domestic and international racing career, but the point was that Shelby was already learning from racing experience, and modifying the Cobra as he went along, to everyone's benefit.

Whatever else was on the grid in the Cobra's first outing, the one that mattered was the other 'experimental' invitee, car 00, the new 327 Corvette – chased here by Billy Krause.

The Cobra's second outing was in the annual Nassau Speed Weeks meeting in December 1962, after which Cobras became a regular fixture at the traditional end-of-season festival.

At this point, every racing Cobra started life as a road car, and once converted fell into the same three categories as in Nassau – works cars, works-prepared/privately entered cars, and fully independent cars. Of the seventy-three leaf-spring Cobras the SAAC *World Registry* listed as having a

period racing history (from 655 leaf-spring cars in total), thirty-three were works cars, twelve works-prepared/privately run, and twenty-eight private entries.

They had basic similarities, but by the nature of motor sport, just as much that was unique to each car. Also by the nature of racing, details on each car changed virtually every time out, as either Shelby or one of the other entrants learned something new. Much of the early effort went into keeping the cars in one piece, which led to improved hubs, steering gear and final-drive mountings. Only once the cars could race without breaking did the emphasis switch to making them even quicker.

A GENUINE RACE WINNER

The Cobra's first full race win (as opposed to a heat win) came in January 1963, at an SCCA Divisional meeting at Riverside, where Shelby entered two cars for Ken Miles and Dave MacDonald. Both were essentially similar to the Nassau cars but with Remington's steering brace, Weber-carburetted engines fed by a cold-air scoop, and dual-brake master cylinders. It was MacDonald who led Miles to the Cobra's first win, and first one-two.

A familiar race number, but no 'experimental' qualification now, as the Cobra was accepted as a production car by the time Ken Miles gave it its first win, at Riverside in January 1963.

It didn't take long for the 260 to evolve into the 289, and for the 289 to evolve from street spec to full race tune, in this case with the maximum-attack quadruple twin-choke Weber option.

Grasping the marketing opportunity, Shelby quickly advertised the availability of 'Riverside Replica' Cobras, identical to the cars as raced except for the option of Halibrand magnesium-alloy wheels rather than the overstressed wire wheels. The 'Replica' cars were offered at $9,000 (plus $500 for the mag wheel option) – but only one car, CSX2017, appears to have been sold as a 'Riverside Replica'.

Most racing customers seemed happy to detail their own specifications – dictated first by what the rules allowed in the relevant class. In SCCA and USRRC 'production' racing, in spite of the name, that wasn't too different from what FIA GT rules allowed in Europe. Internal engine components (except pistons) could be lightened and balanced, cylinder heads and camshafts modified. Silencers weren't required, side exhausts were permitted. Shelby had homologated a wide range of carburettor options, topped by the exotic (and expensive) four-Weber set-up. Internal gearbox and final-drive ratios could be changed, and the clutch could be modified. Racing tyres could be used, as could heavy-duty dampers.

The main restriction was that overall weight couldn't be reduced by more than 5 per cent from the homologated figure. As the Cobra was already pared to the bone, that was more advantage than disadvantage, in that it did not allow heavier rivals to narrow the gap.

FIA regulations were more restrictive than SCCA or USRRC ones in requiring the standard windscreen to be retained. If that sounds trivial, it wasn't: in Europe, the tall, flat roadster screen had the aerodynamics of a barn door.

In smaller races, not everyone took full advantage of what the rules allowed, many cars running close to 'stock'. Typical modifications fell into definite categories: safety modifications like roll hoops, competition seats and full-harness belts; chassis modifications to improve handling and braking (including bigger wheels and better tyres to put more and grippier rubber on the road); and whatever engine modifications were allowed.

Shelby offered plenty of those. By the time the 289 appeared, standard road tune meant 271bhp. Beyond that there was a road/race option (suitable for street use during the week and modest competition at the weekend), plus several levels of full race engine for circuit racing. There were more specialized engines for drag racing – even a complete car prepared specifically for drag racing, the Dragon-snake.

In all engine variants, the main areas for modification were cylinder heads, camshaft, carburation and exhaust system, all to help the engine breathe more efficiently. Road/race engines typically had mildly modified heads with slightly bigger valves and matched, polished ports, plus pistons with valve cutouts to allow higher revs. Full race engines had big valves and ports, modified water passages for better cooling, higher compression, stronger valve springs for better reliability at sustained high revs, and rocker pedestals threaded rather than pressed into the heads. The heads were also held down by stronger studs, and used thin steel-shim racing gaskets. The drag-racing heads were similar, but used the biggest valves and ports of any of the engines, as flexibility wasn't an issue.

There was a huge range when it came to camshafts and carburation, both from Shelby and from outside tuners (who latched onto the Cobra very quickly). The top carb option was the four 48IDM twin-choke downdraught Weber set-up, which was expensive (at more than $1,230 in 1964) but extremely effective both for outright power and driveability.

Customers could also order tubular exhaust manifolds (another big power improver), competition distributor, several types of baffled or larger-capacity sump in steel or aluminium, and a scatter-shield for around the flywheel. One thing Shelby never offered was a dry sump option, but once you'd devised your spec, you could either buy the bits and assemble it yourself (or engage your local speed shop), or buy a complete engine off the shelf.

HOW FAST DO YOU WANT TO GO?

Remember that sign over the speed-shop door? 'Speed Costs Money. How Fast Do You Want To Go?' In 1964, when a complete Cobra road car sold for $5,995, a complete road/race engine (less carburettors) was advertised at $729; a full race engine (again less carbs) at $2,045; and a full race engine including the four-Weber set-up, at $3,295.

Precisely what you got for your money depended on exact specification (and to a lesser extent on individual engines, because there will always be the odd 'demon' one); but it was possible to have over 360bhp from a heavily modified race engine on a single four-barrel Holley, or a reliable 385bhp for a full-house engine with Webers et al. Those full-fat engines were mainly for international racing, and once the 289 Cobra was homologated at the end of 1962, that's where Shelby's focus would be for much of the next three years.

The banking in the background reveals that it's Daytona, in 1963, and the Cobra's first full international outing, first full endurance distance, head to head, as here, against Ferrari's 250GTO. Three Cobras were entered, MacDonald's survived to finish fourth.

Having scored its first race win at Riverside, the Cobra's first international outing (in an international-class race as opposed to overseas) was Daytona in 1963, head to head with Ferrari under FIA Manufacturers Championship GT rules. As well as being the Cobra's first international race, it would be the first time it had been asked to do a true endurance race – three hours in this case.

Shelby entered three cars: for Riverside winner MacDonald, Dan Gurney, and Skip Hudson. The cars had tack-on spats to cover as much of the protruding tyre as demanded by the FIA rules, FIA-spec full windscreens, and Halibrand pin-drive magnesium-alloy wheels – the pin drives proving essential as the original splined hubs had proved themselves unable to cope with the race engines' torque.

At Ford's request, Gurney's car was originally fitted with an experimental all-alloy engine, but had problems immediately before the race and after a quick change back to the all-iron V8, Gurney just made the start as the rest of the field left the grid.

Like the others, that car initially ran well, but dropped out after forty-eight laps with ignition problems (after which Gurney went to help in the pits!). Hudson had the terrifying experience of the flywheel disintegrating and jamming the steering, causing him to spin off. Having overcome an electrical problem, and another in restarting after visiting the pits to cure it, MacDonald got the other Cobra to its first international finish – in fourth place, behind two Ferrari GTOs and a Corvette. Reliability was clearly an issue.

The same held true at the Cobra's next international appearance, at the Sebring 12-Hour race in March. There was one privately entered road car-based Cobra, and no fewer than five factory cars, all with Weber-equipped 289 engines and rack-and-pinion steering for the first time. They also had numerous small body tweaks after Daytona, new instruments and quick-change front brakes, but otherwise looked familiar.

It wasn't a good race for the team. The private entry and two of the works cars failed to finish. Best of the rest was

Phil Hill and Ken Miles in eleventh over-all and a disappointing eighth in GT, with the others way back in twenty-eighth and thirty-eighth.

Gurney did give the Cobra its first inter-national win, at the SCCA Bridgehampton Double 500 endurance race in September 1963, with one of the works 'Le Mans Repli-cas'. But after its early-season failures it was clear that there was much to be done to make the Cobra competitive (and reliable) on the FIA level. While that was addressed, the works cars were largely confined to USRRC and selected SCCA Champion-ship rounds for the rest of 1963. Reliability improved and they won the USRRC Manu-facturers title, plus first and second places in the Drivers Championship for works drivers Holbert and Miles.

Ken Miles' number 16 (shared with Phil Hill) was one of five 'factory' Cobras at Sebring in 1963, but it was a disappointing day, with eighth in class the best they could deliver.

FINDING ITS NICHE

This was the first year of the USRRC Championship (fore-runner of the prestigious Can-Am series). It was open to any 'closed-wheel sports car', and pitted the Cobras against some very specialized racing machinery, but they dominated, with 111 points to Ferrari's twenty-eight and Chevrolet's nineteen.

The Cobra had also started winning regularly in SCCA Production events, first at regional level in southern California, then at divisional level, and very soon at national level. In July 1963, Cobras finished one-two-three in an SCCA A-Production race at Lake Garnett Raceway, Kansas; then Miles put himself into the Modified class (by virtue of adding an oil-cooler to his car) and proceeded to run away from even the most specialized sports racing cars like the Chaparral and the mid-engined Cooper-Monaco.

In June, *Road & Track* magazine had said: 'it is very hard to imagine that any well-prepared, well-driven Cobra will be beaten this year – not by the Corvettes, and possibly not by anyone…' They were almost right. The privately entered

AC entered two 289s with the new 'fastback' hardtop at Le Mans in 1963, the pale green Sanderson/Bolton car and this one for US Cobra dealer Ed Hugus and Brit Peter Jopp – the first Cobras to race in the 24 Hours.

Cobras of Bob Johnson and Bob Brown took first and second in the SCCA A-Production Championship and went on to win both the USRRC Championship and the SCCA S-Production title again in 1964, all with 289s. When the 427 took over, they won SCCA A-Production titles in 1965, 1966, 1967, 1968, and (amazingly) 1973. Mainly thanks to the GT40 and Daytona, the 427 might not have had the greatest international career, but for many years it took a lot of beating on home ground.

With the 427 still to come, for 1963 Shelby had the challenge of making the 289 work on an international level, and there were times when he knew it was an uphill struggle. He was, however, a realist, especially when it came to the biggest race of all, the 24 Hours of Le Mans. In 1963, accepting that he wasn't yet ready to compete against Europe's best, he made the brave decision to wait until 1964.

Nevertheless there were two Cobras at Le Mans in 1963, and they were far from disgraced. They were the first Cobras built from scratch as race cars, by AC on behalf of Shelby. CS2131 (the missing X signified that the car was never intended for export out of Europe) was entered by AC themselves for English driver Peter Bolton and Scot Ninian Sanderson (who had won outright in 1956 with Ron Flockhart in an Ecurie Ecosse Jaguar D-Type). CSX2142 was entered in 1963 by Shelby's biggest dealer, Ed Hugus of Pittsburgh, for Hugus himself and Englishman Peter Jopp.

Before building the actual Le Mans car, AC built a 'Le Mans prototype', on chassis CSX2130, completed in April 1963 and delivered to Jopp for race testing. It was the first Cobra with 'FIA-type' integral bonnet scoop, and front-wing vents for additional cooling. Both 2130 and 2131 were right-hand-drive cars, but CSX2142 was the standard left-hand drive, designated in AC's records as 'American Le Mans car'.

EMBRACING SCIENCE

The biggest difference between prototype and race cars was that the race cars gained a new kind of hardtop: not the old, short, bubble-style, but a new shape that virtually

The 1963 Le Mans hardtop had very little to do with weather protection and everything to do with aerodynamics at a circuit dominated by the high-speed Mulsanne Straight.

AC's 1963 Le Mans entries were sponsored by *The Sunday Times* newspaper, pit-managed by Stirling Moss, and shown off to the media at the newspaper's offices before the race.

transformed the roadster into a fastback – to improve high-speed aerodynamics and give the car a better top speed on the all-important Mulsanne Straight.

Shelby supplied Weber-carburetted engines in a relatively mild state of tune for ample power with long-distance reliability and driveability – giving around 355bhp. AC ran a long 3.31:1 final-drive ratio that gave a maximum speed of 167mph (269km/h) on the Mulsanne, and a best lap of 4 minutes 14.3 seconds. That was well off the sub-4-minute pace of the fastest qualifiers, but there was no fighting science.

They ran on Dunlop alloy centre-lock wheels with wide-section racing tyres that needed front and rear arch extenders to satisfy the FIA rule about covering tyre treads. They had long-range 38gal (173ltr) fuel tanks and large, quick-release, fast-flow filler caps behind the rear edge of the hardtops, which necessitated an extra-short bootlid.

High-speed drag wasn't the Cobra's only aerodynamic issue. During practice, Bolton and Sanderson's car lost its rear window at near maximum speed, sucked out of the hardtop by the low pressure behind the car (rather than blown out by high pressure inside). For the race, the window was held in by supplementary bolts all round.

The Hugus/Jopp car retired during the eleventh hour while in thirteenth place when a connecting rod broke. It was probably about to be disqualified anyway, for taking on oil before it was permitted to do so by the complicated Le Mans rules.

Only thirteen of the forty-nine starters (which included no fewer than eleven Ferraris) finished, and the Bolton/Sanderson Cobra was one of them. Sponsored by *The Sunday Times* and managed (like the other Cobra) by Stirling Moss, no less, it rumbled around steadily and reliably to finish seventh overall (behind six Ferraris), fourth in the GT class – and first home of the three 'British' survivors.

So the 1963 Le Mans effort hadn't been a huge success, but Shelby did commission a short run of 'Le Mans Replicas' both for works use and private customers. Shipped to the USA, they joined the existing Shelby cars to contest the remaining 1963 USRRC and SCCA races, to be replaced in turn by new FIA/USRRC-spec roadsters for 1964. At that point the old team cars were sold off to private entrants; other private entrants had run in FIA events too, but with predictably limited success.

Staying on 'home' ground, Shelby's next major outing wasn't until 1964, by which time AC had sent him five more purpose-built racers – this time specifically for FIA GT competition, where Shelby was still determined to make it work.

Their specification included anything that had been tried and proved so far, plus wider wings to accommodate wider wheels and tyres as the season went on, which also required reworking around the driver's door. They also had a hump moulded into the bootlid to accommodate the notional 'suitcase' which FIA regulations dictated all cars should be able to carry.

The first two of the new cars appeared at Daytona in February 1964, for Dan Gurney/Bob Johnson and Jo Schlesser/Jean Guichet. At one point, another Cobra, driven by Dave MacDonald with Bob Holbert, led by six laps from the chasing pack of Ferrari GTOs, but was put out of the race by a pit fire while refuelling.

FERRARI-CHASING

As might be gathered from the spectacular mid-race lead, that was not, however, an ordinary Cobra. This was the first of the Daytona coupés, whose aerodynamic bodies would eventually help Shelby deliver on his promise of beating Ferrari in Europe.

With the demise of that car, all Shelby salvaged from Daytona 1964 was fourth overall (which was also fourth in GT) for Gurney and Johnson. The bitterest pill was that the three cars that beat it were three of the Ferraris the Daytona had eaten for breakfast before its pit fire. Now, though, Shelby at least knew that the Daytona clearly could run with the best.

Just a few weeks later, at Sebring in March, Shelby introduced another 'different' Cobra alongside the usual 289 roadsters – Miles' first attempt at shoehorning a 427 engine into a leaf-spring chassis, and the start of another direction.

While Miles's 427 eventually broke, the 289 roadsters at Sebring had mixed fortunes. Gurney and Johnson were to drive one car, Bob Bondurant and Lew Spencer a second, and Phil Hill and Jo Schlesser the third. Bondurant and Spencer took fifth overall and second in GT, closely followed by Hill and Schlesser in sixth/third. Johnson was lucky to survive a truly huge, high-speed accident during the night when he ran over the back of a slow-moving Alfa Romeo with no lights on, totally destroying the Cobra roadster.

The blow was softened slightly for Shelby, who had taken several senior Ford executives to watch the race, by Holbert and MacDonald finishing fourth overall in the Daytona, and winning the GT category ahead of the Ferraris. Shelby

By any standards, the Targa Florio road race, in Sicily, was a car-breaking endurance test, and it punished the Cobras badly, including this one driven by Phil Hill.

now knew he could do it, but only with the coupé, not the roadster. Thereafter, in works terms at least, international competition opportunities for the open-topped 289s were strictly limited. But not over. Shelby continued to enter roadsters in FIA races in Europe throughout 1964, now usually alongside the Daytonas, which were already genuine contenders for the manufacturers' title.

Quite often, the roadsters would pick up minor but valuable points towards Shelby's overall championship tally, but in some places they were embarrassingly out of their depth, and nowhere more so than around the punishing roads of Sicily, in the Targa Florio.

Five roadsters (but no Daytonas) were entered for the 1964 Targa, and were quick enough on the mountain roads to lead the race, but not durable enough to finish. The bumpy roads knocked the hell out of the old leaf-spring chassis, and the only Cobra to be classified was the works car driven by Gurney and Jerry Grant, which clung on to finish eighth overall and second in GT. Even that finished with broken rear suspension; another had the same problem; one had a steering breakage; the last had a seized engine caused by a broken oil pipe. Shelby might have taken some consolation

from Porsche beating the usually dominant Ferrari, but it wasn't a race to remember for Cobra.

For the roadsters, that was a familiar story in 1964, although sheer weight of numbers meant they actually won the majority of Shelby's FIA championship points. At Spa their best was ninth overall, sixth in GT for Bondurant and Jochen Neerspach (later European competitions manager for both Ford and BMW); at the Nürburgring, Schlesser and Richard Attwood managed twenty-third overall and another sixth in GT.

As ever, the big one was Le Mans, which came next, but the roadsters were now very much the B Team there as Shelby's major effort went into the now competitive aerodynamic Daytona Coupés. The Daytona delivered, with fourth overall and an emotional GT win, five years after Shelby's overall victory, but maybe just as sweet in his continuing onslaught on Ferrari. Best of the roadsters was a virtually standard car driven by two French amateur drivers to a distant nineteenth. Shelby had entered it largely as a political move, knowing that if the notoriously partisan French scrutineers passed the 'French' car (as they almost invariably did), they could hardly reject his.

On the international stage, for his first attack on the FIA championship, Shelby had some impressive names on the team roster: from the left, engineer Phil Remington, Shelby, Bondurant, Neerspach, Attwood and Schlesser, in the Nürburgring pits.

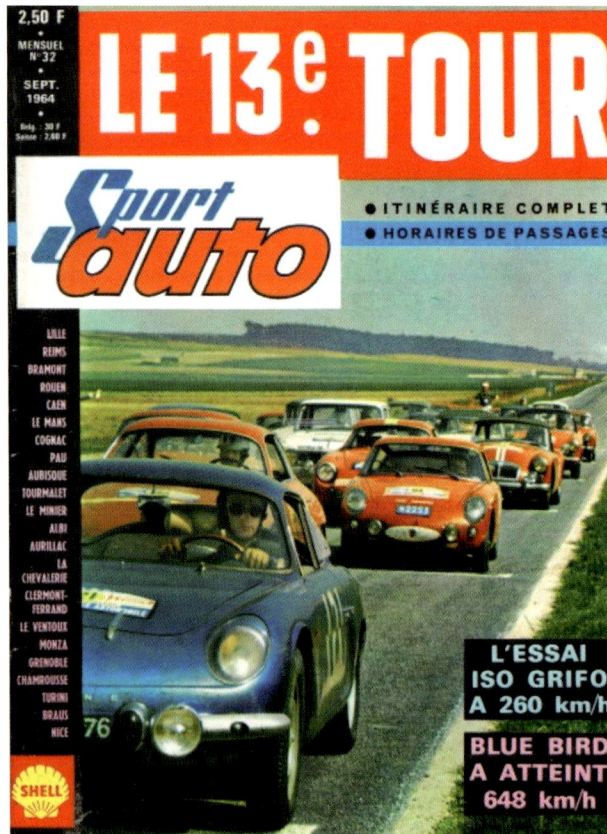

STRETCHING THE RULE BOOK

At this point in the 1964 season, Shelby remained firmly in contention for the FIA GT Championship that was his primary target, but in the end he missed it by just 6.3 points, with 78.3 to Ferrari's 84.6. That involved another piece of Ferrari rule-stretching.

The scoring system was complicated: only the first car of any make scored, on a scale of 9-6-4-3-2-1 for the first six places (as in GP racing at the time). Unlike GP racing (where any car could also score), the points were then multiplied by a 'coefficient', depending on the difficulty of the race (assessed by the FIA). In brief, what Shelby lacked was consistency. They had a disastrous Tour de France (as much a rally as a race) where none of the Daytonas finished. They did better in the RAC Tourist Trophy at Goodwood, headed by the Daytona but with two roadsters backing up. Then Ferrari sent Shelby's hope of taking the Championship fight to the wire up in smoke.

The Cobra was never further out of its comfort zone than in the Tour de France Auto, with its multi-circuit, race/rally format and demanding time schedules.

Confirming Shelby's reasons for wanting to beat Ferrari in the first place, it was another piece of Enzo chicanery that effectively sealed the 1964 GT Championship.

The final round should have been the Monza 1000km (Ferrari home ground) in October. Shelby might even have had a prototype 427 coupé ready for the race, but it never happened. It was cancelled completely after Ferrari cynically engineered a dispute between the organizers and the FIA over the eligibility of his own Ferrari LM. In a nutshell, if Shelby couldn't win points at Monza, Ferrari couldn't lose the title. Again, Shelby was less than impressed but powerless to change anything. It was a title he could and should have won; a clean sweep for his roadsters at the final US championship round at Bridgehampton was scant consolation. The SCCA and USRRC titles were good, but not like beating Ferrari.

So far as the roadsters were concerned, that was in effect the end of the international road. The 427 was a very different proposition in 1965 from the 289 in 1963 – fearsomely quick but ill-suited to long European-style circuits. With the works concentrating on other directions, such development as there was, was done mainly by private owners.

As USRRC racing edged closer to becoming Can-Am (and dominated by big, ultra-specialized mid-engined sports

racing cars), even Miles couldn't keep the 427 roadster in contention. Even in SCCA racing the 427 never appeared in the same numbers as the more affordable (and less intimidating) 289 had – although the 427s that did race usually did so with devastating effect, including those five SCCA A-Production titles. One of the first 427 owners, Hal Keck, won in 1965; Ed Lowther won in 1966; Sam Feinstein was the shock winner in 1973, several years after it looked as though the 427's winning days were over. And he did it with Lowther's old car that had won in 1965.

There were occasional international outings for 427s, too, but now only to individual races, never again as a championship campaign. Most of those were in US-based rounds of the FIA Championships, like Daytona and Sebring; but even previously successful drivers like Keck and Lowther couldn't achieve much at that level. In Europe it was no better. Tony Settember and Ed Feutel campaigned a 427 in several events, usually without finishing. The 427's best ever European result was an outright win for Bob Bondurant and David Piper in the Ilford Trophy at Brands Hatch, against good opposition.

So the 427s were an anticlimactic swansong for the roadster; but at least with the Daytona, Shelby had found his genuine way to attack Ferrari head-on.

Inevitably there has to be a number 98, which more or less defined the rest for the 1964 Cobra works team numbers for the FIA campaign.

CHAPTER EIGHT

THE DAYTONA – SHELBY'S CHAMPION

Successful as the Cobra roadster was, both in national racing and to a lesser extent in international racing, Shelby wanted more. His own racing career had touched the pinnacles: outright winner at Le Mans, F1 driver, multiple sports car champion and record breaker. Shelby knew what it meant to win at the highest level. Then he had that personal agenda: he had openly committed to teaching Enzo Ferrari a lesson in respect.

Ferrari had dominated world sports car racing for the past decade; the Cobra roadster, good as it was, wasn't the car to break that dominance. It was hamstrung by the nature of the sport: the FIA's World Sportscar Championship was global insofar as it included races in America, but dominated by races in Europe. While the Cobra roadster could romp away with any kind of race on a twisty circuit with relatively short straights, those weren't the kind of circuit that dominated the European calendar. On the longer straights of a typical European international circuit, it just wasn't quick enough.

The problem was fundamental. Given adequate grip

AC's 1963 'fastback' Le Mans entries were a step in the right direction, but only a step.

The defining feature of Le Mans, and the biggest aerodynamic challenge of the season in the mid-1960s, the Mulsanne Straight dominated everything else in the days before the chicanes.

and properly chosen gearing, a big power-to-weight ratio and ample torque (such as the light, V8-powered Cobra delivered) would take care of acceleration off the line, and particularly out of corners. With good handling, too, a Cobra was hard to catch between the straight bits.

Maximum speed is not governed by power-to-weight ratio (or torque) but by the outright power required to overcome the forces wanting to keep any body at rest. The power needed doesn't increase in direct proportion to the speed, it increases in proportion to the square of the speed. So adding more power has little effect at the maximum speeds racing cars attain. Even adding lots of power (as in the leap from 289 to 427) obeys the same law of diminishing returns. So while the 427 was even more ferociously quick on any circuit in terms of acceleration, it was little quicker than a 289 on the longest straights.

The compounding problem is that the biggest element the power has to overcome is aerodynamic drag. Simply adding power frequently increases drag – in the case of the 427, from a bulkier car to accommodate the engine, wider wheels to put down the power, and more drag from a necessarily uprated cooling system.

The other side of the coin was shown by AC's and Hugus' 1963 289 Le Mans entries. With no more power than any other 289, those cars with their 'fastback' roofs reached as much as 167mph (269km/h) on the Mulsanne Straight (a flat-out 3-mile blast not yet emasculated by later chicanes). They were easily the fastest 289s to date, but still weren't fast enough to live with cars developed for low drag from the start.

DESIGNING A COUPÉ

Those, without exception, were purpose-built coupés (a step beyond the 289 roadster with add-on fastback). Ferrari had a highly effective coupé in the controversial 250GTO; Shelby knew that if he was to have any chance of beating Ferrari in Europe, he needed a coupé too. Having seen the effectiveness of the 289 fastbacks at Le Mans, Pete Brock was thinking along the same lines, as was development engineer Ken Miles. Impressed by Shelby and the Cobra's progress to date, Ford could see that a modest injection of direct financial support might help Shelby deliver big PR

133

returns for the Blue Oval. So around October 1963, Don Frey suggested that Ford could back Shelby's plans for 1964.

Shelby, Brock and the engineering team were already working on it. They would have liked a few other things, too, like more power and some chassis improvements; but most of all they knew they needed a coupé, and needed it fast. The further complication was the rules: short of devel-oping and homologating an entirely new car (which was out of the question), the FIA only allowed a limited degree of modification ('normal evolutions of type') to an existing one. In Shelby's case that meant the leaf-spring 289. Shelby also knew that however willing Ford and AC were to support the programme in the longer term, if it was to happen in time for the approaching season, they had to do it in-house.

PETE BROCK

In 1961, Californian racer Max Balchowski told fellow racer Shelby that he knew of a young man looking for a job. Soon after, Pete Brock became Shelby's second employee.

Brock was born in New York in 1937, but brought up and educated in San Francisco. In the late 1950s he used to gatecrash classes at the Art Center School of Design in Pasadena, until they told him that the course was by professionals for professionals; if he wanted to attend, he would need to show his portfolio. Once they'd explained what a portfolio was, he went out to his car, spent a couple of hours sketching, walked back in and asked 'is this what you need?' It was, and he enrolled to study car styling more formally.

Around 1957 he joined General Motors to continue his studies. In November, Brock says, he did a sketch for what they called the Stingray racer, forerunner of what became the Sting Ray: 'Bill Mitchell [GM styling legend] said, "that's the direction I want to go". My sketch was almost identical to the car that came out in 1963. Tony Lapine and Larry Shinoda did the refinement, but I feel like I did the original.'

Brock also worked on a project of his own, a small fastback sports car codenamed Cadet, intended to sell very cheaply. He was allowed to build a full-size (non-functional) styling model. When the chairman saw it he said he didn't like small cars, and that was the end of Cadet – except that some see shades of it in GM's later Corvair. Brock left GM frustrated by big company process, just as Shelby would be when he was peddling the idea of his European-style hybrid sports car around the US Big Three.

Brock returned to California and the occasional amateur race outing, first with a Cooper, then various Lotuses, bringing him into contact with Balchowski, then Shelby, who liked the amiable, articulate and obviously talented young man and offered him a job – alongside the only other employee at the time, the telephonist.

His first role was to organize the embryonic racing school, from preparing cars to teaching customers. In September 1964, *Car and Driver* described him as being 'in charge of special projects for Shelby, which seems to include everything from designing letterheads to teaching at the school, designing show-cars to art-directing advertising campaigns…' Brock did design everything from Cobra logos to T-shirts and posters. Inevitably, he also became involved in the Cobra racing programme, and once John Timanus had taken responsibility for the school, he had time to get involved in the Daytona programme.

As Chief Designer, he went to Italy to work with Shelby's old friend De Tomaso on a planned Brock-designed Shelby mid-engined racer. The part-built car was so badly put together that Brock took it away from De Tomaso and Ghia to another coachbuilder. When it was finished, De Tomaso brazenly announced it as the Ghia-De Tomaso, as built for Shelby. Unable, for once, to squeeze backing from Ford, Shelby couldn't take it up, but de Tomaso sent it to another stylist, Giugiaro, who turned it into the Mangusta – Italian for mongoose, deadly enemy of the snake! With backing from Ford, it evolved into the De Tomaso Pantera.

Brock had a torrid time with Shelby and left in 1966, the company having grown a bit too large for Brock's liking, and become in effect Ford's racing research facility, and getting uncomfortably close to the big corporation mentality in consequence. Brock's latest projects, notably the 427 Super Coupé, had been overtaken by the need to get the GT40 right, and by work on the Cobra MkII. He was ready to do something different.

Actually not so different, as he set up Brock Racing Enterprises, heavily involved in SCCA Production racing with a string of Japanese cars. He started with a team of Hino Contessas and switched to Datsuns when Hino was taken

Not everyone at Shelby agreed that it was the way to go. Remington, whose main concern was engines and who had only limited experience of the unique demands of European racing, still believed the goal could be achieved with power. He was a coupé sceptic, but willing to support the development, and even provide someone from his side of the operation who did have more experience of European

over by Toyota. Brock and Shelby had some conflicts when Shelby took over a development contract for a Toyota race team, leaving Brock to retaliate with a well-funded Datsun programme, racing their 2000 Roadster, 240Z and Trans-Am 510 saloons to win two SCCA Production National Championships in 1970 and 1971, in BRE colours. It was close to twenty years before Brock spoke to Shelby again. A planned BRE move into Indy or F5000 racing was less successful, and ended when the F5000 car was wrecked, in Atlanta. 'That was the end of my ambitions to go racing'.

By the late 1970s, Brock was a big name in high-end sports hang-gliders, and helped turn Ultralite into the biggest hang-gliding company in the world: 'I made some good hang-gliders – took the sport from hippies running them off the beach to winning cross-country world championships'. He walked away when increasing legislation overtook the fun.

He started designing aerodynamic body parts for all kinds of cars, and never stopped sketching. One of his first projects of the 1990s saw a partial reconciliation with Shelby as Brock helped design the Dodge-powered Shelby Can-Am racer, as commissioned by the SCCA; but in 1999 he created the Brock Coupé, his version of 'a modern Daytona', initially built with Hi Tech in South Africa – upsetting Shelby again.

In 2008 he launched an aluminium-bodied, aerodynamic car trailer, marketed as the Aerovault.

He returned to the Art Center School as a tutor, and in 2010 they honoured him with a Lifetime Achievement Award. In 2013 he received the Phil Hill Award from the Road Racing Drivers Club, for outstanding services to road racing. In 'retirement', he became a respected journalist and photographer, specializing in endurance racing, working with wife Gayle.

racing and regulations. That was a young New Zealander, John Olsen, who had been working in European racing since the late 1950s, including time with Bruce McLaren before he joined Shelby.

Olsen would contribute greatly to the overall philosophy of the coupé, and by November 1963 the project had started to take physical form. Coincidentally, given the car's future name, Brock and Miles started to plan it around the remains of the 289 leaf-spring roadster wrecked by Skip Hudson at Daytona early in 1963.

DISSENT IN THE RANKS

Much later, in *Car and Driver*, Brock confirmed how much internal antipathy there had been to the coupé idea:

> What was the budget, I asked? 'There was none', [Shelby] replied. But we had to build a car in ninety days to make the season opener at Daytona!
>
> At first, like many of Shelby's ideas, there wasn't much substance to the coupé. But by the next morning, I'd finished some ballpoint-pen sketches.
>
> I had definite ideas on the aerodynamics, my inspiration being an obscure German engineering treatise, written in the late 30s, that described the work of

Pete Brock advocated the aerodynamic approach over Remington's preferred palliative of more power, and it was the Brock philosophy that got the nod.

Phil Remington, left, at Sebring with the roadster, was the third key element in bringing the Daytona to fruition, alongside Brock and Miles.

The simple approach, but it worked: Miles with tape measure checks the 'gallows' over the first Daytona mock-up to determine the lowest viable roof height.

a young aerodynamicist named Reinhard von Koenig-Fachsenfeld. I couldn't read the German text, but the numbers and illustrations were compelling. The proven reduction in drag over conventional forms was so significant that I tried to interest my colleagues at GM, but no one seemed interested in any potential modern applications.

I thought that was a weird response, as we were supposed to be trying to improve the Corvette. Disappointed, I filed the data away in my memory.

Theories were of no interest to Shelby. 'Would it work?', he wanted to know. It would (I hoped). 'OK then, let's build it.'

It was a low-key start. Brock took what was left of the stripped chassis of CSX2008, laid a hefty piece of corrugated cardboard on the outriggers as a temporary floor to support a very basic glass-fibre seat shell, and moved it as far back and as low down as he could within the physical constraints of the chassis. He put in a steering wheel, attached to a short length of steering column, simply tack-welded to a tube attached to the chassis.

Miles, inappropriately dressed in striped jacket and collar and tie, was put into the seat and juggled the steering wheel until it was comfortable for him as a driver and low enough for Brock as an aerodynamicist. Brock then made up a wooden 'gallows' to pass over Miles's head to determine the lowest position for a roofline.

A photograph shows Miles sitting in the 'car', Brock holding his measuring square an inch or so over his head, a shirt-sleeved Shelby looking on. All three are laughing like schoolboys doing something silly, but it didn't turn out to be silly at all.

Miles now took responsibility for the chassis and Brock for the shell, more concerned with what was physically possible rather than future homologation issues. The hope was for the coupé to be accepted as a special-bodied version of

the already homologated roadster without taking them out of the GT class. The FIA regulations allowed that 'evolution', including a modest amount of modification under the skin to facilitate it; but their intention was a lot more restrictive than both Ferrari's and Shelby's interpretations.

Had the FIA not accepted the coupé as a legitimate bodywork variation on the roadster, Shelby would have had only two options, neither of them feasible. He could have run the coupé as a prototype, immediately making it uncompetitive (however good it turned out to be) against more sophisticated, purpose-built mid-engined rivals; or he could have started to build the required 100 cars in a year for production homologation back into the GT ranks. That wasn't going to happen either, even with Ford's support.

EVOLUTION ACCEPTED

The grey area wasn't the body but what was underneath. Fortunately (and maybe surprisingly), the FIA accepted

As with Ferrari's GTO evolution of the 250, there was more to the Daytona coupé than just a new body shape, including the more complex spaceframe elements under the skin.

Miles' new superstructure as being there only to support the new bodywork, and confirmed the coupé's continuing homologation in the GT class. For once, Shelby maybe owed Ferrari, as Enzo's similarly liberal interpretation in evolving the 250GTB into the world-beating 250GTO had established a precedent the FIA couldn't ignore.

Miles' modifications stretched the spirit of the rules every bit as much as Ferrari's had. Yes, it supported the bodywork, but it also gave the old Ace-type ladder frame the torsional rigidity it had never had. A fully triangulated frame now rose from the large-diameter tubes, completely surrounding engine and transmission to form what was in effect a strong, light, tubular backbone. Another pyramid of tubes continued from the part of the frame that now surrounded the gearbox to an apex in the centre of the new dashboard hoop. Another substantial, triangulated hoop behind the driver combined the functions of roll-hoop, body-support and further chassis stiffening. In reality, it was a classic space-frame, entirely in straight tubes with obviously efficient triangulation.

Brock, meanwhile, was visualizing the shell, taping sketches around the workshop walls, gradually distilling them to one integrated design, from which he made a series of working drawings, and from those a wooden buck on which to shape the aluminium panels.

THE SIMPLE APPROACH

Continuing the low-tech approach (no Ford computer here), Brock transferred dozens of quarter-scale drawings to full size by photographing each cross-section, projecting the transparencies onto sheets of plywood propped against the workshop wall, and drawing the outlines onto the wood. Each piece was cut, finished and assembled into the full-size three-dimensional buck, around which the panels could be hand-formed and fitted together. For the first car that was done by the California Metal Shaping company, who hand-shaped the many individual panels, butt-welded them together into a single large shell, and buffed the finished assembly to a suitably smooth finish.

The finished shell had a much lower nose than the roadster's (made possible, on Olsen's suggestion, by tilting the radiator steeply forwards and mounting it in a clever piece of ducting of its own). That would dump hot air directly over the bonnet rather than into the engine compartment, also giving a worthwhile amount of front downforce. The nose was longer, with a much smaller air-intake, and the headlights smoothly fared in, with additional driving lights let into the nose, flanking the grille opening.

The carburettors on the familiar full race 289 V8 would also be isolated from the engine compartment, in their own box, breathing cool air directly through a hole in the bonnet. The side exhausts were neatly recessed into the sills below

For stability Brock would have liked an even more innovative ring-shaped rear aerofoil section, but the classic Kamm tail with its near vertical flat panel was a solid low-drag solution.

They would have loved to have used a 427 engine as well as the slippery bodywork, but the first step, given all the restrictions, had to be the familiar 289.

the doors, and the fuel-filler and air-jack connectors also recessed into the shell. Smoothness was everything.

The rear ended in a classic, square-chopped Kamm-type tail, but Brock had considered an even more radical shape, including a Porsche 959-like 'hoop' spoiler. It appeared on some early drawings, but never on a car. As Brock told *Sports Car International* magazine in May 1990, it was a serious proposal:

> *I was trying to keep the Cobra coupé's roof curvature within a seven-degree slope, to minimize airflow separation, drag and lift. Nevertheless, I felt the new coupé would lift at the rear, so I wanted to use a ring-shaped aerofoil similar to what Porsche adopted twenty years later on the 959. Shop politics were against such a radical feature as there was neither time nor money to experiment, so my ring aerofoil idea was never tried on the Cobra coupé.*

He did find it necessary to add a simple duck-tail spoiler to negate a worrying high-speed tail-lift, and added other detail tweaks suggested by Ford's aerodynamicist, Herb Karsh. There was a small lip ahead of the radiator exit vent (to create a low-pressure area above the vent and extract hot air), while the vent soon lost its original splitter, which restricted airflow. For some circuits, vertical slots were opened up in the outer edges of the concave Kamm tail, for better rear-end cooling; for other circuits they were covered.

Brock was happy to accept advice on such fine-tuning details, but didn't compromise on much else. Even in the face of quite vociferous scepticism, he stuck to the rather bulbous windscreen and roofline as originally conceived.

ANOTHER NON-BELIEVER

A notable sceptic was another visiting aerodynamicist, Benny Howard, who Shelby had invited along to see the car while it was taking shape on the body buck. Brock had never had any formal training as an aerodynamicist, or much practical experience beyond what he'd done on the Sting Ray during his brief stint at General Motors, or at Shelby with the roadsters. But he trusted his instinct and believed in his design.

Howard looked at the evolving shape, talked to Brock about the roof angle in particular, made some quick calculations and suggested to Shelby that even to get it to 160mph (257km/h) would take at least 450bhp. Given that even 400bhp wasn't possible with any reliability from a 289, that wasn't something Shelby wanted to hear. As the 'fastback' roadsters had already achieved 167mph (269km/h) with no more than 350bhp on the Mulsanne, Howard appeared to be suggesting the coupé was a step backwards.

Howard had an illustrious background, but not in racing cars: his speciality was aircraft design (admittedly including racing planes as well as highly successful commercial ones, but in the 1930s). Shelby talked at length to Howard over lunch, then again to Brock. As Brock told Car and Driver, 'Benny said "that'll never work, all that bullshit around the roofline". I said to Carroll, "Benny knows about airplanes. He doesn't know about cars." Carroll looked me in the eyes and said "you better be right…" '

Brock asked Shelby if he'd ever let him down before; Shelby had to admit he hadn't; Brock's design was allowed to proceed unchanged. Also according to Brock: 'Carroll said, "I want everyone to dive in and help build this car for Daytona". That's how it got its name – it was just "the Daytona car".' Whether or not Howard's ideas could have wrung even more from it is a matter of conjecture, but given how well Brock's solution did work, it's unlikely.

Under the skin, the preferred engine used four Weber 48IDA carburettors, a relatively low 11.5:1 compression (for reliability on the typically variable fuel quality found at European circuits), big-valve heads and camshafts designed for a lot of high-speed running. A typical engine to this spec would produce around 380bhp, and the desired reliability.

They kept the four-speed Borg-Warner T10 transmission, with closer ratios, and something like a 3.09:1 final-drive ratio for the longest straights. That gave a theoretical maximum close to 200mph (320km/h). No Daytona ever did that, but, contrary to Howard's predictions, it was a good 20mph (32km/h) quicker than a roadster with similar power.

It used the same Girling discs all round as were used on the GT40 (and later 427s) and had front and rear anti-roll bars as standard. With its longer nose it had much more under-bonnet space than the roadster, and better access, as the whole nose tilted. It had a small flip-up cover so that oil (it took about 2.5gal, or 11.5ltr) could be added without opening the whole bonnet. It had a quick-fill radiator and a long-range 37gal (168ltr) fuel tank. The packaging was tight enough for the steering column to have to thread its way through the exhaust headers on the driver's side.

'THE DAYTONA CAR'

The car ran for the first time on 1 February, at Riverside, with Miles driving. Within a few laps, they knew it was dramatically quicker than any roadster. Brock later talked about how good that felt, after so many people had written off its chances: 'for a while, they refused to work on it, thought it was ugly, called it "Brock's Folly", or "that piece of shit". But then it was 3.5 seconds faster [than the Cobra roadster] at Riverside…'

In fact, at around 165mph (265km/h) on the relatively short Riverside straight it would have been maybe 10mph (16km/h) slower than one of Ferrari's 250GTOs, but the coupé, which weighed little more than a roadster, also maintained the Cobra's traditional advantage of blistering acceleration and nimbleness. With its stiffer chassis and marginally better weight distribution (almost precisely 50/50 front to rear) it handled even better than the roadsters. Another unexpected bonus was that the coupé showed close to a 25 per cent improvement in fuel consumption, and the brakes ran cooler – all big pluses for endurance racing.

There was little time to do any more testing of the Cobra coupé (as it was still more usually called in-house) before it had to face its first race, the Daytona Continental on 12 February 1964 – only eleven days after it first turned a wheel.

Dave MacDonald and Bob Holbert were entrusted with its race debut, and eight hours into the race it was going better than anyone could have hoped, comfortably leading Ferrari's GTOs, with a new lap record to its credit. Then Holbert began to have problems with an overheating differential and came into the pits. Olsen rolled under the car to see if he could identify the problem, as the pit-crew poured fuel in directly above. The problem was nothing more serious than the failure of the small electric pump from diff to oil-cooler; but with Olsen still under the car, fuel blew out

Keeping the big rear window in the car was an issue until they added a few tweaks, and John Olsen found out the hard way not to work under the car while they were refuelling.

of one of the tank vents, poured over the hot diff casing and turned the back of the car into a ball of flame – with Olsen inside.

One quick-thinking crew-member grabbed his ankles and dragged him, already badly burned, from under the car, while others extinguished the fire. Olsen would recover, but while damage to the car wasn't particularly serious, it was enough to put it out of its first race, and rob it of what had looked like a certain debut win.

By the time it got to the next FIA GT round, at Sebring on 27 March, it was repaired and had undergone further testing at Riverside alongside Miles' 427 prototype. In the absence of a wind tunnel, that included airflow testing with tufts of wool distributed over the bodywork and Dave Friedman riding alongside at high speed in the passenger seat of a 289 roadster, taking photographs of how the tufts were behaving – and that was interesting.

PROBLEM-SOLVING ON THE HOOF

One problem revealed in early tests was that the rear quarter-windows (projecting from the bodywork supposedly to scoop air for rear brake cooling) were throwing air out rather than taking it in. Air flowing along the body was separating from the car's sides and leaving a low-pressure area by the windows; the rotation of the rear tyres was pumping air from under the body *out* of the supposed intakes. This was solved by adding small deflectors ahead of the windows, to stop the separation and correct the flow.

One issue that was never really resolved was excessive cockpit heat (a problem even the roadsters suffered). Efforts were made to provide more ventilation but the interior was finished mainly in matt black paint with almost no trim, and it tended to be like an oven. Hacking crude vents into the

In profile it's hard to see any remaining elements of Cobra roadster in the Daytona's far
more slippery shape – and it started its winning streak here at Sebring in 1964.

dashboard, fed by scoops on the front wings and bulkhead, was never better than a partial solution.

At Sebring all the work paid off. Holbert and MacDonald took the Daytona (after its debut, the name had inevitably become official) to a comfortable GT win, and fourth overall. They were followed home by three Cobra roadsters. Beating both Ferrari and the best of the Grand Sport Corvettes made it a good day for Shelby (and Ford).

So the Daytona could win races, and Shelby now looked towards the Championship; but he could hardly contest that with the single car completed to date. So a Daytona 'production' programme had been started. It would only extend to six cars (all of which survive) but Shelby couldn't build even that many without outside help – in particular with the bodywork. That was farmed out to the traditional home of the specialist body builder, Italy. On the advice of Alessandro de Tomaso (car builder, friend of Shelby and one of the people he approached first with the Cobra idea), Shelby went to Carrozzeria Grand Sport in Modena – target one,

to complete another Daytona for Le Mans. According to Brock, the Italians didn't much like the car either: '"that's a terrible-looking thing", they said.'

FIGHT FOR THE CHAMPIONSHIP

Grand Sport had it ready in time for the Le Mans test days, although it wasn't quite as intended. Somehow, the chassis had been delivered to Italy with a body hoop a couple of inches taller than it was supposed to be. The Italians (quite used to working directly with what they were given, and often without scaled drawings) assumed it was an intended modification and built the car around it, with a taller roofline. In the end, it was a fortuitous mistake, as the taller roof made space in this particular car for lanky Californian Dan Gurney, who had trouble fitting into the 'standard' Daytona. So chassis CSX 2299 became 'his' car.

While the second car was being built, the first (on chassis CSX2287) made its European debut, on 17 May in the Spa 500km. In between, Shelby had chosen not to take it to the Targa Florio, as he knew the Sicilian road race was hard enough even on the roadsters and would probably have destroyed the coupé. But Spa, with its long, fast Masta Straight and super-quick lap times, should have been perfect for the Daytona.

It should also have been ideal preparation for Le Mans, barely a month away, but turned into a nightmare. Shelby sent just one coupé, for Phil Hill, but it spent almost as much time in the pits as on the circuit, mainly cleaning clogged fuel filters caused by locally supplied petrol – a common issue when racing in Europe, even at Le Mans.

At the end of the day, all Hill had to show for his efforts was a new GT lap record, at almost 130mph (209km/h). Ferrari took the GT points, while Hill noticed that at very high speeds the tail of the Daytona was getting frighteningly light. That was the origin of Brock's 'ducktail' spoiler, and would be even more important come Le Mans.

Shelby didn't take the Daytona to the 1964 Nürburgring 1000km either (where the GT40 made its debut), as he was busy preparing for Le Mans itself. The preparation paid off, as both cars were ready for the race in June, to be driven by Gurney and Bondurant, and Chris Amon and Jochen Neerspach.

From the start and in the early stages they ran well, right on the pace. Amon and Neerspach had worked their way

Class of 1964: the start at Le Mans, led away by the mid-engined Ferrari LM, chased by front-engined Aston Martin, leading Daytona, number 6, on the outside line, in a very mixed pack.

Daytonas in the Le Mans pit lane in 1964 – showing fully hinging front section for easier access under racing conditions.

to fourth place, then fell foul of regulations: after a routine pit stop, the car wouldn't start on the button, one of the pit crew used an auxiliary battery to get it going, and the car was disqualified. It was a hard penalty to accept, but Shelby was well aware of how closely the FIA was watching him after granting the Daytona its homologation.

The Gurney/Bondurant car continued to lead the class, but during the night it had problems of its own, with a broken oil-cooler, falling oil pressure, and overheating. While the closest Ferrari GTO steadily nibbled into its lead, they nursed it to the finish, and the GT category win. They also finished a remarkable fourth overall, the best a GT car had achieved in an 'open' race at Le Mans, beaten only by three Ferrari prototypes. It was some consolation (and justification of spend) for Ford, too, after the new GT40s had failed.

Having lost one Daytona to a rule infringement, Shelby saw the other one (driven by Dan Gurney and Bob Bondurant) hold off Ferrari for an emotional GT win at Le Mans in 1964.

Both Brock's aerodynamics and Miles's engineering had been vindicated: the Daytona topped 180mph (289km/h) on the Mulsanne Straight, and had averaged more than 117mph (188km/h) for the 24 hours.

Shelby now had a serious chance of taking the GT Championship, which made the next race very important, at another of the super-fast European circuits, Reims.

The cars stayed in France between Le Mans and Reims and were completely overhauled in Ford France's workshops. The race, on 5 July, wasn't the Daytona's day. Gurney and Bondurant retired within the first hour with broken transmission mountings, while Ireland and Neerspach (having already lost time with a broken exhaust) were put out by the same transmission mounting failure at around half distance.

The Championship was now in the balance, with the number of races running out. On 29 August at Goodwood, totally against the odds on a tight circuit that really didn't suit the coupés, Gurney tipped it Shelby's way with another GT class win, and an amazing third overall. Phil Hill had cruel luck again, relegated to eleventh place after spending a lot of time in the pits having a broken oil line repaired.

That should have left three races to resolve the title fight: the road-based Tour de France in September, which most definitely wouldn't suit the Daytonas; the ultra-fast Monza 1000km, scheduled for October, which equally definitely would; and the finale, on US home-ground at Bridgehampton. There was everything to race for.

The Tour de France was a unique event, or series of events: a near 4,000-mile (6,400km) mix of eight races and eight hillclimbs, linked by open-road sections, with demanding average speed requirements, taking competitors all across France over a period of more than a week. More in hope than expectation, Shelby did enter two Daytonas, for Bondurant and Neerspach, and French drivers Maurice Trintignant and Bernard Saint-Auban. There should even have been a third car, but a catastrophic sequence of events meant it didn't start.

Both cars that did started well and won races in the early stages, but neither finished the whole event, as the team, with no experience of this sort of thing, struggled to keep them running within the allotted service times. Vastly more experienced Ferrari cleaned up, and left France with what would turn out to be a winning lead in the Championship.

Three more coupés were under construction as Shelby planned to go all out at Monza; one was to be something even more special for next season – a heavily modified Daytona with 427 V8 shoehorned in. That car was almost completed while the next two 289s weren't; then the third of the 'normal' coupés was badly damaged in a transporter accident en route to the Tour de France. So the 427-engined car (already in Italy where it had been bodied as usual by Grand Sport) was hastily converted back to 289 spec in order that Shelby could still have three Daytonas ready for Monza.

Daytonas versus Ferrari GTOs in the Tour de France Auto 1964 – a turbulent interlude.

LOCAL SOLIDARITY?

But Monza never happened. Ferrari perfectly timed his protest about the non-homologation of his mid-engined 250LM as a 'production' car to force a showdown between team, FIA and Monza organizers. The FIA refused to accept the LM even when Ferrari threatened to withdraw completely from the Championship if they didn't accept it. The Monza organizers (only a few miles down the road from Maranello) conveniently averted the ensuing showdown by cancelling their race anyway.

The big loser, of course, was Shelby, who could no longer win the 1964 Championship, whatever happened in the final round. Once again, he probably drew his own conclusions about Ferrari's ethics, Italian solidarity, and motor sport politics.

Shelby didn't even take the Daytonas to Bridgehampton, so in spite of taking maximum points with the roadsters he had to settle for missing the title by just 6.3 points, with 78.3 to Ferrari's 84.6.

THE 1965 SEASON

By 1965, with the 427 project taking shape, and the GT40 occupying all Ford's attention and a lot of his own, life was

What a difference a year makes: compare this shot of the Daytona at Sebring in 1965 with the car's first outing at the same circuit in 1964. It's all in the detail.

THE 427 SUPER COUPÉ

The reasoning was simple: the 289-engined, leaf-spring Daytona coupé's vastly improved aerodynamics delivered a massive gain over equivalent roadster performance. So what might a coil-sprung 427-engined 'Super Coupé' deliver?

Pete Brock started looking for answers late in 1964, but on a strictly limited budget as Ford's primary spend was now on the GT40, and a new mid-engined direction. Brock, on the other hand, felt brute 'Super Coupé' power might yet trump GT40 sophistication, even for outright wins. And having calculated that a front-engined, coil-sprung 427 coupé might reach 215mph (346km/h) on Le Mans' all-important Mulsanne Straight, he knew that even a GT40 would have a real fight on its hands.

He had already had one false start, earlier in the year with a project based on chassis CSX2601, in the middle of the Daytona series. That had gone to Italy to be bodied as a 427-engined leaf-spring Daytona, but before the 427 was fitted it was re-assigned as a 289-engined replacement for its sister car, CSX2300, which had been damaged en-route to the Tour de France. At which point Brock went back to the drawing board and to ideas of a coil-spring car.

The initial plan was for it to be built as the Daytonas were, with chassis from the USA being bodied in Italy, with hand-formed aluminium shells. But Ford had a better idea.

Peyton Cramer was a young Ford accountant assigned to Shelby around 1964 as 'general manager', tasked with tightening up process in Shelby's previously rather ad-hoc build, sales and dealer programmes, and generally looking after Ford's investment.

Wearing a similar hat for the GT40 programme, early in 1965 he was at British specialist coachbuilder Harold Radford, in north-west London, to see why it was costing so much for them to finish the GT40 interiors. When he mentioned the 427 coupé project, Radford offered to take it on at a knock-down price, with the proviso that they kept the GT40 contract, too. Realizing this was probably their only option, Shelby and Brock (reluctantly) agreed to the proposition, and Brock's working drawings and quarter-scale clay model were sent to Radford, along with engineless chassis CSX 3054, completed by AC early in 1965.

Radford would need additional specialist staff to do the job, but that aside it didn't appear particularly complicated, and Shelby and Brock looked forward to the kind of fast turnaround they had come to take for granted from Italy. What they got instead (while purposely keeping their distance) was progress reports, but little actual progress – until one of Shelby's racing people dropped in on Radford one day during a UK trip and found that even what little *had* been done had not been done very well.

Shelby and Brock were quickly summoned to see what might be done, and found that Radford had used unsuitable materials, by-passed drawings, and were building a bigger, heavier car – and not even close to the expected standards.

Resisting their first instincts to bale out, and with unexpected support from Ford who were simultaneously realizing that the GT40 was not going to be a winner out of the box and that the 427 might be a viable stopgap, they threw Radford, and the Super Coupé, a lifeline.

Ford again threatened to take away the GT40, Radford promised to get their act together, and Brock stayed on to supervise what was now intended to be finished in weeks. But with the best racing fabricators already committed for the season, Radford again got second best, and although Brock gave them almost another three months slack, he ultimately had little alternative but to take the project (also around five times over-budget) back to base. Where unfortunately (and ironically thanks mainly to Shelby and John Wyer) Ford were seeing light at the end of the GT40 tunnel, meaning the returned Super Coupé languished.

They never did complete it, but it passed through several would-be saviours in the late 1960s and 1970s until it was bought by Craig Sutherland and completed in 1980 by respected fabricator Mike Dopudja, with help from a much happier Pete Brock.

The single right-hand drive car looked bigger than the Daytona, a little less clean-cut and lithe, but purposeful. It had odd rectangular headlights above the central air intake, a distinctive recessed rear window above a classic Kamm tail, two massive fuel fillers and a large air-slot, and a transparent front-roof panel, apparently for better visibility on the high Daytona banking. But it never ran in anger, so how it would have fared against the GT40 (and the rest of the class of 1964–66) remains an open question.

becoming complicated for Shelby. There should also have been another 427 coupé for 1965 but wasn't. Ferrari's Monza manipulations may have robbed Shelby of any chance of winning the 1964 FIA GT Championship, but it had made him all the more determined to beat him in the end. By the start of 1965, five Daytonas were completed with a sixth on its way. Shelby used all of them, to devastating effect, taking six GT wins and two second places from eight starts, fielding as many as five of the six cars together on one occasion – at Le Mans, of course.

It may have been a disappointment for Shelby that Ferrari pulled out of the Championship in mid-May, after another of his traditional protests – this time because the FIA had refused to homologate his new 275GTB even though he had built the requisite 100 by then. Shelby rose above it, though, reasoning that Ferrari had made his own decision, and the Daytona finally *had* 'whipped his ass' in the first three races of the Championship before Enzo took his ball out of the playground.

At Daytona in February they finished one-two-three in

After the GT win in 1964, 1965 wasn't the Daytona's year at Le Mans, the best result from the five cars entered being eighth overall, and second in class for Dick Thompson and Jack Sears.

the GT category and an impressive second, fourth and sixth overall, led home by Schlesser and Harold Keck. They were beaten for the outright win only by a GT40; another GT40 split second and fourth, and only a Porsche, not a Ferrari, in fifth stopped a Ford-powered clean sweep.

Sebring, in Florida in March, was unseasonally wet – wet enough to go down in Sebring history as the race where the small, production cars almost beat the big prototypes, simply on the strength of the conditions. The Daytonas finished one-two-three-four, Schlesser winning again, this time partnered by Bob Bondurant. After just two races, the sour taste of 1964 was sweetened a little by 1965's early points tally: Shelby 28.8, Ferrari 4.8.

Better still, Shelby went to Monza in April and showed what might have happened if they'd raced there six months ago. Only two Daytonas were entered, but took first and second places, for Bondurant and Allen Grant.

Ferrari flounced out immediately before the Spa 500km in May, but ironically, with his works cars gone, Bondurant's Daytona was beaten into second place in GT by a Ferrari GTO privately entered by Briton Peter Sutcliffe, while Sir John Whitmore in the other Daytona didn't finish. That was one of only two 1965 races where the Daytonas ran but didn't take the GT win. The other, unfortunately, was Le Mans, the one that counts most of all.

Between Spa and Le Mans, the Daytona had extended its winning streak at the Nürburgring 1000km, with another one-two-three, led by Bondurant and Schlesser, together for the first time since Sebring. Bondurant set a new outright GT lap record for the most demanding circuit in the world, which said much for the Daytona's all-round excellence.

It's possible that the problem at Le Mans was that Ford and Shelby's loyalties were finally too conflicted. With the GT40s now managed by Shelby's old mentor John Wyer, Ford desperately wanted to win overall, and focused their efforts accordingly. Le Mans was awash with Ford personnel and Ford money, so for once the Daytona was the bridesmaid, and it suffered. Of the five entered, only one finished,

driven by Dick Thompson and Jack Sears to eighth overall and second in GT. Anywhere else that would have looked respectable, but in the glare of Le Mans 1965 it was a minor disaster – especially as the race was won by a Ferrari 275LM; an American-entered one, at that.

FINISHING THE JOB

The blow was softened just a couple of weeks later, emotionally enough on 4 July, Independence Day. That was the day when Shelby finally clinched the FIA World Manufacturers Championship for GT cars, with another one-two finish, at Reims. Yet again, Bondurant and Schlesser delivered the win. Anywhere on the European title trail where the Daytona hadn't seemed appropriate, the roadsters had done their bit by steadily picking up points, if never winning. But it was the Daytona that had done the trick, as the car that had dominated most of the last two seasons.

They ended as they began, at the Coppa di Enna in August, with a final one-two from the two cars entered, led yet again by Bondurant. Then the Daytona was retired.

Its race record had been short but spectacular. The six cars raced across just two seasons between them, the final pair not being completed until 1965. They ran to a total of thirty-six entries in fifteen races – seven in 1964, eight in 1965. They won the GT category three times in 1964 and missed the title by a whisker after Ferrari's shenanigans. On the way to the 1965 Championship they won six times. When Shelby retired the Daytona at the end of 1965 it was mainly to concentrate on helping Ford thrash Ferrari again at the next level, in the outright Championship with the GT40.

However, cars like the Daytona were nearing the end of a glorious reign. Science was about to overtake the brutal and relatively crude sports car relying on power alone. Ford led the shift, while Shelby called an end on the Cobra's international racing career. But he walked away with the satisfaction of knowing he'd achieved what he set out to do.

CHAPTER NINE

THE COBRA FRINGES

The final Shelby 427, chassis CSX3360, was shipped from AC in late December 1966, via Shelby to a New Hampshire Ford dealer, who didn't sell it until March 1968. As such, it was the last built, but not the last sold, as a couple of others languished in dealers until at least August 1968. This was indicative of the state of the Cobra market by this time, and the date is significant. Those 'final' cars were sold a couple of months after new Federal emissions and safety legislation took effect in the USA, which would have meant the Cobra in its original form would henceforth be unsaleable.

Notwithstanding its rebirth as an icon, the Cobra had reached the end of its 'natural' life, and now it was gone – overtaken by a changing market, changing regulations, and a newer generation of sports car alternatives. With the rose-tinted spectacles of nostalgia, it's hard to imagine how easily it was allowed to slip away, but it was. Even Shelby himself wasn't burdened by sentiment: rather than emasculate the Cobra to satisfy new rules that apparently frowned on performance and mechanical simplicity, he preferred to let it go and move on.

The AC 289 was the last of the authentic 'first generation' Cobras, satisfying the European market after sales had stopped in the USA, but ultimately running out of time.

AC did build a few more Cobras, a final short run of COB6- and COX6- cars, along the lines of the earlier Cobra Britain and Cobra Export numbering system they'd used on the AC-badged leaf-spring chassis. The final COB/COX production (starting with chassis number COB6101 in June 1966) ran to just thirty-two cars, with what was actually a great specification, combining small-block V8 and coil-spring chassis (although, predictably enough, several were retrospectively converted to 427 spec).

SILVER SCREEN STRANGENESS

As the Shelby contract had now ended, and as Ford had owned the Cobra name since 1965, this short run of cars were sold as AC 289s. Even among those thirty-two, the final five were a long way from being authentic Cobras (although several later morphed into 'genuine' cars). The five in question were built early in 1968, on chassis numbers COX6128 to 6130, plus COB6131 and COB6132 (where the '1' indicated coil-spring chassis, '0' having meant leaf-spring). They were built for Hollywood giant Paramount Pictures Corporation, to appear in the 1969 film *Monte Carlo or Bust* (released in the USA with the even cornier title, *Those Daring Young Men in Their Jaunty Jalopies*).

It was the kind of film that used to be called 'zany', and starred usual 1960s comedy suspects like Peter Cook, Dudley Moore, Tony Curtis and Terry Thomas. Film-lovers' bible *Halliwell's Film Guide* summarized it thus: 'Accidents befall various competitors in the Monte Carlo Rally. Rough-edged imitation of *The Great Race* and *Those Magnificent Men in Their Flying Machines*, much feebler than either but with the waste of a big budget well in evidence'.

AC gratefully accepted their slice of that $10 million budget. The film cars were built on stretched coil-spring 427 chassis. The first three (COX6128/6129/6130) were on 135in (3,429mm) wheelbases, half as long again as the standard 90in (2,286mm) 427. The others were on 117in (2,972mm) wheelbases. The first three were given 'vintage' sports bodies – caricatur-

ing a late 1920s Mercedes-Benz SSKL, with comically long bonnet, three flexible external exhausts (odd for a V8), swoopy wings and huge headlamps. They weren't pretty, but those three at least appeared in the film. The final two (COB6131 and 6132) were also given 'vintage' bodies, but not used in the film – which wasn't made in Hollywood but by Paramount Studios UK, near London, where the cars were delivered.

The plot didn't bear much resemblance to the real Monte Carlo Rally (even in the late 1920s, or when AC won it in 1926). It involved a winner-takes-all wager pitting terribly British Army officers Maj. Digby Dawlish and Lt Kit Barrington (Cook and Moore) against brash American Chester Schofield (Curtis), who had won half an automobile factory (and his rally car) in a poker game. The stake is the lost half of the company; the list of stereotypes is completed by German, Italian and French entries, 'wacky' modifications to the cars, plus the mandatory love interest (Susan Hampshire). We won't spoil it by giving away the ending…

According to the SAAC *World Registry*, Brian Angliss later converted 6128, 6131 and 6132 into '427 roadsters'. That was symptomatic of how something that couldn't possibly have been considered a Cobra when it was built could retrospectively be represented as one, purely on the strength of a chassis number belonging to the original series. SAAC didn't have much time for such conversions: 'any attempts to build these chassis into Cobra roadsters would have no historical justification'.

Surely the strangest Cobra sibling of all? One of the stretched-wheelbase coil-spring chassis dressed in caricature 1930s sports car clothing for the film Monte Carlo or Bust.

REPLICAS AND CLOSER COUSINS

The last genuine AC 289/COX car was completed in late February 1969 and originally sold in Italy, but even that wasn't quite the end of the line. Almost before the real thing went out of production it was possible to buy replicas (SAAC pointedly preferred 'kit cars'), on both sides of the Atlantic. Most were glass-fibre-bodied, some more convincingly accurate than others; most were pretty crude under the skin, some, in fairness, were well engineered (and appropriately priced). The choice of engines was almost as wide as the choice of colours, from authentic 289 and 427 Ford V8s to the ubiquitous Rover (née Buick) V8, and Jaguar sixes and twelves.

None was a real Cobra, but such was demand (and

The quality of Cobra replicas ranges from the sublime to the ridiculous. The British-built **DAX** is one of the better ones, for both build quality and visual accuracy. It also had a genuine **Cobra** (and **AC**) link, with **Ace** chassis designer John Tojeiro acting as engineering consultant.

This **DAX** interior shows how it's possible to evoke the spirit of the **Cobra** while
adding a few welcome creature comforts, even a touch of luxury.

so limited and increasingly expensive the genuine supply)
that the Cobra became the most copied car in motoring
history. There are Cobra replica builders today who have
been in business for over forty years, and built more
cars than AC and Shelby ever did. Fifty years after the
real thing appeared, the replica market continues to
thrive, and eligibility for show classes and race series of
their own even lent a degree of legitimacy to the better
examples.

Carroll Shelby, unsurprisingly, had his opinions – but not
always as negative as might be imagined. In 1983 he joined a
Road & Track replica road test, and without actually criticiz-
ing the cars, remarked that he couldn't understand why the

hell anyone would want to build a replica of a car that was
already twenty years old when he built it.

Whatever he thought of replicas, Shelby also built
plenty of post-Cobra Cobras of his own in the coming
years, pushed the boundaries of provenance to breaking
point while doing it, and eventually fell foul of the law – as
described in Chapter 13.

The emerging fact was that, a decade after the real thing
stopped production, the Cobra was more missed than it
had been when it stopped. Prices were spiralling as collec-
tors realized there really weren't many cars around, there
was money in the market again, and if you bought a 'classic'
Cobra, modern regulations didn't matter.

The clue is in the number of carburettor throats: not the usual eight but a dozen, identifying this
particular **DAX** as being powered by a 450bhp Jaguar V12 – an interesting alternative.

AND THEN THERE WERE THESE

If we accept all these CSX/COX/COB cars and their derivatives (wacky racers included) as the 'mainstream', there remain a small number of other cars that are directly linked to the main line, even authentic Cobra under the skin, but somehow or other out of the standard scheme of things – usually in numbering as well as specification.

Two of those defined as outside the numbering system but legitimately Cobras, within the original timeline, were HEM-6 and A-98, both built by AC Cars for racing in Europe.

HEM-6, built for the 1964 season, was a right-hand-drive leaf-spring car built to full FIA racing sports car specification, including cut-down doors and FIA-style flared wheelarches. It was sold, less engine and gearbox, to British entrant CT 'Tommy' Atkins, and raced by both Roy Salvadori and Grand Prix driver Chris Amon during 1964. Salvadori (Shelby's winning co-driver in the 1959 Aston Martin Le Mans victory) finished third with HEM-6 in the supporting GT race at the 1964 British GP meeting at Brands Hatch. It had a long and active racing career that took it all the way through to qualifying as a historic racer, and along the way was also road registered, as GPG 4C.

The other AC-built car, again based on a 289 leaf-spring chassis (but like HEM-6 outside of the standard numbering scheme) was A-98, the AC Cars Le Mans coupé, built specifically for the 1964 race.

European-spec competition roadsters did tend to be a bit more conservative than their American cousins. This is one of the best, the ex-Tommy Atkins, ex-Chequered Flag 289.

The cockpit of the ex-Atkins 1964 roadster is as understated as the exterior – bar a few racing essentials like big rev counter and mandatory kill and fire-extinguisher switches.

Wheelarch extensions cover wider rubber as required by FIA regulations, while slots give better brake and final-drive cooling, and bumpers give way to quick-lift jacking points.

A-98 – THE AC LE MANS COUPÉ

Having won the 2-litre class with the Ace at Le Mans in 1959 (the year Carroll Shelby won outright for Aston Martin), AC continued to contest the 24 Hours into the 1960s, including running one of the two 'privately entered' Cobras in 1963 while Shelby was delegated by Ford to sounding out possibilities for the future GT40.

Already aware of the importance of high-speed aerodynamics (and in particular low drag) at Le Mans, AC's 1963 'fastback' entry was an interim step between the barn door-like roadster and Shelby's ultra-slippery Daytona Coupé that would appear in 1964. It was effective so far as it went, and finished seventh overall, that year's Best of British.

They knew, though, as did Shelby, that even more effective aerodynamics were the key to Le Mans success, and committed to another step for 1964 – a true coupé.

Like Shelby's Daytona coupé (and Ferrari's GTO), it took advantage of the loophole that allowed an 'evolution' of an already homologated model (even if that amounted to a bit more than the FIA rule-makers had intended), to keep its status as a production GT rather than a GT prototype. So the AC Coupé was more than just a new shape, as its new body was used structurally to make the car (based on the proven 289 leaf-spring chassis) stiffer, which clearly benefited handling as well as speed.

The body was designed (more than just styled) by AC's Alan Turner, and was longer and lower than the usual Cobra with a hardtop, or AC's 1963 Cobra fastback. Its nose wasn't unlike the GT40 and the roofline and tail not dissimilar to Ferrari's Kamm-tailed GTO; but its most distinctive feature was small, Mercedes SL-style 'eyebrows' over each wheel opening, designed to separate airflows over upper and lower body sections.

It was rolled out in the pre-race April Le Mans tests and (like the Daytona) showed an alarming tendency for the tail to lift at high speeds. Like the Daytona, it addressed that with a similar spoiler added to the top edge of the tail. That helped, but before the race the AC Coupé also had to deal with braking and cockpit-cooling issues.

After solving one late engine problem back in Britain just before the race, A-98 was given a final shakedown on the morning of 14 June 1964, six days before the race started. It proved capable of around 185mph (298km/h), notoriously on Britain's M1 motorway rather than on Le Mans' Mulsanne Straight. There was no motorway speed limit at the time, but the newspapers heard about the (early-morning, almost zero-traffic) run and made a big thing of it. Questions were asked in parliament; the Ministry of Transport officially 'recommended' that in future motor manufacturers (and they weren't only looking at AC) ought not to use Britain's motorways for speed-testing.

The Coupé went to Le Mans in British Racing Green, for Jack Sears and Peter Bolton. With a 355bhp 289 V8, it recorded 180mph (289km/h) on the Mulsanne, identical to one of the Daytona coupés and only 6mph (9.5km/h) slower than the other. Unfortunately, while the Gurney/Bondurant Daytona won the GT class and finished fourth overall (behind three Ferrari prototypes and ahead of two GTOs), the AC Coupé was wrecked in a major accident in the sixth hour – also involving Baghetti's Ferrari and tragically killing three spectators.

AC's plan to continue development and build a series of perhaps a dozen more cars were abandoned. The badly damaged A-98 was returned to the UK, dismantled and stored for many years at AC, before being acquired by British Cobra enthusiast Barrie Bird in the early 1970s and eventually restored to precise 1964 Le Mans spec during 1984.

THE ITALIAN JOBS

Alongside HEM-6 and A-98 there were a small number of otherwise normal Cobra chassis that never had Cobra bodies, but which over the years formed the basis for various show cars and prototypes – some just for display, some as possible Cobra replacements.

Two of them were commissioned by Shelby in 1966, from styling house Ghia of Turin, later acquired by Ford, via De Tomaso, as part of turning the Mangusta into the production Pantera. The Shelby chassis were numbered CSX50001 and 5002, again breaking with the convention of numerical '2' prefixes for leaf-spring cars, '3' for coil springs, and '6' for export. In spite of their significance as one-off Ghia cars, and

A-98 was a unique car with a unique, out-of-series identification number. It was AC's next step forward after the relative success of their 1963 Le Mans fastbacks, for the 1964 race.

Italian styling house Ghia of Turin produced two styling exercises based on the Cobra chassis in 1965, both with classically mid-1960s Italian lines. The first was a pure roadster …

… the second had a removable hardtop. The interiors, as seen in this hardtop version, were considerably more luxurious than any 'real' Cobra, but they were never more than show cars.

further underlining the extraordinary prices commanded by 'real' Cobras, both later went the way of almost everything else with the magic CSX chassis number, to re-emerge as '427s'.

One was originally built as a pure roadster, the other had a removable hardtop. Both had quite stylish and luxurious interiors with considerably more comfort options than the spartan Cobra – including wind-up windows!

The two Ghia Cobras were unveiled at the Turin Show in November 1965, reflecting the mid-1960s shift towards sharper edges, more modern-Italian than the curvy Cobra, with tall windscreens and rectangular headlamps. The line never progressed beyond the two show cars, but they typified the styling class of 1965, and bore a resemblance to the Frua-bodied AC 428 that AC built on the stretched 427 chassis after Cobra production ended. Ghia also designed and built a body for Willment, for a road-going coupé cousin to the Willment racing coupé, built on a 1965 chassis.

That car, the AC 428, is more properly regarded as a Cobra follow-on rather than a true Cobra variant, as described in Chapter 10. There was also a 'missing link' between Cobra and AC 428 in the shape of another car with anomalous chassis number – MA-200. AC Cars built that late in 1963, based on a leaf-spring chassis stretched by 6in (152mm), with a one-off body that suggests they were already thinking along the lines of a more civilized roadster. The 'MA' prefix apparently referred to AC's Polish-born designer Z.T. Marcewski – the man who John Tojeiro had taken out and frightened in the prototype Ace.

Following AC's brief for a slightly softer, less rabid, more comfortable European cousin for the Cobra, Marcewski devised a car with strut-type rear suspension and wide-angled wishbones (improving luggage space as well as ride comfort), and a steering rack mounted above and behind the front suspension.

The '-200' relates to the early plan to use a strange choice of engine – a 2-litre flat-6 AC engine designed by Alan Turner in the early 1960s. They actually built a few examples of it, but they weren't very promising, with rough running and a tendency to break altogether – so not ideal for a new car. Inevitably, they fell back on the bombproof Ford 289 V8 to get the car onto the road. The angular, Italianate lines led a lot of people to think, wrongly, that it was a 428 prototype. Registered 6000 PE, it was used as a company car by AC Sales Manager Jock Henderson, but had a catalogue of problems, with overheating, and the complex chassis and rear suspension changes. It's questionable, anyway, whether Ford would have been happy to supply engines for a car that, had it happened at the time, might have competed with the Cobra. So that was as far as MA-200 went, although the one-off prototype, being just different enough from a Cobra-in-the-making, escaped the familiar fate of being re-configured.

If nothing else, the angular lines of MA-200, the one-off 289-powered roadster built by AC and used as a director's car, showed what a tough act the real Cobra shape was to follow.

THE PLUG-IN ALTERNATIVE

Strangest of all the not-quite-Cobras was the EFX series, from a programme that didn't start until after the original Cobra went out of production, and never had Cobra bodies, or much else to let them be designated true Cobras in any meaningful sense.

In 1969, Electric Fuel Production Inc. of Ferndale, Michigan, were looking for a basis for an experimental, electric-powered car, and approached an independent engineering consultant by the name of Bob Negstadt – the same Negstadt who, in 1963, had helped Klaus Arning, with Ford's computers, to design the suspension for the coil-spring Cobra.

Perhaps rightly given the scale of the challenge, Negstadt suggested to Electric Fuel Propulsion that instead of spending a large proportion of a limited budget on starting from scratch, they could do worse than adapt a 427-type chassis to their needs.

Still having the tooling to hand, AC built eight special chassis for the company, each virtually identical to the out-of-production original except for modifications between the large-diameter main chassis tubes – to accommodate a large package of batteries along the length of the car, including the space where the engine would have been.

Because the lead-acid batteries were considerably heavier than even the big-block engine, and as the electric motor (driving the rear wheels) was rather less powerful, they had slightly stiffer springs and a slightly higher rear axle ratio.

Their biggest problem was that they were conceived rather too early for viable electric technologies, so they went no further. Except, of course, that most of them eventually re-emerged as 'new' 427s, or as parts donors for badly damaged 427s. Yet again, they show the lengths to which some people would go to get even that close to a 'real' Cobra.

CHAPTER TEN

AC AFTER THE COBRA

During the lifetime of the Cobra, none of the main protagonists, Shelby, AC or Ford, made much money out of it. But AC, in particular, became the bridesmaid. True, Shelby had conceived the idea, brokered support from Ford, resolved design issues, and fostered the image-building competition career. It was Shelby, too, who took the Cobra to the American market, without which it couldn't have survived. On the face of it, AC 'only' built the car; and only the UK ever really thought of the Cobra as an AC rather than a Shelby.

But it was AC who had spent a decade creating the Ace, without which there would have been no Cobra, AC who listened to Shelby's proposals when others wouldn't, AC who built and shipped chassis to demanding schedules and budgets, and AC who supported every subsequent stage of development. Yes, the Cobra project rescued AC, kept it alive as the 1960s began, but it didn't make AC rich, or even secure. Once the Ace (and Aceca) had ended production in 1963, all AC's sports car eggs were in the Cobra basket; yet by then, AC were in reality little more than a supplier to Shelby. When Shelby refocused on the GT40 and Shelby Mustang, when Ford cut the financial lifeline, and when a changing world moved the sports car goalposts in the mid-1960s, the Cobra's own days were numbered.

After it died, Shelby *did* capitalize on his Cobra heritage for the rest of his life, and Ford made far more from the

There's a lot of Cobra under the skin, in the coil-spring chassis and big-block Ford V8 power, but the AC 428, styled by Frua, shows just how far away you can get from the Cobra's character while still having links to the Cobra. It didn't enjoy the oil crisis.

Cobra name than it ever had from the Cobra proper. AC, meanwhile, drifted into convoluted reorganizations, splits and mergers, changes of name and ownership, and threats of extinction. But AC didn't go away.

THE AC 428

Even with Shelby and Ford support, the Cobra itself would have been a hard act to follow. Without the benefit of Shelby's vision or Ford money, it was a near impossibility. After shipping that last 427 export chassis (CSX3360) in late December 1966, AC faced an uncertain future. But even while still building road-spec Cobras for Europe, they explored new

directions. The first (and closest to the Cobra in character) of these was a luxurious grand tourer, the Frua-bodied AC 428, previewed at London's Earls Court Motor Show in October 1965.

Derek Hurlock had considered asking Bertone to create a similar car before being introduced to coachbuilder Pietro Frua by Hubert Patthey, AC's Swiss distributor (and former Le Mans Ace driver). In early summer 1965, AC sent Frua a 96in (2,440mm) chassis stretched from the 90in (2,290mm) coil-spring 427, but otherwise essentially identical. Frua hand-built a steel body over traditional wooden bucks (without detailed drawings or styling models), and it was welded to the chassis, which was then returned to AC for running gear and trim.

In fairness to AC (and Frua), the 428 was one of the better-resolved potential successors, and fifty years on its crisp, clean lines still have a certain style.

As with the styling, AC did as much as they could inside the 428 to distance it from the spartan Cobra, but the stylized automatic transmission lever says a lot for its character.

The first car, CF1, was completed so quickly that there were suggestions that Frua maybe drew on other designs from his portfolio, but the 428 was a handsome car, in either variant – convertible or fastback coupé; and the first coupé was the fourth car built.

CF1 appeared at the 1965 Earls Court Show as a dark-red convertible (alongside a road-spec AC 289 and competition 427). It looked more road-ready than it was, as Hurlock, Turner, Davison and Jim Bennett faced much testing to make it work. In particular, with its steel body and 'luxury' trim, an AC 428 was significantly heavier than a 427, at around 3,250lb (1,474kg), so demanded uprated springs and dampers. The 428 was also very sensitive to tyre spec, and that occupied their thoughts more or less for the life of the car.

The show car apparently had a 6250cc (381cu in) V8; the next two or three had the pukka 427; all subsequent cars had the less exotic, less expensive 428. CF1 originally had a Ford four-speed manual gearbox but alternated with a Ford automatic during development, and while the manual was always available, the overwhelming preference was always the Ford C6 auto – mainly because the manual option entailed a heavy clutch action, just as the 427 Cobra always endured.

The AC 428 looked good, and became a comfortable, relaxed, untemperamental, easily maintained tourer, with decent weather protection (unlike a Cobra), and a top speed north of 145mph (233km/h). Its downsides were familiar to any low-volume manufacturer. Build quality from Frua

was variable; splitting the build process between Italy and England wasn't ideal, and further hurt by strikes in Italy in 1969, by which time around fifty cars had been built. AC had expected many more, and planned to transfer body manufacture to the UK once they'd passed around 150 cars, but that never happened.

By 1969, at £5,573, an AC 428 cost more than an Aston Martin DB6, a Jensen Interceptor, and most worryingly of all, it was two-and-a-half times more than an E-Type. AC had lost the cost-sharing benefits of Cobra chassis production and tougher legislation was looming, as was the energy crisis, death knell of many a big gas-guzzler. Production ended in 1971 after just eighty-one cars – fifty-one convertibles and thirty coupés. Thoughts of a Frua-designed two-door saloon were also stillborn, so in effect the last tenuous link between Cobra and any AC successor (notwithstanding the MkIV) was ended.

THE DIABLO

Derek Hurlock would have loved AC to have continued as a sports car manufacturer, but as the company limped from one financial precipice to the next in the later 1970s and into the 1980s, it only happened in a limited way, starting in 1972, when Hurlock saw a one-off prototype built by Peter Bohanna and Robin Stables – the Diablo. It was a

With more resources to develop it, the mid-engined ME3000 could have evolved into a pretty good car, but only as a Cobra alternative, never as a successor.

mid-engined coupé with the odd choice of a (front-drive) Austin Maxi engine and gearbox behind the cockpit.

Hurlock may have seen it as the 1972 equivalent of Tojeiro's precursor to the Ace, so AC re-engineered the prototype around a 3-litre Ford V6 (mated to their own five-speed manual transmission), and turned it into a compact and neat-looking two-seater, which they launched at the 1982 London Motorfair, as the AC ME3000. Sadly, it never managed to turn its apparent potential into a commercially viable proposition. It struggled to satisfy Type Approval requirements, AC's dealer outlets were fast disappearing, and they ended up trying to develop the ME3000 in production, Cobra-fashion, with customer as test driver. It went into production in 1979, but only sixty-eight examples were built before AC cried 'enough' in 1984, by which time they had bigger problems to worry about.

LIFELINES CUT

In 1976, new safety legislation had brought dangerous anomalies like AC's invalid carriage face to face with the real world, so they lost even that much-ridiculed but financially crucial lifeline. All AC now had left alongside any potential Cobra successor was building commercial trailers and making bodywork for other people's cars.

The story of Brian Angliss and the AC MkIV (the closest true successor to the Cobra) is told in Chapter 11, but AC's company story now started to become even more complicated. For many years, precisely who owned which parts of the company, which names (or rights to use them) and when was quite a jigsaw. Production in Thames Ditton stopped in 1984 as the historic High Street premises were sold for redevelopment. The 'old' company continued as a service operation in the nearby '21st Century' works in Summer Road. Rights to use the AC name and badge under licence, and to build the mid-engined ME3000 were sold to a new company, AC (Scotland), run by David MacDonald, in Hillington, Glasgow, where they built around thirty ME3000s before going into receivership in 1985.

To their credit, AC (Scotland) had made an effort to redevelop the car, under the guidance of respected former BRM engineer Aubrey Woods, as the Alfa Romeo V6-powered

The nearest thing to a legitimate run-on, the MkIV, was controversial but well respected.

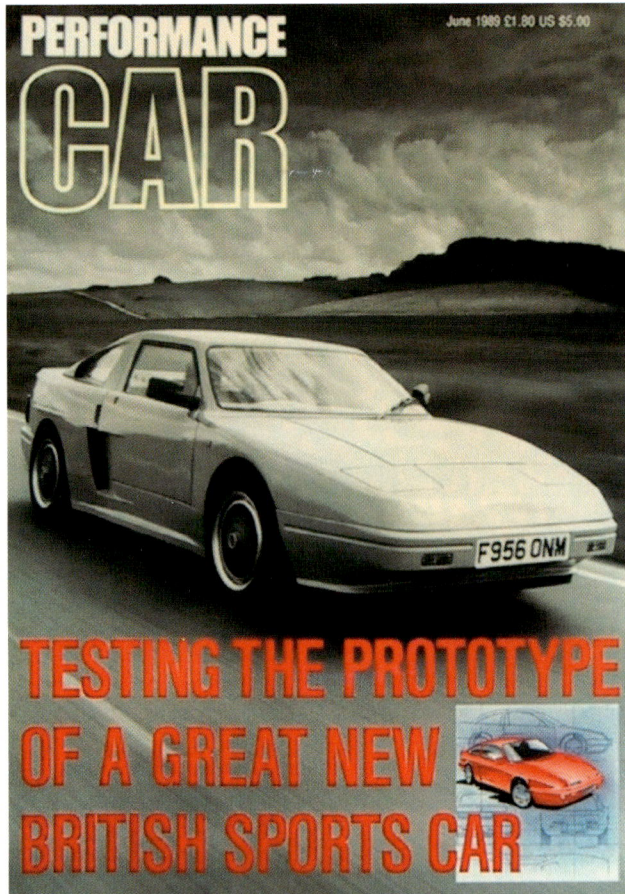

As the twists and turns in the company story continued, the Ecosse, evolving from the **ME3000**, was another brave effort thwarted mainly by funding struggles.

ME2500. After the money ran out, the operation was re-financed by John Parsons, another former racing driver (with Ford) turned marketing expert. With Parsons as chief executive and Woods in charge of design, AC (Scotland) was restructured again as AC (Ecosse), relocated to Knebworth, Hertfordshire, and in June 1989 relaunched the mid-engined coupé as the Ecosse Signature, with turbocharged 2-litre Fiat engine.

THE END OF A GENERATION

In 1986 (after fifty-six years of ownership but with Derek in failing health) the Hurlocks finally sold the car-building

side (with full ownership of the AC name, as distinct from simply a licence to use it) to Brian Angliss, and the remainder (now largely comprising property interests) to one William West, who was never involved in the car story. Ford in turn bought a controlling interest in AC Cars (in October 1987, for £1.3 million) and were happy to continue working with Angliss, as MkIV production climbed steadily towards the 100-car mark.

AC enthusiasts were happy, and Ford revealed plans to build a turbocharged 4-cylinder Cosworth version of a new Ace, after a major redesign by Angliss. In 1988, the production element was moved to a purpose-built 90,000sq ft factory on the historic Brooklands site, where AC forged its competition history in the 1920s and 1930s.

Ford then dropped a bombshell, announcing in May 1990 that it intended to liquidate AC Cars Ltd, because of what it described as 'a stalemate' between themselves, Angliss, and the company who were to assemble the reborn Ace in volume. Angliss announced that he would fight the liquidation, but it was clear that if anything was to survive the crisis it would only be the MkIV – now including a (very) limited-edition lightweight version with even more power, known as the S/C, evoking another old Shelby 427 theme.

THE ACE REBORN

The AC twists and turns continued alongside it, principally with that new Ace, whose story started in 1986 with a concept car called the Ace of Spades, unveiled at the

Just as there would never be a 'new Cobra', there were only ever the glimmers of a 'new Ace', and after almost a decade of on-off development, it faded away in 2000.

Birmingham Motor Show. At this point it was a Ford/Angliss project, with Ford Scorpio V6, four-wheel drive transmission, and pretty dull styling by Ford, which ensured it disappeared fairly quickly. But the Ace idea resurfaced in 1991, when Angliss commissioned UK design consultants IAD to create a body for a new purpose-built front-engined chassis, to be built by Autokraft.

By 1993, after further development, it gained EEC Type Approval and appeared at the London Motor Show. In 1994 it reached production, was quite well reviewed, and even appeared at the Detroit Motor Show in 1995. It was another project, though, overtaken by changes in ownership, as Angliss sold out in 1996 to Alan Lubinsky, who carried on building his version alongside the final true MkIVs. For

1997 it had a 5-litre V8 with modern emissions equipment, a claimed 140mph (225km/h) top speed, all-independent suspension, ABS brakes and a luxurious specification including power-operated soft-top. Unfortunately, attempts to cut costs killed the Angliss Ace's reputation for quality, and production ended in 2000 (with a proposed Aceca coupé version barely getting off the drawing board.

COBRAS GO INTERNATIONAL

On Lubinsky's watch, AC now hived off production in several directions, always with the 'Cobra' as the carrot for the licensee. In 2006, a handful of 'MkVs' was built in

Post-Angliss, in 1996 the AC baton was picked up by Alan Lubinsky, who took the line (in nomenclature at least) through MkV to this MkVI, with many a twist and turn.

Malta, before that operation returned to the UK with abortive plans to build MkII and III Aces. In 2009, more successfully, Lubinsky licensed Gullwing GmbH in Germany to build a Cobra 'MkVI' which has stayed in production in small numbers. In 2012, Sir Jeremy Mackenzie, former British General and former Deputy Supreme Allied Commander of NATO Forces in Europe arrived at Lubinsky's AC Group tasked with rationalizing the licensing arrangements, which now also included the Brooklands Motor Co., who promised a series of very faithful, very expensive Cobra 'continuations', alongside an arrangement with Hi-Tec in South Africa to build the Superformance coupé Daytona clone.

It all seemed a far cry from southeast London and three-wheeled delivery vans, but above all AC's survival showed the enduring legacy of one car, the Cobra.

Remember Shelby's friend Max Hoffman and the Mercedes 300SL gullwing in the mid-1950s?
This is the Gullwing interpretation of the Cobra from the latest company connection.

CHAPTER ELEVEN

AC MkIV AND THE ANGLISS YEARS

While Shelby and AC's links were long gone by 1982, you could still have bought something closer to an authentic Cobra than any 'outsider' replica (however well done), yet not the 'real thing'. The all-new AC MkIV was very faithful to the original, above and below the hand-crafted aluminium shell. What's more, it legitimately carried the AC badge, with full approval from Ford, who were otherwise notoriously sensitive about misuse of any Cobra heritage.

It was created by Brian Angliss, who described it as 'what Shelby might be building if he was still building Cobras today'. Angliss meant it as a compliment, but Shelby didn't concur,

was less magnanimous than Ford about Angliss' right to do it, and started a long campaign of more or less open hostility to Angliss and his 'Cobras'.

In fact soon after the MkIV was introduced, Shelby took action against AC Cars and Angliss in the US District Court in Los Angeles – leading to all parties jointly announcing that AC and Angliss acknowledged Shelby as manufacturer of all 1960s AC Cobra automobiles in the USA, and the only person allowed to call his car a Cobra. Thus the MkIV was only ever an Autokraft or AC MkIV, never a Cobra, but no less a car for that.

Difficult to fault the quality of Brian Angliss' 1990s interpretation of the Cobra, the MkIV, beautifully built with original tooling on original bucks, and truly in the Cobra spirit.

The conjunction of names came and went, but there was a time when AC and
Autokraft worked together without attracting the lawyers.

A GENUINE EXPERT

Angliss was both well known and well respected as a specialist Cobra restorer. In the mid-1970s, when he began
to restore his first Cobra, his business was struggling to
source many of the parts he needed, so he started to make
them himself, from body panels to chassis components.
Other owners soon became aware of that, and once he had
covered his own requirements, Angliss started to sell re-
manufactured components to other restorers, or to owners
direct. He renamed his company Cobra Parts (or CP), with
small workshops in Chessington, Surrey, close to AC's long-
time home in Thames Ditton.

In time, Angliss was making enough key parts to build
complete cars, possibly as replacements for originals that
had been so badly damaged by accident or neglect as to
be economically unsaveable by other means. In most cases
an original would become a donor for major components
– in some cases its key donation was a legitimate chassis
number.

In 1974, having had extensive access to a customer's 427
for extensive study and measurement, Angliss built his first
complete car from parts, and followed it with a couple more.
He scrupulously identified them as his own, having no intention to pass them off as originals. Unfortunately, a couple
of early customers were less conscientious, which would

MkIV authenticity included the correct-pattern Halibrand wheels.

kraft (later just Autokraft), with premises on the industrial estate at Brooklands, again close to Thames Ditton. By 1978, while continuing his restoration and parts business, he saw an opportunity to build complete cars in a small series, and made contacts with a Chicago-based classics dealer who was interested in becoming backer and sole US importer.

Early in 1980, Angliss shipped the first batch of twelve cars, almost identical to the original 427. By using genuine 427 engines he hoped to have them officially accepted as rebuilt cars, and as such exempt from current Federal Type Approval requirements – the continuation of the more stringent rules that had been partly responsible for the 'real' Cobra's demise more than a decade earlier. Unfortunately the authorities didn't share Angliss' view and the cars were impounded for some time before being released.

cause Angliss many problems that, in fairness, weren't of his own making.

AC Cars themselves had absolutely no reservations about Angliss' integrity; he had an excellent working relationship with Derek Hurlock, to the extent of being appointed as sole supplier of authorized replacement AC bodies and panels.

Angliss' business continued to grow, evolving as CP Auto-

AIMING FOR FEDERAL APPROVAL

Unlike Shelby and AC, Angliss accepted the challenge to update the necessary areas of the car to allow it to be 'Federalized'. That would include statutory 5mph (8km/h)

Following tradition, the MkIV offered a choice of classic or modern engines, so long as they were by Ford, from this readily available 302 Boss Mustang V8 to the authentic 1960s 427.

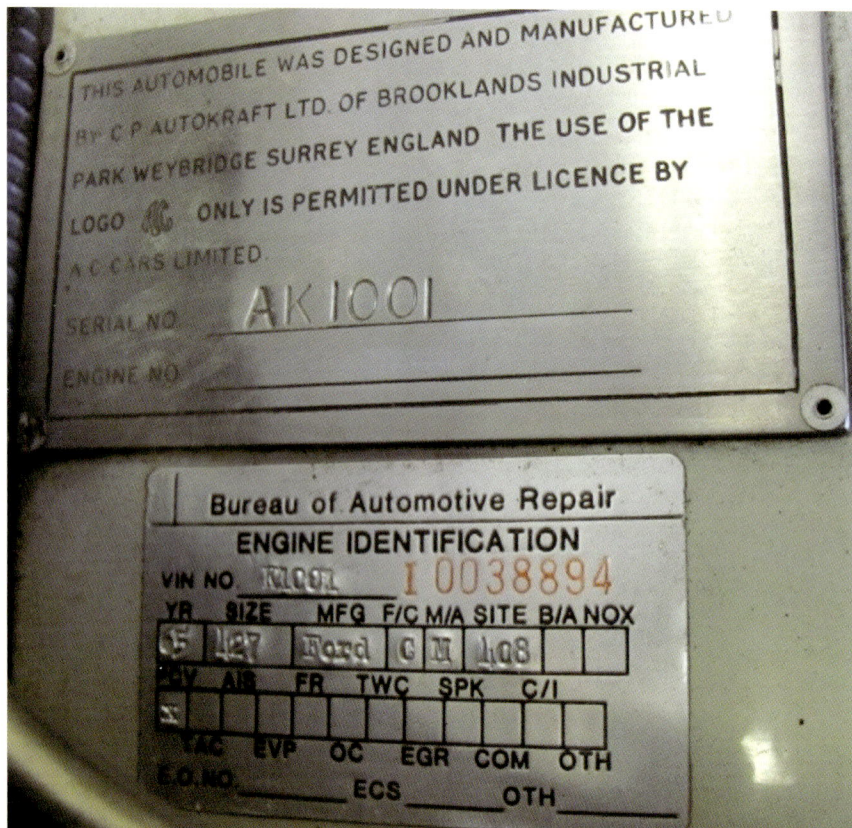

The chassis plates tell a considerable story of a particular moment in MkIV history: AC's relationship with Autokraft, a manufacturing base at Brooklands, and the use of a period 1965 427 V8, certified by the **US Bureau of Automotive Repair.**

bumpers (neatly done with visually standard bars on shock absorbers hidden within the chassis), side-intrusion protection, high headrests, and re-siting the fuel tank behind the cockpit for better rear-impact protection. There were many other detail changes: the body-supporting tubular superstructure was beefed up, the shell was formed from heavier-gauge sheet, and the cockpit was more spacious, improving occupant protection.

The chassis remained virtually identical to the original (including the classic Salisbury rear axle) and differed significantly only in suspension bushing and spring and damper settings – all better to suit modern tyres (on replica Halibrand magnesium wheels). By now, Angliss had also bought a significant range of original assembly jigs, wooden body bucks, stamping dies and other tooling from AC, further endorsing 'authenticity'.

Shrewdly, Angliss had rejected the softer option of using the readily available Rover (née Buick) V8, but was pragmatic enough to adopt already certified running gear from Ford. Initially that meant the 352cu in (5766cc) Windsor V8 with five-speed Ford manual gearbox. Later it more

usually meant the 302cu in (4948cc) Boss Mustang V8; but Angliss always offered a range of options, up to and including the authentic 427.

Sourcing engines brought Angliss into direct contact with Ford, with oddly mixed reactions. Edsel Ford II and Mike Kranefuss (of Ford Special Vehicle Operations) were enthusiastic; others were less so, notably most dealers, who couldn't get excited about reviving the old 'Cobra' as a prestige Ford to compete with the modern Corvette.

In spite of that, and of the ongoing challenge of 'Federalization', of Angliss' admitted inexperience in the American market, and his split with the original Chicago backer, the project was making real progress, while still enjoying the aura of legitimacy.

NAMES AND LOGOS

Beyond Ford's support, in February 1982 AC Cars granted him the rights to use the AC logo and build 'Cobra-shaped cars' for the next twenty-five years – in return for a licensing fee and authority for AC to inspect and approve the quality of the product.

Angliss therefore started production of the next batch of cars, intended to go on sale from early 1984. Logically enough he called them the AC MkIV – following on from the MkI (the 260), MkII (the 289 with rack-and-pinion steering) and the MkIII (coil-spring 427).

Also in 1984, although US dealers had been notably reticent about Edsel's offer of AC MkIV franchises, Ford Motor

Brian Angliss' other passion was flying, from commercial helicopters to his own restored Hawker Hurricane. This MkIV shared hangar space.

Credit agreed to provide customer finance to purchase a MkIV, which was a massive breakthrough for the project. Less positively, having rejected several other applicants as unsuitable, Angliss opened for business in 1985 with only eight US dealers (none of them, remarkably, on the west coast), a thin response following a direct-mail approach to the approximately 5,600-strong national network.

While Shelby nursed his personal issues with Angliss and the AC MkIV, the car was almost universally praised for its engineering quality, excellent workmanship and finish. It was further admired as being the closest contemporary equivalent to an authentic Cobra, from design to performance. Most remarkably, Shelby eventually bought four of them – one for himself, one for each of his three children!

SAAC, on the other hand, while including the MkIV story in the *World Registry*, were careful to clarify on what basis: 'the AC MkIV is an exciting car in its own right' they said, 'and it is probably as close to being a Cobra as it can be without the Shelby American pedigree. But it is not – and cannot ever be – a genuine Cobra, simply because it was not produced within the original Cobra's time frame'. More colourfully, they added, 'on the Cobra family tree, the AC MkIV is a limb that hangs out there, all by itself'.

In 1984, *Car and Driver* tested an early 300bhp, 352cu in (5773cc) MkIV and recorded 0–60mph in 4.4 seconds, 0–100mph in 11.2 seconds, a standing quarter in 12.8 seconds, and a maximum speed of 140mph (225km/h) – none of which would have looked out of place in any early 289 test. They also commented that the handling was much improved, and concluded:

> As a high-performance toy it's hard to beat. Modern exoticars may be a bit more practical, and several have more refined handling, but few enjoy the AC's heritage. Still fewer can touch its performance and head-turning ability, and none can match its craftsmanship. For a car nut, the MkIV presses all the right buttons.

An impressive endorsement.

Even in Lightweight form, the MkIV was a bit more civilized than the original, but faithful.

BACK TO MARKET

The first customer cars had actually been delivered in mid-1985, and retrospectively, Angliss' first twelve MkIVs (the ones that ran the gauntlet of official approval) became known as Series 1, the next twenty-five, partly 'Federalized', became Series 2, and the next generation, fully Federalized, became known as Series 3.

Continuing the theme of legitimacy, and notwithstanding Shelby's earlier injunction against it, in 1987 Ford granted Angliss the right to use the jealously guarded Cobra name. Everywhere, that is, except in the USA, where Ford, as owner of the name (whatever Shelby might think), didn't want to risk the product liability implications of an outside user.

Ironically, the MkIV survived for longer than Mks I to III, and even evolved, although it didn't always improve. In 1987 (still partnered with Ford), Angliss launched a more 'affordable' version with 250bhp 302cu in (4942cc) Ford V8, claiming a top speed of 134mph (216km/h) and 0–60mph in 5.2 seconds. At the 1990 Geneva Show, he took the opposite direction and created the MkIV Lightweight, with weight down by around 260lb (118kg) to 2,360lb (1,070kg) and power up to 370bhp, with alloy heads and Holley four-barrel carburettor. Dropping the catalytic converter meant the Lightweight no longer satisfied Federal regulations, so couldn't be sold in the USA, but other versions of the MkIV had been. Come 1993, the MkIV Lightweight was re-engineered to satisfy both EEC Type Approval and US Federal requirements, so it could be sold more or less worldwide again. And by 1996, 480 MkIVs of all versions had been built.

By that time, Angliss had ended his relationship with Ford, and was moving towards severing his AC links. The divorce from Ford started in May 1990, with unease over MkIV production, and saw Angliss buying their holdings in 1993 before selling AC Cars Ltd in 1996 to South African-born Alan Lubinsky. Under the umbrella of AC Cars Group, Lubinsky took it on roller-coaster ride described in Chapter 10, always with ersatz Cobras in the mix.

Those included a small group of cars tenuously included in the MkIV story, but a far cry from what retrospectively looked like the golden days of Angliss' tenure. In 1997 Lubinsky launched the Superblower, with aluminium body and supercharged 320bhp 302cu in (4942cc) Ford V8, but only twenty-two would be built. Even further from the 'classic' MkIV were the CRS and 212 S/C, both introduced in 1998. The CRS (for Carbon Road Series) was another 'more affordable' exercise, with composite body and 225bhp V8, of which thirty-seven were eventually sold. Wackiest of all was the 212 S/C, with a twin-turbocharged 3506cc Lotus V8 allegedly producing 350bhp, but a million miles from the classic Cobra concept of big, low-tech engine. The market voted with its feet, and only two were built. For the MkIV, the most legitimate final link to the authentic Cobra, the game was already over.

It looks like a Cobra, but under the skin the 212 S/C was way out of the mainstream, with a twin-turbocharged 3.5-litre Lotus V8. With only two built, it was clearly a step too far.

CHAPTER TWELVE

SHELBY AFTER THE COBRA

Throughout his life, Carroll Shelby would remain synonymous with the Cobra, and through originals, recreations or 'continuations', Shelby would bring 'authentic' Cobras into the market for more than fifty years. But Shelby also had a life outside of Cobra. Even as the 'first generation' ended production in 1966, Shelby was looking at what might come next – and neither racing nor the Cobra name were ever far away.

In 1963 and 1964 he built a short run of mid-engined 'King Cobras' for the potentially lucrative Can-Am series, putting full race Cobra engines into Cooper-Monaco sports racing chassis imported from the UK. The Shelby King Cobras had drivers of the calibre of Ken Miles, Ronnie Bucknum, Richie Ginther, Bob Bondurant and Parnelli Jones, but despite early promise they weren't very successful and only eight examples were built.

Shelby was also involved with Dan Gurney's All-American Racers in the early 1960s, before AAR made its mark in GP racing; but his next big thing after the Cobra was another collaboration with Ford under the Total Performance banner, the GT40.

THE FORD PAYROLL

Like the Cobra, the GT40 had echoes of confrontation with Enzo Ferrari. By 1962, Lee Iacocca, champion of the Cobra and prime mover behind Total Performance, had set his sights on Ford winning in disciplines as diverse as Indianapolis, NASCAR, rallying, F1 and endurance racing. The European Cortina programme would take care of rallying, providing engines for Indy, and the Cosworth V8 for F1

The only real connection is the name, and the fact that the King Cobra chassis came from the UK (from Cooper) to be fitted with a Ford V8 engine by Shelby. Dave MacDonald leads Dan Gurney en route to winning the *Los Angeles Times* GP in 1963.

Indianapolis was one element of Ford's Total Performance programme, and they won it with conventional V8 power. In 1968 Shelby looked at Indy with this turbine-powered four-wheel-drive car, and built two cars, but they never ran at the Brickyard, as rules intervened again.

would deliver single-seater domination, while the Cobra and title-winning Daytona coupé would attack endurance racing. But the ultimate aim was outright victory in the 24 Hours of Le Mans, and that need a far more specialized car.

There is an old adage that, however good you are, it takes three years to win Le Mans, and it's remarkably prescient. But Iacocca didn't want to wait three years, so he tried to broker the ultimate short-cut by buying out serial winners Ferrari.

In mid-1962 Ford offered $18 million for 90 per cent of Ferrari's shares, with rights to all Ferrari's patents and designs, under the company name Ford-Ferrari, to be managed by Ford with Enzo as Vice President. The new operation would build Ford-Ferrari road cars and Ferrari-Ford racing cars. Ferrari would retain 90 per cent of (and oversee) the racing division. During due diligence, Ford's offer was reduced to $10 million, but negotiations continued and Shelby's Ford ally, Don Frey, was despatched to Maranello to complete the deal. In the end, it foundered on Enzo Ferrari's distrust of big-corporation bureaucracy and his own pride: he still wanted total control of the racing side; and while Ford were willing to accommodate that, Ferrari also insisted that Ford could race only via Ferrari-Ford.

That would have meant ending links with the Indy and NAS-CAR teams, no F1 Lotus-Fords, and no Cobras in endurance racing. Whether or not the latter was a direct dig at Shelby (already a thorn in Ferrari's side), it was one more reason

for Ford walking away. Success with the likes of Lotus and Shelby had transformed Ford's image, and although Ferrari soon tried to reopen negotiations (and would continue to do so in coming years), Ford had already decided to emulate Shelby and commit to beating Ferrari rather than joining him.

Within days, Ford conceived Ford Advanced Vehicles to develop their own GT programme, and recruited Shelby to steer them towards their Ferrari-beating sports car. To that end, in June 1963 the Cobras at Le Mans were run independently (by AC and Hugus), leaving Shelby free to go fact-finding for the nascent Ford programme.

They based their prototype GT on one of the cars Shelby studied after that fact-finding Le Mans trip, an English Lola, designed by Eric Broadley. Shelby co-ordinated the US sides of the operation with the European part run by his old Aston Martin mentor, John Wyer, and would become distributor for the planned customer cars.

The GT programme started slowly and shakily as the Ford-powered Lola GT evolved into the Ford GT40 in 1964, but Ford honour was propped up by the Daytona, running Ferrari close for the GT title. For 1965 the GT40 appeared in Shelby colours, significantly improved by much the same team at Shelby that had developed the Cobra and Daytona. They started winning almost immediately, and although it *did* take three years for Ford to win Le Mans outright, from here on the GT programme, led by Shelby and Wyer, was a runaway success.

Even while the Cobra was in production, Ford had diverted Shelby to a major role in the GT40 programme – in this case at Le Mans in 1965, overseeing last-minute aerodynamic tweaks.

While running Cobras, Daytonas and GT40s, Shelby added another income stream from Ford in the production Shelby Mustang. Ford launched the basic Mustang (the original 'pony car', conceived by Iacocca to tempt a younger, sportier market) in 1964. While it was a youthful alternative to Chevrolet's Corvette, it wasn't a real sports car, so Ford called Shelby again. Ray Geddes (another of Shelby's desk-based Ford allies) suggested Iacocca should see Shelby about improving the Mustang's image, and Iacocca enthusiastically agreed.

As with many 'Total Performance' decisions, the subtext involved motor sport. If Shelby could contrive a two-seater version and if Ford would build at least 100 examples, they could get a performance Mustang accepted by the SCCA as a sports car rather than as a saloon. Enter the Shelby GT-350.

It did take Ford a while to win Le Mans with the GT40, but Shelby was still very much part of the operation when the 427-engined MkIV won in 1967.

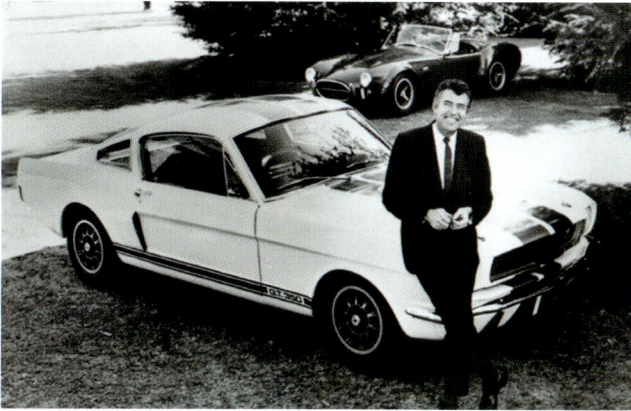

He usually managed to scrub up well for the publicity shots, even to the extent of suit and tie. The **GT350** became another Shelby legend, and, of course, massively outsold the **Cobra**.

THE GT-350

This time, Shelby didn't dream the name, and it had nothing to do with capacity or performance. Struggling for something to call the car, Shelby looked out of the office window and asked chief engineer Phil Remington how far he thought it was to a nearby building. Remington guessed about 350 feet: and the car had a name. It also had the 'Cobra' word and Brock's snake-bite logo on its engine and steering wheel, but it was never called a Cobra.

Again, Miles did much of the development, Brock did the cosmetics and Ford's Klaus Arning (soon to develop the coil-spring chassis for the 427 Cobra) was also on the team. In much the same way as AC did for the Cobra, Ford supplied the basic car while Shelby added a powertrain from the Cobra parts bin, eliminated weight where he could, and added sporty flourishes. The cars were completed at Shelby's impressive new premises at Los Angeles airport, the

GT-350 was homologated in January 1965, and went on sale a few weeks later.

The new premises showed how Shelby had grown, and while it had all started through the Cobra, the Mustangs would make far more money for Shelby than the Cobra ever did, both through substantial numbers of production cars and a good number of competition cars that quickly started to dominate their class in SCCA racing.

Shelby briefly offered a Paxton-supercharged version of the car, but the most famous variant started with a quite different role. The GT-350H was created for car-rental giant Hertz, and Shelby originally hoped he might sell them a few dozen cars. He eventually received an order for 1,000, to sit alongside Hertz Corvettes for Hertz Sports Car Club members to rent.

Hertz soon found that they were renting a lot of GT-350Hs out over weekends, a suspicious number of which were coming back with near-extinct brakes and tyres, and some (it was said) even showed under-carpet signs of having had a roll-cage temporarily installed for the weekend. The GT-350H was promptly nicknamed 'Rent-A-Racer', and even image-conscious Ford didn't seem to think that was a negative.

It was a brave move by Hertz commissioning a bespoke version of the GT350 for their 'Club' customers, and all you need to know is that the GT350-H was quickly dubbed 'Rent-A-Racer'.

In 1966 Shelby prepared a four-seat Mustang for the SCCA's new Trans-Am saloon class, and started winning regularly there, too. In 1967 he added the 428-engined GT-500 – not so much a faster car but a less stressed, more refined one. It increased production again, but Ford's focus was already shifting from performance towards (less expensive) cosmetic packages, so the emphasis on the Shelby Mustangs was starting to fade.

By 1968 Shelby's relationship with Ford was changing. Mustang production was being phased out of Shelby to in-house Ford, as Ford started looking for more control, with their own workforce and more direct input into specifications, which increasingly differed from Shelby's thoughts. Although they were pondering a showroom successor to the Cobra, it was more likely to come from Ghia or De Tomaso than from Shelby, as Ford had a different kind of car in mind. And that led eventually to De Tomaso's Mangusta and Pantera.

Shelby was constantly thinking about a Cobra successor, while also pursuing links with other manufacturers; for 1968 he would set up a three-car production racing programme with the Toyota 2000GT, which triggered an acrimonious split with the faithful Brock. In 2013, Brock told *Car and Driver* magazine, 'I had a contract with Toyota to race 2000GTs in '67, but Carroll scooped me on that deal. He would never admit it and never apologised for undercutting me like that. We became enemies, didn't really speak for twenty years…'

The Lone Star, a joint venture with GT40 collaborator Len Bailey in the UK, was technically sophisticated but dynamically flawed, and never made it past the prototype stage.

There was a degree of poetic justice in that: Shelby's efforts with Toyota bombed; Brock, through Brock Racing Enterprises, found another Japanese partner in Datsun (later to be Nissan) and engineered their multi-title winning 2000 and 240Z racing sports cars.

DIVERSIFICATION

Shelby had other concerns. Shelby American was now big enough to be split into three elements, as Shelby Automotive and Shelby Parts and Accessories moved manufacture and supply to Michigan while Shelby Racing stayed in California. At the same time, Shelby was doing less and less work for Ford. Late in 1969 they announced a 75 per cent cut in their racing budget, which effectively ended the racing links with Shelby, while Shelby himself negotiated an end to the Mustang operation, ostensibly because legislation was making the cars harder to build. In reality, both the car and the associated bureaucracy were headaches Shelby no longer needed: growing issues with being recognized by the authorities (especially in California) as a separate entity from Ford made him uneasy.

While he still had the remnants of Ford backing, Shelby did try another mid-engined Can-Am project, the Cougar-Cobra. The unconventional car was developed in England by Len Terry but didn't work. Shelby also dabbled with another putative road/race Cobra successor, tentatively dubbed 'Lone Star'. The plan was for a mid-engine, monocoque-chassis, 289-powered open car, with all-independent coil-and-wishbone suspension and a lift-off hardtop. Again it was developed in England (this time by Len Bailey, who played an important part in the later GT40 programme), but the bulbous-looking, evil-handling Lone Star was abandoned after one prototype.

BEWARE SNAKE, ENTER TIGER

Far more successful was the Sunbeam Tiger, a Ford V8-engined version of the Sunbeam Alpine, which Shelby created while he was still working on the Cobra and GT40 programmes, and for which he always retained a considerable affection.

It was another Anglo-American collaboration, this time with Rootes Group, which was just becoming the British outpost of Chrysler. The Tiger deal was brokered by US-

Creating the Sunbeam Tiger was one of Shelby's more successful diversions, putting the 289 Ford V8 into a modified Sunbeam Alpine, built in Britain by the Rootes offshoot of Chrysler.

based Sunbeam executive Ian Garrad, and on a shoestring budget Shelby developed the car in a matter of weeks. Chrysler didn't seem to mind that it had rival Ford's 'small-block' V8, and the car was introduced at the New York Show in April 1964.

It was never as iconic or as viscerally fast as the Cobra, but was much more refined, even more affordable, and a fine, quick car in its own right. Like the Cobra it started with the 260 V8 (originally with 164bhp) and in 1967 it adopted a 200bhp version of the 289 – but that was the last year of Tiger production. Shelby never actually built it: he organized the powertrains and other modifications, but the cars were built in England, by Jensen. Having 'Powered by Ford' on the flanks of a Chrysler partially contributed to its downfall as

the American parent group gained influence over the British subsidiary. They built just over 7,000 examples, which was a respectable number, but in the end politics won.

After parting with Ford and these various false starts, by the early 1970s Shelby's direct links with the industry were tenuous, but his automotive-based business was still very active and had many tentacles. Carroll Shelby Enterprises marketed magnesium wheels for cars and motorcycles, he had a Lincoln/Mercury dealership, and maintained his Good-year race-tyre connections. He also had extensive property interests, marketed a fearsomely hot Shelby-branded chilli mix, organized hunting trips to Africa, and farmed thorough-bred horses and exotic birds (not chickens) on a huge ranch in east Texas, close to where he'd grown up.

"You don't just start it...you unleash it!"
—says Carroll Shelby

Carroll Shelby describes a run in the new V-8 powered Sunbeam Tiger: "Turning the key is like cracking a whip – she roars into life like her tail's on fire. The best of both worlds is here – British sports car knack and American engine know-how. It's one of the hottest, fastest machines I've ever driven. Yet for all the power and zip the big V-8 pours on, the Tiger sticks close to the road, low, snug, safe. You get the feeling there's a lot held in reserve,

too. It's a great package for the money."
Want to know what "go" feels like? Test a Tiger. It's packed to the teeth with a roaring Ford Fairlane V-8. And this 8-fisted powerplant moves! We engineered the chassis, brakes and suspension especially to handle all this action. Beats many cars costing $1500 more. Grab a Tiger by the wheel for just $3499* and hold on—it's alive!

V-8 powered **SUNBEAM TIGER** by Rootes of England

*East FOE, White walls optional extra. For information write to Rootes Motors, 505 Park Avenue, New York, N.Y., or 9830 West Pico Blvd., Los Angeles, California.

GIVING BACK

He bought a share in another Texan cattle ranch, some 200,000 acres around the abandoned mercury-ore mining town of Terlingua, near the Rio Grande and the Mexican border, sharing part of its boundaries with Big Bend National-al Park.

In the mid-60s, two or three times a year, Shelby used to take friends to the area (often in his own DC-3 plane) for boys-behaving-badly weekends, hunting, eating, drinking, riding motorcycles, generally unwinding. Buying the land grew out of that. In 1965 one of the group, Bill Neale, designed a coat of arms for the as yet fictitious Terlingua Racing Team: a 'black rabbit rampant', under a blazing sun, with three feathers (representing the three Native American tribes that originally lived on the land), all on a yellow shield.

In February 1965 Ken Miles raced the first Shelby GT-350R for the first time, at Green Valley Raceway, near Dallas. They stuck Terlingua Racing Team badges on it, and it won. The team now actually existed, albeit in a very ad hoc way. Officially and unofficially the team logo appeared on cars around the world. They did run Jerry Titus in Trans-Am in 1967, but also used to sneak badges onto any car that stood still in a paddock for long enough. So Terlingua 'appeared' everywhere from Indianapolis to Le Mans, and

TOP: **Shelby was justifiably proud of the Tiger, and more than happy to endorse it even if his name never appeared on it. 'Want to know what "go" feels like? Test a Tiger.'**

LEFT: **Wilderness playground, Texas-style – Terlingua, 'Where Rainbows Wait For Rain'.**

**Shelby, in the centre, and friends,
ready to unwind in Terlingua.**

for well over forty years the Terlingua Racing Team was a bit of a legend.

More seriously, in March 1966, Shelby, with another of the original group, Dave Witts, helped turn part of the ghost town and surrounding scrub into the Terlingua Boys Ranch, a sort of outward bound school for young people, teaching everything from farming to auto and aero engineering to underprivileged boys – and promoted through the Terlingua Racing Team. It operated for a few years, but eventually, in the words of logo designer Bill Neale, 'fell apart, for many reasons, most of them political'.

Shelby also helped found what became a world-famous chilli cook-off in Terlingua, starting in 1967 (and still running every November). Terlingua's 'Ghost Town Texas' later became an anarchic vacation destination resembling an

**Bill Neale's badge for the originally fictitious
Terlingua Racing Team – rabbit rampant, blazing
sun and three feathers for three native tribes.**

old-time pioneer town, and Terlingua was also a location for Wim Wender's iconic 1984 film, *Paris Texas*.

Through all this, Shelby's health was frequently an issue, and he underwent several heart operations; but he wouldn't give up work, and was ever ready to take up the challenge if and when the mainstream auto industry beckoned again.

A DIFFERENT SNAKE

In 1978, Shelby's former Ford mentor, Lee Iacocca, frustrated by Ford's tamer image in the 1970s, had migrated to the top spot at Chrysler – on the face of it a risky move, joining a company with massive problems and few signs of improvement. By giving Chrysler a sporty slant again, 'car guy' Iacocca turned it around. In 1982 he brought Shelby into the fold, offering him an R&D operation of his own to inject that sportier life into the corporation.

Necessarily, Shelby's early mandate was low budget and low key, but as Iacocca's ideas showed promise it moved from simple window-dressing to quite sporty small and front-drive cars for the Dodge division. Shelby's name soon

appeared on all manner of Dodges, from compact front-drive Shadow-based CSX to big Shelby Dakota pick-up. In 1986 he created America's most extreme 'hot hatch', the turbocharged front-drive Omni-based Shelby GLHS. Between 1983 and 2000, Shelby would base hot cars on the Charger, Daytona, Lancer, Spirit and Durango. But even Chrysler always kept one eye on the man in the street who was now the target customer, rather than the old wannabe racer – so Shelby had to be realistic.

His name hit the headlines properly at the January 1989 Detroit Show when Chrysler showed a spectacular concept sports car, badged Dodge Viper – a brutal-looking two-seater roadster with side exhausts and massive 8-litre (488cu in) V10. 'Viper' alluded to their idea of a 'Cobra for the 1990s', and Shelby was credited for his input.

Public reaction gave Chrysler the confidence to commit to production, aiming for the kind of image boost Ford had reaped from the Cobra, on a similarly tight budget (millions of dollars rather than the hundreds of millions of a typical full-scale programme). Hence an off-the-shelf engine (based on a truck unit) and simple solutions wherever complexity could be avoided. It was the kind of operation Shelby liked: a

It wasn't as glamorous as most of Shelby's creations, but his much-modified Omni for the Dodge division of Chrysler became America's hottest hatchback.

Old Ford mentor Lee Iacocca brought Shelby into the Viper programme, and was careful to make the most of the association when the car went into production.

small team (no more than fifty people, led by Chrysler President Bob Lutz, another real 'car guy'), minimum bureaucracy, a small but adaptable budget, and a prototype facility that could also build the first cars.

In May 1990 Chrysler Chairman Iacocca announced that the Viper would go into production by the beginning of 1992, diluted as little as possible from the 1989 concept. They were as good as their word; with Shelby's input, the 'Cobra for the 1990s' was born.

Just before it was launched, in June 1991, *Exotic Cars Quarterly* tested one against an original 427 Cobra, found many parallels, and noted the sibling links:

The Viper is what's coming up next: give the Iacocca and Lutz duo credit for that. There are no more new Cobras, just new Vipers on the way in less than a year. Give most of the credit to Carroll Shelby, though. Seeing the two machines together you'd think he never stopped building Cobras but decided simply to name the latest version after a different snake.

A decade and a half later, several generations down the road, the Viper is still going strong.

By the time it did reach production, Shelby's personal life had taken another major turn. Having lived most of his life with heart problems, from childhood and even through his racing days, in June 1990 he finally had the heart transplant he'd needed for many years. He had been waiting so long for a suitable donor that when it happened, he simply said 'when you hear those words, "I think we found you a heart", there's nothing so sweet'.

Predictably enough, once recovered, Shelby resumed work at a pace that would have tested most 67-year-olds even without heart issues. In May 1991, less than a year after his transplant, Shelby drove the Pace Car for the Indy 500 – the Viper. In 1989 he had been honoured by his old school, Woodrow Wilson High, celebrating its sixtieth anniversary by inviting Shelby into its Hall of Fame. In 1991 and 1992 he was inducted into the Motor Sports Hall of Fame of America, then the International Motor Sports Hall of Fame.

He committed himself to giving something back. In May 1991 he created the Carroll Shelby Heart Fund, followed later in the year by the Carroll Shelby Children's Foundation. In 2009 those would evolve within the Carroll Shelby Foundation – supported by merchandising (mostly with Shelby's autograph), by corporate and private sponsors (including Ford) and in his lifetime through personal appearances. Team Shelby, the Shelby American Automobile Club (SAAC), Shelby Mustang and Shelby Dodge clubs all included the Foundation as an active participant in and beneficiary from events such as their national and regional conventions.

There would be times when, like most of Shelby's life, the charitable Foundations attracted controversy, including accusations (led by *Automotive News*) that, especially in the early years, giving fell some way short of income. They battled through the criticisms (citing initial investment to create 'perpetual endowments'), announced that the Carroll Shelby Foundation donated over $450,000 in cash and other gifts in 2010, and restated the aim of 'providing financial support for children and medical professionals to help overcome life-threatening health issues worldwide and promoting continuing educational development'.

In May 1991, less than a year after his heart transplant, Shelby drove the Viper Pace Car for the Indianapolis 500, possibly laying a few Indy ghosts after previous confrontations.

Those initiatives focused on acute coronary and kidney care, and included funding for medical facilities in developing countries such as Ecuador, significant contributions to the Children's Medical Center in Dallas, and establishing the Carroll Shelby Automotive Technology Center at Northeast Texas Community College.

COMPLETING THE 'BIG THREE'

When Shelby's relationship with Chrysler ended he flirted briefly with General Motors, completing his unique achievement of collaborating with each of the Big Three. As ever, he was pondering a Cobra successor, but his inside track at GM ended prematurely when his main supporter, Oldsmobile boss John Rose, resigned in 1996 over internal disagreements at least partly involving the Shelby project. What became the Shelby Series 1 sports car did materialize,

After his health issues, Shelby committed himself to giving something back.

Having worked with Ford on the Cobra, Mustang and GT40, and Chrysler on the Tiger, Viper and others, Shelby completed his 'Big Three' link with GM and the Shelby Series 1.

however, and with an Oldsmobile connection, but it would also be the only designed-from-scratch, Shelby-built car in his entire portfolio.

The idea had been kicking around, according to the motoring press, since 1994, but didn't go into production until 1998, after Shelby's split with GM. In the meantime, Shelby had endured further serious health issues; in 1996 his son Michael donated a kidney to his father and back he bounced. Originally, the Shelby Series 1 was to use a 4-litre (244cu in) Oldsmobile engine designed for the Indy Racing League. As Shelby's relationship with GM changed and production delays dragged on, it switched to Olds' 4-litre 4-valve L47 Aurora production engine, giving 320bhp, about 60bhp less than the race-based version. The rest of the car, though, was technically sophisticated: a chassis mainly of bonded aluminium honeycomb; a glass-fibre/carbon-composite body; clever all-independent suspension; and a 'front-mid' engine with six-speed ZF manual transaxle at the rear, linked by a torque tube, for near-ideal weight distribution.

But it was overweight (mainly because of body quality issues), prone to mechanical and electrical problems, and late. Shelby started taking $25,000 deposits against a planned price of around $100,000 and allegedly received 225 orders. As delays dragged on, the price increased to $135,000 by late 1999 and eventually to over $180,000 (for the base model; the supercharged option added another $20,000). Several deposit-payers made legal noises, but the car did go into production, and between 1985 and 2005 they built 249 in the main run.

Being a Shelby project, it was more complicated than that. In late 1999, as Shelby struggled to build and deliver cars, Venture Holdings Corporation of Fraser, Michigan (a large parts supplier run by Larry Winget) bought into the project, in effect taking over from Shelby American Inc., with financial, technical and administrative support, improved build quality, and actually delivering cars – through a small network of fifteen Shelby Series 1 dealers.

For reasons completely unconnected to Shelby, Venture Holdings went bankrupt in 2004, setting the project back to square one. Shelby cannily bought it back (at a fraction of stock value) through a new company, Shelby Automobiles Inc. What he couldn't do was to sell cars as before, because the 1999 Federal certification had now expired and he couldn't afford the changes needed to renew it. His answer was to sell the few cars (around a dozen) he could assemble from remaining parts as 'component cars', delivered to customers without engines and transmissions, to bypass the whole-car certification requirement. They had a familiar feature, a CSX[5000] number (where Venture cars all had seventeen-digit VINs).

Aside from reliability issues, the few Shelby Series 1s that got as far as magazine tests were well received: 170mph (274km/h), 0–60mph in about 4.1 seconds (claiming sub-3.5 for the near-600bhp supercharged option), and fine handling. The downsides, though, technical and commercial, meant it was all over by 2005.

ON TWO WHEELS

Alongside it, Shelby launched an even more exotic detour – a Shelby motorcycle. The Titan Shelby Series 1 two-wheeler was announced in 2000 and built by premium custom-bike specialists Titan, of Phoenix, Arizona. It was way over the top, with a 112cu in V-twin (by S&S) at a time when Harley-Davidson's biggest was 88cu in. It looked good for its day, in a classic low-rider way, with sculpted aluminium tank and lower fairing; and while it was reportedly violently quick off the mark, it was also a refined cruiser.

As a marketing ploy, Shelby offered the bike to customers for the car, and apparently sold twelve that way. *Car and Driver* magazine sensed another Shelby twist: 'the bike is free', they said, 'it's Carroll Shelby's signature on the tank that costs $48,250'.

It was a version of familiar comments. There's no pretending Shelby was everybody's cup of tea, and there were probably as many who thought of him as a schemer and bully as thought of him as a hero – especially in the business world.

In their 1991 comparison of Cobra and Viper, *Exotic Cars Quarterly* alluded to Shelby's reputation: '...one of the least timid of men. Don't let the carefully created and well-honed image of a good ol' Texas boy wearing bib overalls deceive you: Shelby is one shrewd cookie, not averse to earning money or getting publicity for himself and/or his products'.

In 2013, *Car and Driver* asked Pete Brock what Shelby had been like as a boss.

> *Well, he could be suave with women. But [Ford racing manager] Jacques Passino once told me, 'that old chicken farmer is so dumb that I have to have three lawyers around me or I'll lose my wallet and my pants… Man, he could lay that Texas accent on so thick you couldn't understand a word, then he'd fly to Detroit and speak perfect English.'*

Alongside the four-wheel Series 1, Shelby commissioned the two-wheeled Titan Series 1, offered alongside the car in a 'buy one, get the other' marketing ploy.

THROUGH THE COURTS

Especially in later years, Shelby was notoriously fond of confrontation and litigation about anything he saw as compromising the Shelby 'brand' – including his long-running arguments with AC. He also attracted incoming litigation. The detail would fill a book of its own, but there were some notable headline conflicts.

Three of them, in the mid-2000s, were loosely linked, via Jon Wilhelm of Wilhelm Motor Works, Unique Performance, and Denice Halnicki. Very briefly, Jon Wilhelm conceived the idea of adding (considerable) value to 'ordinary' Mustangs of suitable vintage by converting them into 'continuation' Shelby GT-350s. In 2002 Shelby agreed to licence the project, and Wilhelm subcontracted building of prototypes to be followed by production cars. In 2005 Shelby sued Wilhelm for 'intentionally and wilfully counterfeiting and infringement of trademarks' (to whit Shelby and GT-350). Wilhelm counter-claimed that Shelby had breached the original verbal contract by not completing the licencing process – which Shelby said was because he'd never seen the prototypes. And so on. In 2007 the courts found for Shelby's claim and awarded him $250,000, but also found for Wilhelm's

counter-claim, and awarded him $250,000. Both had spent a good deal more in legal fees.

Wilhelm had contracted some of the 'continuation' production to Unique Performance, of Farmers Branch, Texas, again apparently with Shelby's approval. Unique allegedly took orders for up to $300,000,000-worth (!) of 'Shelbys' but were plagued by customer complaints about non-delivery, or build quality, or mechanical issues, until Federal authorities authorized police raids after irregularities with duplicated or non-existent VIN numbers. Unique went bankrupt and Shelby severed all connections.

Denise Halnicki was the widow of H.B. 'Toby' Halnicki ('The Car Crash King'), creator of the customized 1967 GT-350 Mustang Fastback 'Eleanor' from the film *Gone in 60 Seconds* – a big-budget 2000 remake (starring Nicolas Cage and Angelina Jolie) of an obscure 1974 B-movie. The plot involved a master car-thief coming out of retirement to take the challenge of stealing fifty specific cars in four days. 'Eleanor' was one of the cars, and attracted a cult following in its own right. Of course, many people made 'replicas', but Denise Halnicki sued Shelby for copyright infringement, and for licencing Wilhelm and Unique to build 'Eleanor' looka-likes. In 2008, Shelby lost this one outright.

189

One of several triggers for litigation in Shelby's post-Cobra life, 'Eleanor' was the Mustang star of the film *Gone in 60 Seconds*, but Shelby had to face copyright issues.

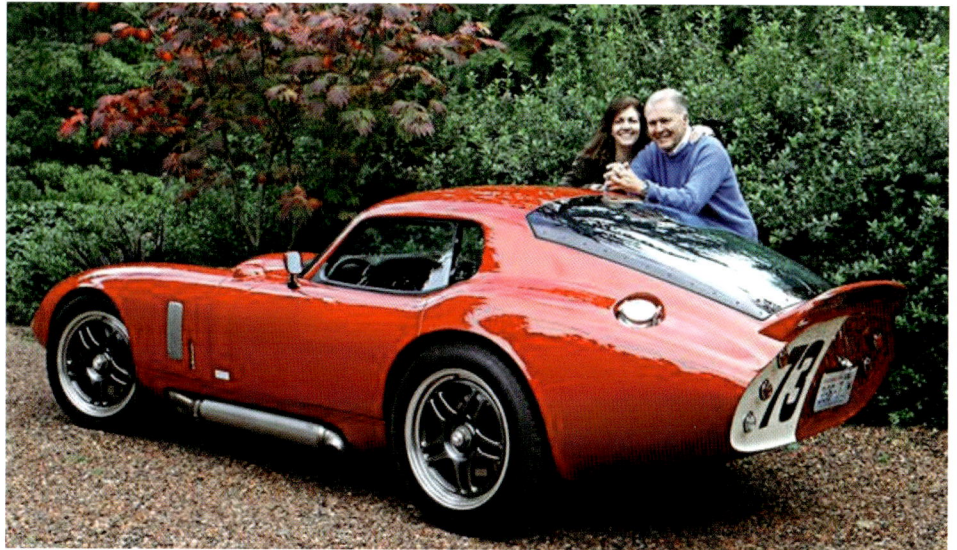

Shelby was just as difficult when Pete Brock (here with wife and business partner Gayle) re-created the Daytona in the handsome, beautifully engineered Superformance coupé.

Equally strange was a dispute with aftermarket company Kar Kraft, who claimed the right to keep and use a batch of GT-500 badges it had bought from Ford. In 2007 Ford declined to support Kar Kraft's claim and in this case sided with Shelby.

In 2003, Pete Brock created a modern, re-engineered version of the Daytona, originally known as the Brock Daytona Coupé. Shelby objected to Brock selling the Coupé under his own name, or later as the Superformance Brock Coupé, built by Superformance in Port Elizabeth, South Africa, then licenced Superformance to market it as the Shelby Daytona Coupé – which was even acknowledged in the SAAC Registry.

One of Shelby's most astonishing fall-outs, in 2007, was with SAAC itself, founded in 1975 and in effect 'official' recorder of everything Shelby, through the *Shelby American World Registry*. The first edition of the registry was published in 1982, becoming the definitive record of every car Shelby ever built, including Mustangs and GT40s as well as Cobras. The second edition, published in 1987, drew on a now-massive archive assembled by SAAC (with full support from Shelby himself) including factory documents, build records, sales and shipping invoices, and information on virtually every individual car.

A highly readable as well as incredibly detailed mix of background and car history, it was and is the ultimate sourcebook on Shelby production. Between the *Registry*'s tireless research and SAAC's many events, no organization did more to spread the Shelby word than

SAAC, and on the face of it Shelby and SAAC were joined at the hip.

But in 2007 Shelby turned on the Club, refused to renew its licence to use the Shelby name, even started to refer to it sneeringly as 'the group formerly known as the Shelby American Automobile Club'. His stated reasons for the schism were that the Club hadn't returned documents, merchandise and personal memorabilia he'd lent them, hadn't provided proof of liability insurance, or statutory financial information, and hadn't produced a new edition of the *Registry* since 1997. He argued that 'the SAAC has 5,000 members who pay almost $250,000 in dues each year. There are advertising revenues, sponsorships, and money made at the SAAC annual convention. In return, from what I can tell, members receive just one mediocre publication and a couple of classified advertising newsletters'. He also claimed that SAAC hadn't paid its nominal $1 annual licensing fee for nine years.

In November 2007, Shelby proclaimed that an annual Ford car show held in Tulsa, Oklahoma, would in future be known as the 'Team Shelby Nationals', and that Team Shelby was now 'the only club officially recognized by the factory for all vehicles built by Shelby'.

RECONCILIATION?

In January 2009, *Car and Driver* suggested they had buried the hatchet:

When we last left the story ... lawsuits were flying... 'Mostly, though,' [Shelby told them] 'I wanted [SAAC] to return to being more of a club than a for-profit organization'. Shelby also announced that his company would be partners in a new club, Team Shelby.

But on August 8, the SAAC announced that 'an agreement was signed, putting behind us the turmoil and uncertainty that accompanied this legal conflict ... as the result of some very hard work by people from both organizations', including Shelby himself and Shelby Automobiles President Amy Boylan... six months later, all seems to be going well. 'Everybody's happy,' Boylan said ... 'SAAC and Team Shelby are coexisting in harmony.'

However much he irritated some people and however many toes he trod on, the industry mainly gave Shelby the benefit of the doubt. In January 2008, 800 guests attended his eighty-fifth birthday celebrations in Las Vegas; in 2009 he received the Automotive Executive of the Year Lifetime Award; in 2011 he added Lifetime Achievement Awards from *Automotive News* (former critics of the Shelby Foundation) and from the Washington Auto Show; and also in 2011 he was honoured by the World Children's Transplant Fund.

Through it all, the cars kept coming – the latter-day Cobras and the non-Cobras, re-creations, rebirths, 'continuations' or otherwise.

In 2003, having played a prominent part in Ford's 100 Years of Racing Festival in 2001, Shelby again renewed his Ford connections, starting with the GT40-clone Ford GT that would help Ford celebrate its corporate centenary. In January 2003 the Ford Shelby Cobra Concept appeared at the North American Motor Show in Detroit. In August, Ford announced another new line of Shelby-Fords. In December, Shelby Automobiles was founded (the name was changed to Shelby American in 2009). In March 2005, the 2007 Shelby GT-500 Mustang made its debut at the New York Auto Show, and over the next few years, as with Dodge, many Fords would carry the Shelby name – including numerous variations on the Mustang themes, from GT-500KR to Hertz GT-H to Supersnakes.

For as long as his declining health permitted, Shelby continued to make appearances for Ford and for his charities, while Shelby American headquarters, next to Las Vegas Motor Speedway, became a popular visitor attraction for Shelby fans.

CREATIVE TO THE END

In February 2007 Shelby announced another motorcycle project, a limited-production high-performance 'bike jointly developed by Shelby Automobiles and Bill Rucker's custom-bike specialists Rucker Performance, who would build it.

Back in the Ford embrace in 2003, at the unveiling of the Shelby Cobra Concept at the Detroit Auto Show, flanked by William Clay Ford on the right and styling chief J. Mays on the left.

Like the short-lived Series 1 Titan, it was powered by an S&S V-twin (an even bigger fuel-injected 128cu in 'X-Wedge'), promising 160bhp (or more with the optional supercharger). This would sit in a lightweight frame (all-up weight was quoted as just 550lb/250kg) with air suspension, ceramic brakes, electronic gearshift, carbon-fibre wheels and upper body, and Superform aluminium panels.

An initial run of twenty-five, each custom-finished to customer's spec, were promised before the end of the year. The long, streamlined, low-slung dragster-inspired prototype looked stunning in pictures, but those were a lot easier to find than an actual bike.

Then there was a Shelby powerboat – the special edition Donzi 22 Shelby GT, (built by powerboat specialists Donzi of Kemah, Texas) powered by an inboard big-block 496cu in 425bhp Mercury V8 with stern drive and capable of 80mph (129km/h), but that was another limited-edition project, with fewer than fifty built over the next few years.

Carroll Shelby died on 10 May 2012, officially from pneumonia, the inevitable outcome of his lifelong struggle against heart disease. He died in Baylor Hospital, Dallas, only about 110 miles (177km) west of where he'd been born, in tiny Leesburg, Texas.

A few years before, facing up to the effect recent disputes may have had on his public image, Shelby told *Car and Driver* that he knew he wouldn't live forever, and that his main

Shelby's second motorcycle project, unveiled in 2007, was even more extreme than the first.

concern now was 'to make sure his legacy was in order and in the hands of people who had his best interests at heart'. Specifically, he told them, 'I don't care how people remember me. But I just want to make sure they have the story straight'.

He maybe didn't need to worry too much: far more people still think of Carroll Hall Shelby as a hero than as a villain. Being Father of the Cobra atoned for many other sins.

Even towards the end of his life, Shelby was never far away from one or other of his icons.

CHAPTER THIRTEEN

SHELBY COBRAS AFTER THE COBRA

Immediately after the Cobra's short but spectacular 'first life', Shelby had no problem walking away; but the Cobra kept coming back like an itch to be scratched. A money-making itch, of course, but the Shelby Cobras kept coming until the day he died, and even outlived him.

THE 'GHOST' COBRAS

Like so much else in his life, they courted controversy, and none more so than the first of the carry-on-Cobra exercises, Shelby's notorious 'counterfeit' cars.

In the late 1980s, Shelby spotted a gap – literally. The gap (gaps) was in the 427 chassis numbering sequence, between CSX3055 and 3063, and most importantly from CSX3064 to CSX3100. Very simply, it was the gap between the competition 427s and pure street 427s, and the fact that the sequence picks up again at 101 is a clue to why.

Originally, AC were to supply the first 100 coil-spring 427s to satisfy FIA GT homologation requirements. Having missed the cut-off date after delivering just over fifty cars, they switched production from race to street, leaving the notional 'homologation' numbers open, in theory to be built fairly soon, to complete the process. But they weren't.

Or not until Shelby, with Cobra values rocketing, realized there were forty or so unused numbers waiting to become complete cars. In 1992, an original 427 S/C with competition history had sold for $550,000; an 'ordinary' street 427 for more than $200,000. Shelby's deception was that the bare chassis and other parts actually existed, in storage, so any build would result in a 'legitimate' car in the series.

But they didn't exist. AC had never built them, let alone shipped them to Shelby for future use. Shelby identified a loophole in the California vehicle licensing system that allowed the licensing agency (the California Department of Motor Vehicles) to issue a duplicate title for a vehicle without the vehicle being presented for inspection, and without its identification actually appearing in the department's database – solely on the strength of a written declaration of ownership from the claimant, in this case Shelby.

In reality, having been granted forty-three duplicate titles, Shelby had the 'matching' chassis built from scratch, by McCluskey Ltd, of Torrance, California, during 1991 and 1992 – reproducing even the rough welds and cuts of an original AC chassis. From the McCluskey chassis, using rebuilt 1965 engines and transmissions, Shelby built the 'missing' 427s.

In 1993, the *Los Angeles Times* investigated, AC confirmed that they had never built the chassis in question, and Shelby had little option but to admit to the truth. In February 1993 the *Times* reported that he had completed nine cars, offered them at $500,000 each, and sold 'at least four'. They also say he blamed his nemesis Brian Angliss for triggering the issue (to protect the value of his own MkIVs) and (post heart transplant) that he claimed to be paying any profits to his Heart Fund. The cars became part of Cobra folklore, but in time many people just accepted the episode as another example of Shelby's 'colourful' character. In truth, it was a straightforward fraud.

HONESTY RETURNS

It didn't stop him building new Cobras, but from now on they would be designated 'continuation' cars, starting a new (and therefore legitimate) numbering series of their own. That started with the CSX4000 series, distancing them from the last of the original CSX numbers, CSX3360, built in December 1966 before the 'run-out' series of COB/COX cars.

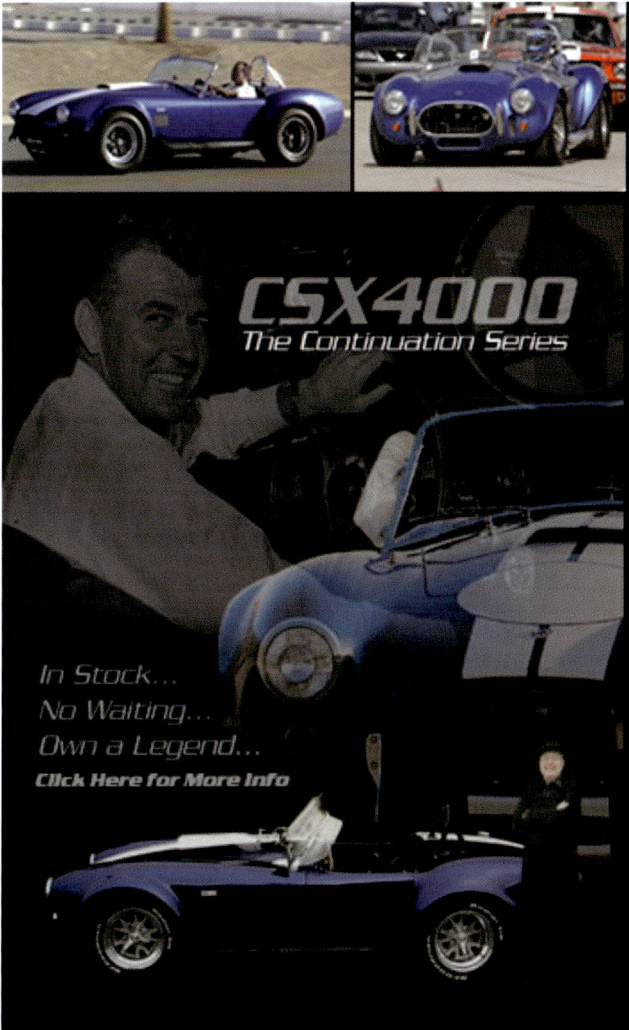

Apparently undeterred by the controversy of his original 'continuation' series involving the unbuilt 'homologation' chassis, Shelby reprised the name for his later **CSX4000** series.

The CSX4000 series was introduced in 1995, as a 'continuation' of the 427 S/C roadster, to be built in Las Vegas by Shelby Automobiles Inc., a subsidiary of Carroll Shelby International Inc. Interestingly, the early 4000 series cars used the left-over McCluskey-built 'counterfeit' chassis, then moved to newly built frames and panels from a variety of suppliers. Legally (because of the original design and running gear), they could be titled as 1965 models, and sold as 'rollers', with drivetrains to be installed by (or for) the customer – which exempted them from some current legislation that they could never meet. The CSX chassis number

'authenticated' each car, and each came with a Manufacturer's Statement of Origin, signed by Shelby himself up to his death. He was obviously keen to make the point that these were legitimate new cars, not in any way counterfeits!

Mechanically, they closely resembled the original coil-spring 427, but with stronger chassis tubes, improved cast and forged parts, better engine and cockpit cooling, and modern brakes. They offered glass-fibre, carbon-fibre or aluminium bodies, and a choice of engine specs. With an alloy-block Shelby Cobra 427 they claimed 0–60mph in less than 4 seconds and a standing quarter-mile in around 12 seconds – all proper Cobra territory.

In October 2003 Shelby announced that the glass-fibre version would be built under licence by CAV, in Cape Town, South Africa, still as a 'turnkey-minus' package, ready for each customer to fit their own engine and transmission, with an 'introductory' price of $39,995. 'Our goal', Shelby Automobiles said, is 'to provide collectors and enthusiasts with an alternative to the kit-car imitation Cobras'. SAAC did document the CSX4000 series (and later continuation cars), including the CAV-built cars starting at CSX4751. The CSX6000 series, also known as the Shelby Big Block 427 Cobra, was simply a continuation of the 4000 'continuation', after they ran out of 4000 numbers. That took almost twenty years and several different suppliers, with CSX4999 completed in 2009.

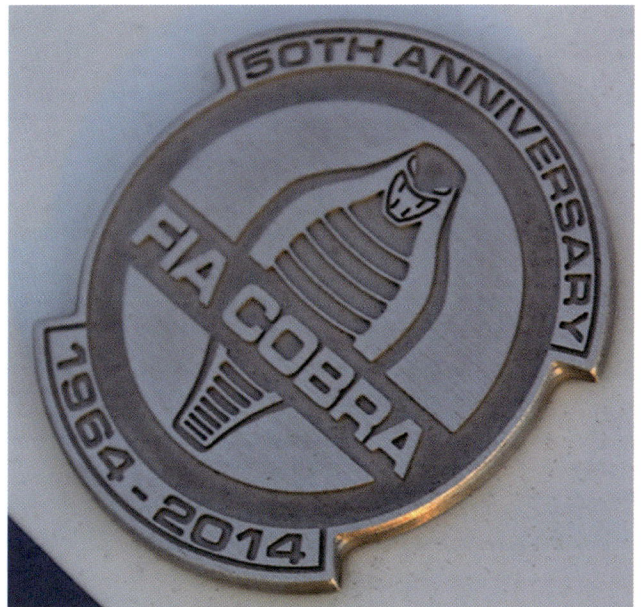

Not one of Brock's, but the original is there in the fiftieth anniversary badge.

ABOVE: **Fifty years on, the classic simplicity is the defining feature of the modern 289, with the wire wheel option completing the period look.**

LEFT: **In a limited edition of fifty cars, the fiftieth anniversary FIA version of the CSX7000 series is distinguished by the iconic pale metallic blue with yellow nose hoop and racing roundels.**

Next up were the CSX7000 and CSX8000 series, respectively continuations of the FIA race-spec 289 and street model 289 roadsters. Both reproduced the original leaf-spring chassis, with minimal changes where they couldn't be avoided, and where better materials or components were available. There was the usual choice of engines, while the 7000 FIA series was alloy-body only, and 8000 'street' glass-fibre only. For an authentic period look, the 8000 came with wire wheels, and optional soft-top.

CELEBRATING FIFTY YEARS

In January 2014, at the annual Barrett-Jackson auction in Scottsdale, Arizona, Shelby Automobiles unveiled the 50th Anniversary FIA version of the CSX7000 series, strictly limited to a run of fifty cars, all finished in iconic pale metallic Viking Blue with yellow 'FIA' stripes and white racing roundels. They had the stripped-out, black-finished competition interior, and original-pattern knock-off alloy wheels. Ex-drivetrain, prices started at $94,995 for a glass-fibre-bodied car or $159,995 for an aluminium one.

Finally there was the CSX9000, Shelby's 'authorized' version of the Daytona coupé, like all the others as a rolling chassis clothed in glass-fibre or aluminium.

Every one of them continued to sell strongly (as the slogan on one brochure said: 'In Stock; No Waiting; Own a Legend'). The Cobra *still* refuses to roll over.

Shelby's own 'authorized' version of the Daytona coupé, the **CSX9000**.

CHAPTER FOURTEEN

OWNING AND DRIVING

The good news is that almost any version of the Cobra is good to drive, and surprisingly easy to live with. The bad news is that unless you already have one in the garage, or have a very healthy budget indeed, you may have left it rather late to start shopping.

The Cobra long ago became 'desirable', for rarity, usability, and maybe most of all for the pure romance. Between February 1962 and August 1968, a total of almost exactly 1,000 were built – 655 leaf-spring cars, 348 coil-springs. According to chassis records, 577 of the 260/289 leaf-springs were sold purely as road cars; only 260 coil-springs (plus most of the thirty-two non-export COB/COX cars) were strictly for the road. The rest, in one way or another, were competition cars, and any competition history is likely to mean a further premium. From being relatively affordable in its day, any Cobra is now a big-ticket item.

THE RIGHT TIME TO BUY?

In the late 1960s, when the Cobra wasn't long out of production, you could have bought a decent 289 for less than £1,500. From there, the asking price headed exponentially upward. In the early 1970s, you could still have found a Cobra for £2,000–£3,000, and probably felt you were paying quite a lot for it. By the mid-1970s prices had reached around £7,000 for a good car; by the early 1980s a good 289 with provenance was maybe £12,000–£13,000 and the rarer 427 had passed £20,000. Five years later £30,000 was a more typical starting point, and the Cobra had already firmly staked its claim as a 'collectible'.

Except for very early days when the Cobra was just another car for sale in the *Motor Sport* or *Road & Track* classifieds, price rapidly became a function of provenance, and of rarity. The market also had an in-built geographic skew: the vast majority of cars were initially sold in the USA, and stayed there. In Britain, there were probably no more than

eighty Cobras in the original car park, and only a handful of 427s. The days of looking for a Cobra in the USA on the grounds of price, however, are long gone: today's Cobra market is worldwide.

By the time the first version of this book was written, in the mid-1990s, a typical price for a good 289 with no special history was as much as £150,000; a genuine 427-engined 427 maybe double that. In 2014, you might find an early 260 for less than $700,000, or a 289 from $800,000–$900,000; any 427 will be well into seven figures, from maybe $1.2 million for a simple 427 roadster to $1.8 million for a 427 S/C, and north of $2 million for a full-competition 427, with an upward sliding scale for added history. In 2012, Barrett Jackson sold one of the two original 'Supersnakes' for $5.5 million including premiums.

Not much point, either, looking for a basket case, or fixer-upper. Cobra values and limited supply have been an issue for long enough that almost any car now coming to market is in Condition A. Or even better, untouched original. But not garage-find.

Desirability and value do mean that most of the cars built survive. Many, inevitably, have at some time or other suffered accident damage, and not always minor; very few were ever considered beyond salvation. And thereby hangs another cautionary tale, about just how original and authentic is 'original and authentic'.

HOW GENUINE IS GENUINE?

Almost anything that ever had any kind of Cobra chassis number (including fringe claimants like the electric-car chassis and Paramount Films long-wheelbase chassis) were long ago rebuilt into 'Cobras', in name at least.

The Shelby American Automobile Club devised a detailed and well-reasoned set of definitions to cover virtually any category of car, and thirty-odd years on they hold good. In

Now heading north towards $2 million, the 427 S/C was a very good investment indeed at the time.

SAAC terms, 'original' described a car whose main frame tubes and any pieces carrying the serial numbers have neither been replaced nor altered. The relevant numbers identify both chassis and major body parts as original, and there are numerous pieces which should carry such identification numbers, including the chassis itself, bonnet and boot catches, door hinges, transmission tunnel, and rear bulkhead.

SAAC's next category is 'original/restored', referring to a car having had less than half its original superstructure or bodywork replaced (that is, more than half remaining), but not losing the main frame tubes or other pieces carrying serial numbers.

'Original/rebodied' defines a car that has had more than half its original superstructure or bodywork replaced (say following accident damage), but again, not including the main frame tubes or other critical components carrying factory identification numbers.

'Replica', so far as SAAC's definitions are concerned, means a car that has been rebuilt substantially to original specifications (even including replacement of the main frame tubes) but in which some part of the original car existed prior to the rebuild, and for which documentary evidence, such as a traceable bill of sale, can be produced.

To a greater or lesser degree, any car falling into those categories (even 'replica') is essentially a legitimate Cobra; some formerly heavily damaged competition cars in particular will fall into the 'lower' definitions while still having perfectly legitimate, even comprehensively documented histories. Perversely, some might even have added value *because* of honourably won battle scars, rather than in spite of them.

Outside all those 'official' definitions are a number of categories that may aspire to legitimacy but can better be described, in truth, as forgeries. By virtue of the relationship between value and simplicity, including readily available major elements like engine and transmission, a Cobra isn't a particularly challenging car to fake quite well.

Some 'fakes' are imitation without intention to deceive. That substantial industry grew up (and continues to thrive) making kit cars, replicas, lookalikes that make no attempt to duplicate 'real' detail under their (usually) glass-fibre skins. Such cars are, fairly obviously, such ad hoc constructions that there is very little likelihood of their being passed off as the real thing – especially in what is now a sophisticated, seven-figure-plus market.

It should be said, too, that the AC MkIV, which actually is very much a Cobra from the ground up, never made any attempt to pass itself off as 'original' or 'authentic'.

There have been less scrupulous copies, up to the level of outright fraud. These may have been created around a notion of genuine but non-numbered parts, yet still claiming a genuine provenance. Such provenances have been based on a 'genuine' number whose record is either non-existent or so vague as to be open to fraudulent claims of ownership. Other cars have been created from zero, without a nut or bolt that has ever been near an authentic Cobra; as an extension of the way cars previously described have claimed provenance, even some of these fraudulently attempted to adopt a 'real' identity. The SAAC colourfully described the last category as 'air cars'.

The author once pointed out to Shelby, post transplants, that with somebody else's heart and kidneys, by the SAAC's definition he was no longer an 'original' Shelby, as he no longer had totally matching part numbers. He enjoyed that.

It should be very difficult to be fooled by a non-genuine Cobra. Notwithstanding spats with Shelby himself, the old AC chassis records and SAAC's impeccably researched *Registry* offer far more detail than is readily available for almost any other classic car, and the SAAC in particular is a very helpful resource. But *caveat emptor*: most of the old deliberately fraudulent Cobras were gradually exposed for what they were, but with values as they are, there will always be the temptation in some quarters to add by whatever means to the Cobra car pool.

MAINTAINING A COBRA

Once found and funded, a Cobra is a relatively undemanding car to live with. Where every significant component on a 1960s Ferrari or Lamborghini, say, can be a nightmare to trace and replace, the majority of the Cobra's major driveline elements are nothing more daunting than Ford or Jaguar/Salisbury. That said, if you have a Cobra in the garage, fifty years on, even some major items (like genuine 427 engines) are becoming scarcer, so you won't quite be shopping for spares at the local motorist DIY.

Even most purpose-built elements are relatively simple fabrications (consider how and where the car was built), so there should be no horrors in maintaining or replacing things like tubular chassis elements, superstructures or mountings. Always with the proviso that you need to be aware of what parts carry identification numbers, and what that implies.

The most challenging area is probably the body, but specialist coachbuilders work to exactly the same standards (sometimes on the same reclaimed bucks) as the craftsmen who built it in the first place. It's best done properly, by those who work to high levels of skill and craftsmanship, and increasingly with an appreciation of the historic importance of virtually any car that has survived this far. They will charge appropriately, but in the context of a Cobra's modern value, it is still a cost-friendly classic. There's no reason at all why any Cobra that's on the road now shouldn't stay there indefinitely.

It is also, essentially, a reliable car in 'everyday' use. Its development problems were engineered out as the Cobra went along, and such modifications (including those made retrospectively) shouldn't be seen as compromising originality, simply part of the car's life.

Corrosion problems were fairly limited, and by now, most historic ones will have been eradicated. There was always the possibility of rust in the main frame tubes, but it was never a common problem and the tubes are strong. It's worth remembering, too, that the majority of Cobras probably spent their early lives in friendly environments, and perhaps later in storage. One area that did suffer to a greater degree was rust in the outriggers from the main frame, or chemical reaction where the aluminium body shell meets the steel frame. Any issue is likely to be minor, however, and readily curable by injections of money and craftsmanship.

Mechanically, none of the Cobras had major issues – especially in road use. Even in advanced states of tune the Ford V8 (big-block and small-block) is inherently strong and reliable – given proper maintenance and a degree of mechanical sympathy. The whole Cobra philosophy, remember, was based on lazy, lightly stressed power from a big engine in a lightweight chassis, rather than on highly tuned exotic engineering.

Cobra transmissions are similarly reliable: they are designed to cope with a known level of power and torque, so they are rarely overstressed. Lower gear synchromesh may get tired after large mileages, but it is rare for any Cobra gearbox to break in normal usage; if it does, it isn't a difficult thing to repair or replace. The same applies to the final drive, which was so far within its capabilities on the 260/289 that it survived unchanged into the 427, still with something in reserve (as could be seen in competition).

DRIVING A COBRA

In a nutshell, and especially now that most cars are prepared to a high initial standard, a well-maintained Cobra driven with the understanding that heavy-handedness will mean unnecessary mechanical stresses, should present few running problems.

A Cobra is not 'precious' in the pejorative way that more esoteric classics are precious and demanding. Any Cobra can genuinely be enjoyed for its simplicity and still staggering performance just as it was fifty years ago, *because* of what it is.

It's a simple car. It has two seats, full stop. Inside as well as out, a 427 is a few inches bigger than a 289, but even a 289 allows a comfortable straight-armed driving style, unlike many early 1960s sports car contemporaries. The pedals are small by modern standards (but with the AC logo cast in, they're non-slip). The big catch is that there isn't much space in the footwell (because of the width of the transmission tunnel) so in the 427 in particular the pedals are heavily offset.

You could never call it luxurious. There's thin carpet and leather seat coverings, but little or no additional trim, not even external door handles, just a catch or leather-cord pull inside each door. The door itself is a thin aluminium skin on a basic tubular frame, with an elasticated map-pocket if the car isn't a totally stripped-out racer.

The seat backs are low by modern standards, with little or no shoulder support, but they're well-shaped for lower-back, hip and bottom support. They look flat and thinly padded but are more comfortable than they look, especially for the shorter journeys that a Cobra nearing pension age is now likely to do more often than not.

It isn't a bad-weather car. Aside from the challenge of taming the performance on a slippery surface, weather protection is rudimentary, even by the standards of the day. The hood is a laughably old-fashioned frame-and-cover affair that's challenging to put up quickly, and which flaps and leaks once you have. Many restored cars have addressed that with better modern materials and fittings, but a Cobra hood is what it is – crude.

Even on a 'fully equipped' road car, the Cobra's racing alter ego is never far below the surface. Instrumentation and switchgear are comprehensive, but scattergun in their layout. The 289 and 427 dash layouts are essentially identical, with the proviso that many cars (especially anything with any competition link) have personalized instrument and switch layouts – again an intrinsic part of the car's 'originality'. If it's needed, it will be there: the larger dials, behind the steering wheel in a flat panel, are speedometer and tachometer; in the centre of the dash are smaller gauges for battery charge, fuel level, water and oil temperatures and oil pressure. There's usually a clock, too. All the instruments are classic round-faced, chrome-bezelled, easy-to-read, white on black. The switches are a bit less intuitive: a spread-out mix of push/pull and toggle switches, typically without any original labelling, but any owner will quickly know their own car.

On a 289, the gear lever is short and set well forwards on top of the transmission tunnel; on a 427 it is usually a long lever reaching forwards from where it emerges from the tunnel, further back than on the 289. It's the standard Ford sedan lever turned back to front from its 'normal' position – so another easy-maintenance item.

So long as you apply the hairy-chested, unassisted 1960s sports car norm rather than modern power-with-everything saloon standards, the controls aren't particularly heavy. As soon as you start the engine, though, there's little doubting its character. There's none of the sewing-machine smoothness or overlaying mechanical clamour of multiple cams and complex valvetrains working in delicate unison. A Cobra V8 (even a small-block) is a big, simple engine, with uncomplicated power and torque that rocks the whole car whenever you blip the throttle. It doesn't whirr, it thumps.

Its performance is huge, but with a dual personality. Even a 427 with its immense flexibility and two-stage carburettor control can be pleasantly docile at low speeds, when it will rumble around in almost any gear you choose, heavier

Aero-screen behind the full windscreen, roll-cage braces, easy to find kill switches all define a racing alter ego for John Atkins' 289, driven by the author.

It's all subjective, but did any car ever shout 'sports car' louder than the **Cobra**?

through the wheel but not impossibly so, and quite manageable even in crawling traffic.

Given an open road, Cobra performance is everything the testers raved about fifty years ago. By any standards, its acceleration is remarkable, but in the context of the car's age it is unmatched: 0–60mph in close to 4 seconds and 100mph in a blink over 10 seconds still feel formidable – especially in such a simple car, where you feel more or less everything and are isolated from almost nothing.

CHOICE OF PERSONALITIES

Of course, there's a difference in feel between 289 and 427, but mainly in degree rather than in basics. The 289 is a bit

lighter and more responsive than a 427, while the 427 is more stump-pullingly flexible in mid- to top-range performance – although all some way out of the realms of normal experience in an older car. Impressive as the standing-start acceleration is, the most defining characteristic is the colossal mid-range flexibility that makes the gearbox a bonus rather than a necessity.

Given the surplus of power and torque over available grip from relatively small 1960s tyre footprints, cornering power is good and the handling is predictable and quite forgiving – which isn't a bad thing. The weight distribution is very slightly rear-biased, but so slightly that you'd be hard pushed to notice. More important is the rear-drive character.

Set up for the road, a Cobra tends to initial understeer, the nose pushing on as you turn into a corner, largely under the influence of the big V8 mass in the front, which would be quite happy to keep going in a straight line. Once the car settles into a corner there is a more neutral feel with ample feedback through steering wheel and seat of the pants (an old tester's cliché, but real enough). Not surprisingly, the dominant option is power-induced oversteer, the sheer grunt of the V8 happily pushing the tail out mid-corner with a suitable application of throttle. But the steering is so quick and the chassis so willing to respond that a reasonably skilled driver can use that to advantage rather than fear it – with the option to adjust line on the limit by a combination of throttle and steering inputs.

Where there is a noticeable difference between 289 and 427 is in the ride: the leaf-spring 289 chassis had minimal suspension travel, and a very firm ride, so on anything but a billiard-table surface you would enjoy the control but feel the inherent harshness. A coil-spring chassis has longer, slightly softer suspension travel with better compliance, which allowed a surprisingly good compromise between road and competition needs.

Probably more than in any other area of dynamics, any time you talk about brakes, you must do so in the context of period. The biggest noticeable difference between any old car, however sporty, and any new car, however mundane, is in how it stops. For its time, the Cobra stopped very well. The brakes were big and powerful, the car was light, and the tyre contact patch (again by the standards of the day) was big enough to get the braking force onto the road. With standard pads, solid discs and not a great deal of assistance, they take a big push, but they work, and have solid, progressive feel.

All in all, a Cobra isn't a demanding car to drive, and even a quite ordinary driver, with an appropriate degree of respect for what lies beneath, can exploit a good deal of its performance without massive worries. To find the last bit, though, is much more challenging, with obvious consequences if you get it wrong, but enormous satisfaction when you get it right. It doesn't have many secrets, it just requires a bit of understanding.

That, above all, is what keeps the Cobra up there among the sports car icons: its simplicity and singleness of purpose will flatter an ordinary driver and reward a skilled one. Its ultimate appeal is in its lack of mechanical complexity, its basic balance of power, lack of weight, and driver involvement. When changing legislation and changing customer demands made a car like the Cobra obsolete, we lost a very special generation.

The last word: it could only ever be this one.

INDEX

Page numbers in *italics* refer to illustrations.